LEO STRAUSS AND THE THEOLOGICO-POLITICAL PROBLEM

This book, by one of the most prominent interpreters of Leo Strauss's thought, is the first to address the problem that Leo Strauss himself said was *the* theme of his studies: the theologico-political problem or the confrontation with the theological and the political alternative to philosophy as a way of life. In his theologico-political treatise, which comprises four parts and an appendix, Heinrich Meier clarifies the distinction between political theology and political philosophy and reappraises the unifying center of Strauss's philosophical enterprise. The book is the culmination of Meier's work on the theologico-political problem. It will interest anyone who seeks to understand both the problem caused by revelation for philosophy and the challenge posed by political-religious radicalism in current events. The appendix makes available for the first time two lectures by Strauss that are immediately relevant to the subject of this book and that will open the way for future research and debate on the legacy of Strauss.

Heinrich Meier is Director of the Carl Friedrich von Siemens Foundation in Munich and Professor of Philosophy at the University of Munich. The author of seven books, including *Carl Schmitt and Leo Strauss: The Hidden Dialogue* and *The Lesson of Carl Schmitt: Four Chapters on the Distinction between Political Theology and Political Philosophy*, he is also the editor of Leo Strauss's *Gesammelte Schriften*. In 1997 he received the Peregrinus Prize from the Bavarian Academy of Sciences in recognition of outstanding work in the humanities, and in 2005 he was awarded the Leibniz Medal of the Berlin-Brandenburg Academy of Sciences.

Marcus Brainard earned his Ph.D. in philosophy in Germany and is the translator of Heinrich Meier's *The Lesson of Carl Schmitt: Four Chapters on the Distinction between Political Theology and Political Philosophy*.

T0371530

MODERN EUROPEAN PHILOSOPHY

General Editor

Robert B. Pippin, *University of Chicago*

Advisory Board

Gary Gutting, *University of Notre Dame*
Rolf-Peter Horstmann, *Humboldt University, Berlin*
Mark Sacks, *University of Essex*

Some Recent Titles

Daniel W. Conway: *Nietzsche's Dangerous Game*
John P. McCormick: *Carl Schmitt's Critique of Liberalism*
Frederick A. Olafson: *Heidegger and the Ground of Ethics*
Günter Zöller: *Fichte's Transcendental Philosophy*
Warren Breckman: *Marx, the Young Hegelians, and the Origins
of Radical Social Theory*
William Blattner: *Heidegger's Temporal Idealism*
Charles Griswold: *Adam Smith and the Virtues of the Enlightenment*
Gary Gutting: *Pragmatic Liberalism and the Critique of Modernity*
Allen Wood: *Kant's Ethical Thought*
Karl Ameriks: *Kant and the Fate of Autonomy*
Alfredo Ferrarin: *Hegel and Aristotle*
Cristina Lafont: *Heidegger, Language and World-Discourse*
Nicholas Wolsterstorff: *Thomas Reid and the Story of Epistemology*
Daniel Dahlstrom: *Heidegger's Concept of Truth*
Michelle Grier: *Kant's Doctrine of Transcendental Illusion*
Henry Allison: *Kant's Theory of Taste*
Allen Speight: *Hegel, Literature and the Problem of Agency*
J. M. Bernstein: *Adorno*
Robert M. Wallace: *Hegel's Philosophy of Reality, Freedom, and God*

LEO STRAUSS AND THE THEOLOGICO-POLITICAL PROBLEM

HEINRICH MEIER

TRANSLATED BY MARCUS BRAINARD

CAMBRIDGE
UNIVERSITY PRESS

CAMBRIDGE
UNIVERSITY PRESS

32 Avenue of the Americas, New York NY 10013-2473, USA

Cambridge University Press is part of the University of Cambridge.

It furthers the University's mission by disseminating knowledge in the pursuit of
education, learning and research at the highest international levels of excellence.

www.cambridge.org
Information on this title: www.cambridge.org/9780521699457

First published 2006
Reprinted 2007
First paperback edition 2007
Reprinted 2007 (thrice), 2008

A catalogue record for this publication is available from the British Library

Library of Congress Cataloguing in Publication data

Meier, Heinrich, 1953–
[Das theologisch-politische Problem. English]
Leo Strauss and the theologico-political problem / Heinrich Meier ; translated by Marcus
Brainard.
p. cm. – (Modern European philosophy)
Includes bibliographical references and index.
ISBN 0-521-85647-7 (hardcover)
1. Religion and politics. 2. Christianity and politics. 3. Theology. 4. Political
science – Philosophy. 5. Strauss, Leo. I. Title. II. Series.
BL65.P7M4513   2005
181.06 – dc22   2005008117

ISBN 978-0-521-85647-8 Hardback
ISBN 978-0-521-69945-7 Paperback

Seth Benardete

1930–2001

Tanto amico nullum par elogium

CONTENTS

PREFACE TO THE AMERICAN EDITION

Leo Strauss found his task in the recovery of political philosophy, and, like no other philosopher of the twentieth century, he engaged in the confrontation with the challenge of revelation. Both are intimately bound together: the grounding of political philosophy and the confrontation with faith in revelation are two sides of one and the same endeavor. What is at issue in both is the rational justification and the political defense of the philosophical life. For this issue, Strauss introduced the concept of the theologico-political problem.

To realize his endeavor, Strauss drew on the entire tradition of political philosophy, which he traced back to its Socratic beginning and whose history – in its continuity, as well as its turns and breaks – he made the object of penetrating studies. Strauss affirmed the tradition when he grasped philosophy as a way of life, and he returned to its Socratic origin when he reawakened the awareness that philosophy has to prove its rationality elenctically, in confrontation with the most demanding alternative. But like every philosopher, he chose the ways and means, the concepts and the rhetoric, that in his judgment were best suited for his task. These included deliberate deviations from the tradition. One was, for instance, his exposure of the exoteric-esoteric art of writing, of which philosophers had availed themselves for more than two millennia. In Strauss's oeuvre, it is given an emphasis that is without example in the history of philosophy. And this holds no less for the concept of political philosophy itself, to which he gave prominence as no other philosopher had before. In his writings, Strauss made the concept a focus of attention. He used it in 1936 in the title of the first book he published in English, *Hobbes' Political Philosophy*, and in the title of his last book, posthumously published in 1983, *Studies in Platonic Political Philosophy*, as well as in the titles of nine essays from the years between 1945 and 1971.[1] Together with Joseph Cropsey, he edited the monumental *History of Political Philosophy*, which first appeared in 1963 (and then in a revised and expanded version in 1972) and to which a number of his students contributed. Yet even before that, he had given a collection of his own essays the programmatic title *What Is Political Philosophy?* The title of the book, from 1959, raised the concept of political philosophy to the level of classical distinction: it made the cause[2] of political philosophy the object of a Socratic question, a cause for which the concept was missing in Socratic philosophy.[3]

If Strauss granted the concept "political philosophy" a weight and visibility that it had never had before, he did so neither to put philosophy in the service of politics nor to encourage that it be put in the service of politics but, quite the reverse, in order to sharpen the understanding of the tension that by necessity exists between philosophy and the political community and to demand emphatically and to promote vigorously philosophy's reflection on its political presuppositions and its rational foundations. And if he dealt more intensively than any other philosopher of his age with the biblical position of faith, he did not do so in order to clear the way to a "Jewish philosophy," which for him was just as much a wooden iron as was a "Christian philosophy": on the contrary, because he took radically seriously revelation's claim to truth, he insisted on the incompatibility of faith in revelation and philosophy.

When, in looking back on his path of thought, Strauss named the theologico-political problem as the theme of his studies, he said in almost as many words that his entire work revolved around philosophy as a way of life and that he had its justification in view. If philosophy is able to justify its right and its truth only elenctically, it has to concentrate on that way of life that might defeat its own answer to the question of

---

1 "On Classical Political Philosophy" (1945), "On a New Interpretation of Plato's Political Philosophy" (1946), "Political Philosophy and History" (1949), "On the Spirit of Hobbes' Political Philosophy" (1950), "On the Basis of Hobbes's Political Philosophy" (1954/1959), "What Is Political Philosophy?" (1955/1959), "The Liberalism of Classical Political Philosophy" (1959), "The Crisis of Political Philosophy" (1964), "Philosophy as Rigorous Science and Political Philosophy" (1969/1971).

2 The German word *Sache* is difficult to translate in a uniform way. Although 'cause' is the best rendering here, elsewhere in this book it is also translated as 'matter at issue', 'issue', or 'substance' (translator's note).

3 The concept does not occur in Plato's and Xenophon's writings. In Aristotle, we find φιλοσοφία πολιτική just once in *Politics* III, 12, 1282b23 (William of Moerbeke translated the important passage as *philosophia politica*). In *De oratore* III 109.4, Cicero speaks of political philosophers (*politici philosophi*). The Emperor Julian cites the concept πολιτική φιλοσοφία in *Epistulae* 61 c. 23.

what is right. If philosophy is able to demonstrate its rationality only by knowing how to repel and refute the most powerful objection to philosophy, it has to seek out that objection and make it as strong as it possibly can, as strong as only philosophy can make it. It is in this sense that Strauss turned to the political life and the life of the obedience of faith in his theologico-political treatises. It is in this sense that he sought out the challenge of revelation and made it strong for philosophy. For there is no more powerful objection to the philosophical life imaginable than the objection that appeals to faith in the omnipotent God and to his commandment or law.

The present book seeks to elucidate the unifying center of Strauss's philosophical endeavor by making the cause at which his endeavor aimed its own. The four chapters of the book are closely connected with the writings that I have published over the past two decades, and they bring to a provisional conclusion the confrontation that I conducted in *Carl Schmitt and Leo Strauss: The Hidden Dialogue*[4] and *The Lesson of Carl Schmitt: Four Chapters on the Distinction between Political Theology and Political Philosophy*.[5] Chapters I and II address Strauss's philosophy directly, whereas Chapters III and IV deal with two concepts whose distinction is imperative for the clarification of the theologico-political problem.

Chapter I is a tripartite treatise.[6] The first part, "The Theologico-Political Problem,"[7] states what the problem involves and which approaches to its solution Strauss's oeuvre contains. It explains how and why the challenge to, and the critique of, the philosophical life posed by politics and religion must be grasped as *the* theme of Leo Strauss's work and why Strauss takes the philosophical refutation of faith in revelation to be a theologico-*political* problem. The commentary "On the Genealogy of Faith in Revelation" attempts, by way of an example

---

4 Translated by J. Harvey Lomax (Chicago: University of Chicago Press, 1995). The American edition was based on *Carl Schmitt, Leo Strauss und "Der Begriff des Politischen". Zu einem Dialog unter Abwesenden* (Stuttgart: J. B. Metzler, 1988; expanded ed., 1998).

5 Translated by Marcus Brainard (Chicago: University of Chicago Press, 1998). The translation was based on *Die Lehre Carl Schmitts. Vier Kapitel zur Unterscheidung Politischer Theologie und Politischer Philosophie* (Stuttgart/Weimar: J. B. Metzler, 1994; 2d ed, with an afterword, 2004).

6 The original German version was published as *Das theologisch-politische Problem. Zum Thema von Leo Strauss* (Stuttgart/Weimar: J. B. Metzler, 2003).

7 The lecture was first given at the international symposium "Living Issues in the Thought of Leo Strauss" at the Carl Friedrich von Siemens Foundation in Munich on June 19, 2002.

that is more than an example, to show how the four approaches
that "The Theologico-Political Problem" outlines for the encounter
with faith in revelation are to be developed. The essay "Death as
God" presents observations on a revealing note by Strauss on Martin
Heidegger. This brief text glances at a philosopher on whose thought
the theologico-political problem cast its long shadow – without its ever
having been a theme of any importance to him, or rather because it
was not a theme of any importance to him.

Chapter II presents reflections on "The History of Philosophy and
the Intention of the Philosopher."[8] It seeks to make understandable
why Strauss engaged in historical research ranging from Heidegger
via Machiavelli and Alfarabi to the pre-Socratic philosophers in order
to answer questions that are inseparable from the theologico-political
problem, such as "What is the right life?" "What is the good?" and
"*Quid sit deus?*" – questions that are by no means intrinsically historical
questions. For anyone who seriously studies his oeuvre, the focal point
becomes the intention that the philosopher Strauss pursues when he
directs his undivided attention, so it seems, to the history of philosophy and presents his philosophy in the guise of interpretations of past
writings.

Chapter III, "What Is Political Theology?"[9] traces the incisive change
in the history of the concept "political theology" caused by Carl
Schmitt's 1922 writing of the same name, and gives a nonpolemical definition of the concept, which shows it to be the symmetrical countercon-
cept to "political philosophy." The concluding Chapter IV, "Why Political Philosophy?"[10] identifies the place accorded to the confrontation

8 The lecture was delivered on November 16, 1994, as the conclusion of the lecture series
   "The Legacy of Leo Strauss," which the University of Chicago organized in honor of
   Strauss on the twentieth anniversary of his death. Seth Benardete had opened the series
   with the brilliant lecture "Strauss on Plato" in autumn 1993. The German version of my
   lecture was published in *Die Denkbewegung von Leo Strauss. Die Geschichte der Philosophie
   und die Intention des Philosophen* (Stuttgart/Weimar: J. B. Metzler, 1996), 17–43.
9 First published in *Interpretation: A Journal of Political Philosophy* 30, no. 1 (Fall 2002), 79–
   91. It is reprinted here with kind permission of the editor. The original German version
   was published in Jan Assmann, *Politische Theologie zwischen Ägypten und Israel* (Munich:
   Carl Friedrich von Siemens Foundation, 1992; 2d, expanded ed., 1995), 7–19.
10 First published in *The Review of Metaphysics* 56, no. 2 (December 2002), 385–407. It
   is reprinted here with kind permission of the editor. The original German version was
   published in *Warum Politische Philosophie?* (Stuttgart/Weimar: J. B. Metzler, 2000; 2d ed.,
   2001). The English version was presented as the Georges Lurcy Lecture at the University
   of Chicago on May 4, 2000. The German version was read as my inaugural lecture at
   the University of Munich on February 16, 2000.

with the theologico-political problem in the inner structure of political philosophy.

The Appendix makes two lectures by Strauss that are highly relevant to the subject of this book available for the first time.[11] "The Living Issues of German Postwar Philosophy,"[12] from April 1940, gives an extremely instructive account of the intellectual milieu and the philosophical discussions in Germany during the twenties and thirties, the period in which Strauss first set out on his path of thought. More than two decades before his well-known "autobiographical preface" from 1962, Strauss outlined in the lecture he gave before the Creighton Philosophical Club at Syracuse University[13] an intellectual autobiography of his early years, where the emphasis was on his confrontation with historicism and his encounters with both Nietzsche and Heidegger. In "The Living Issues," Strauss takes up the concept "political theology" and employs it in a precise sense for the first time (5 recto). It comes as no surprise that the concept that Strauss uses only rarely, and therefore all the more significantly in his published writings,[14] occurs after

11 Both texts will be included in Leo Strauss, *Gesammelte Schriften,* vol. 4. They are published with the kind permission of Professor Joseph Cropsey, literary executor of the estate of Leo Strauss.

12 The manuscript is located in Leo Strauss Papers, Box 8, Folder 14, Department of Special Collections, University of Chicago Library. It is written on eight oversized sheets of paper. Sheets 1 through 7 are written on both verso and recto, but sheet 8 only recto. The fair copy is in ink with corrections and additions in pencil. My transcription follows the wording of the manuscript; any deviations from it are recorded in the editorial notes. The orthography – which is partly British – has also been retained.

13 That is clear from the following note in the *Philosophical Review* 49, no. 4 (1940), 492: "The Creighton Philosophical Club held its thirty-ninth meeting at Syracuse University, on April 27 and 28. Dr. Leo Strauss, now lecturing at Hamilton, Colgate, and Amherst, read a paper on 'The Living Issues of German Postwar Philosophy' with special reference to Husserl's phenomenology, and Dr. Julius Kraft of Rochester University read one on 'The Philosophy of Existence', with special reference to Heidegger and Jaspers." My thanks to Emmanuel Patard, Paris, for drawing my attention to this note.

14 The most important passage in the published writings reads: "We are compelled to distinguish political philosophy from political theology. By political theology we understand political teachings which are based on divine revelation. Political philosophy is limited to what is accessible to the unassisted human mind." *What Is Political Philosophy? And Other Studies* (New York: Free Press, 1959), 13. Cf. "Marsilius of Padua," in Leo Strauss and Joseph Cropsey, eds., *History of Political Philosophy* (Chicago: Rand McNally, 1963), 227 and 236 (reprinted in *Liberalism Ancient and Modern* [New York: Basic Books, 1968], 185 and 193). In the manuscript *Die Religionskritik des Hobbes*, Strauss had spoken in 1933–34 of the "tradition of theological politics, which appeals to *revelation,*" and contrasted it with the "tradition of philosophical politics." *Gesammelte Schriften,* vol. 3 (Stuttgart/Weimar: J. B. Metzler, 2001), 270.

a discussion of *Der Begriff des Politischen* and unmistakably in reference to Carl Schmitt.

Under the title "Reason and Revelation," Strauss gave a lecture at the Hartford Theological Seminary in Hartford, Connecticut, in January 1948 in which he dealt with the theologico-political problem in a more outspoken way than at any time before or after. There are several lectures in which he took up the biblical alternative to philosophy. The best known are the two lectures held on March 13 and 15, 1967, at the City College of New York and published under the title *Jerusalem and Athens: Some Preliminary Reflections* in the same year.[15] The lecture "On the Interpretation of Genesis," which was made available posthumously,[16] was presented at the University College of the University of Chicago on January 25, 1957. The first public treatment of the theme I know of dates from November 13, 1946, when Strauss spoke in the General Seminar at the New School for Social Research in New York on "Jerusalem and Athens."[17] The three texts from 1946, 1957, and 1967 overlap extensively since all three center on an interpretation of the book of Genesis, the account of the creation of the world and the story of the fall of man, or – in the case of the first lecture – culminate in such an interpretation. The text published in the Appendix differs from all Strauss's other published and unpublished treatments of the theme with which I am familiar both in the overall approach that Strauss chose and in numerous arguments, hints, and examples he gave. However, we do not know exactly what Strauss said to the theologians in Hartford. For we are faced here with two manuscripts: On the one hand, with the lecture "Reason and Revelation" written out at least up to page 9 verso; on the other, with a text that begins in the form of shorthand notes and, as it develops, overlaps partly with "Reason and Revelation," a text for which I have chosen the title "Notes on Philosophy and Revelation"

15 The City College Papers no. 6 (New York: The City College, 1967), 28 pp. Strauss included this text from 1967 in *Studies in Platonic Political Philosophy* (Chicago: University of Chicago Press, 1983), 147–73.

16 First published in *L'Homme: Revue française d'anthropologie* 21, no. 1 (January–March 1981), 5–20.

17 I have in my possession a copy of a typescript with the title "Jerusalem and Athens. (Lecture to be delivered in November 1946 in the General Seminar.)" comprising twenty-seven typed and three additional handwritten pages, as well as a later version of its first part with the title "Jerusalem and Athens. (Lecture to be delivered in the General Seminar on November, 13, 1946)." comprising five typed pages with handwritten emendations by Strauss.

and placed after "Reason and Revelation."[18] Whereas Strauss did not write a concluding part for "Reason and Revelation," the "Notes on Philosophy and Revelation" lack an opening part. They start abruptly under the heading "The Biblical argument." Strauss noted at the top of the first page, "(typescript p. 22 para 2 ff.)." The reference points to the typescript of the lecture "Jerusalem and Athens" from November 13, 1946. Indeed, the ten points in which Strauss develops the biblical argument on the first three pages of the "Notes" contain a compressed, partly refined and expanded version of the presentation given in "Jerusalem and Athens" on the last six pages of the typescript and the two pages of handwritten additions to the text. It is possible that we have in the "Notes on Philosophy and Revelation" the first version of the Hartford lecture. In that case, Strauss would have begun afresh, writing the talk "Reason and Revelation" and then drawing on the argumentation and the conclusion of the "Notes" in order to supplement the unfinished talk. It is conceivable that Strauss read the talk up to page 9 recto or 9 verso and continued with page N 3 recto or N 3 verso. Another possibility is that he wrote the "Notes on Philosophy and Revelation" in 1947 for an occasion about which we know nothing and then used them for the Hartford lecture as just described. Regardless of how Strauss may have used the two manuscripts in Hartford, given the line of thought that they both contain and the period in which they were written, it is certain that they are closely connected and need to be studied together.

To conclude this preface, I want to address two questions that arise from a statement I make in "The Theologico-Political Problem" and that I do not discuss there. They concern the institution of the philosophical school, which has played an important role in the reception of Strauss's philosophy. In the essay, I remark that the sole political act of consequence that Strauss brought himself to launch was to found

18 Both manuscripts are located in Leo Strauss Papers, Box 11, Folder 13, Department of Special Collections, University of Chicago Library. "Reason and Revelation" comprises twelve sheets, which are numbered 1–4 and 4a–11; with the exception of the last sheet, on which there are only ten lines, both sides of all the sheets have been written on. The fair copy is in ink, and additions are in pencil. The second manuscript comprises five sheets in a somewhat smaller format, which are numbered 1–5 and are written on both recto and verso. The fair copy is in ink, and there are numerous additions in pencil.

a school, which the offer of a professorship in political philosophy at the University of Chicago in 1949 provided him the opportunity to do. I add that Strauss surely was aware of the price he had to pay for making this political decision. What can move a philosopher to found a school? And in what sense does that founding involve a political decision?

The school has uncontestable advantages for the development of a comprehensive teaching, for the pursuit of a research project, and for the formation of an interpretive approach. It makes it easier to test philosophical arguments and to experiment with rhetorical figures. It makes possible both the thorough differentiation of an edifice of thought in directions and the application of an interpretation to objects, the pursuit or execution of which would surpass an individual's powers. In the best case, the semipublic sphere of the school permits the combination of the playful treatment of possible answers that presupposes the release from the demands of public self-assertion, and the serious involvement with the true questions that requires agreement about the fundamental points of a common agenda. The institution of the school helps to gain an audience for a new orientation of philosophy and to lend it stability. It is the means of choice when the aim is to found a tradition and thereby to make it more likely that an oeuvre will remain accessible to future generations. The school offers, not least, the possibility of making some citizens familiar with philosophy and educating them in such a way that, when they later assume responsibilities in the commonwealth, those citizens will treat philosophy favorably or at least respectfully and, if necessary, grant it protection and support.

Strauss used all of these advantages of the school. He also took the opportunity – following Plato's and Aristotle's example – to foster the politically gifted and the gentlemen among his students. As a citizen of the United States of America, he was loyal to the country that had given him refuge from persecution. He showed himself to be a friend of the liberal democracy that allowed him to lead a philosophical life. He prompted a number of his students to investigate the historical, constitutional, and political foundations of the United States and encouraged them to defend those foundations. He respected their patriotism and taught them to understand the dignity that is proper to the political life. Yet he made it clear: "patriotism is not enough";[19]

---

19 Cf. *Xenophon's Socrates* (Ithaca, N.Y.: Cornell University Press, 1972), 179.

and he – no less than Socrates, the citizen of Athens – left no doubt about the fact that he did not consider the political life to be the best life.

The founding of a philosophical school, however, becomes a political decision not only insofar as the founding makes it possible to exert a salutary influence on the commonwealth – no matter how mediate, no matter how variously refracted that influence may be. It is a political decision already insofar as the school like the commonwealth comprises quite different natures, it too consists of philosophers and nonphilosophers who (bound together to varying degrees) cooperate in different ways, and therefore the central determinations that apply to the tension between the political community and philosophy remain valid in the relationship of the school to philosophy. For the school, no less than for the commonwealth, it holds true that different addressees have to be addressed differently, that they grasp the teaching differently and pass it on differently. The school demands political action and is fraught with political risks.

If the school gains a larger audience for the philosophical teaching, it also contributes to strengthening and oversimplifying the doctrinal content of philosophy, to emphasizing everything that allows of being taught and reduced to formulas, and, without any in-depth confrontation with the cause or the matter at issue, can be repeated, applied, and communicated. And if the school is able to exert some political influence, then it is in danger of accommodating philosophy to a particular regime or underscoring its closeness to this regime in such a way that the philosophically gifted in the future or in other regions of the world who have a genuine philosophical interest in that teaching must once again loosen the link to that political regime in order to free the teaching from the odium of being bound to an order prevailing at a certain time and in a certain place or being subservient to an ideology.

The founding of the school will be successful only if the teacher adapts his oral teaching to his students' ability to understand. It is very likely that he will entrust his farthest-reaching reflections, his most profound thoughts, and his most challenging considerations to his carefully written books. Members of a school, however, are inclined to value the oral tradition more highly. They tend to overestimate or to regard as absolutely indispensable what for them was of enormous significance. This may explain in part why the school is so susceptible to apologetic tendencies regarding the teacher's philosophical radicality, why precisely in its orbit his thought is often rendered innocuous, and why pieties of all kinds are able to take root there.

Strauss was as familiar as anyone with the problem of the school and the tradition in philosophy. He knew the history of Platonism, of the Aristotelian, Epicurean, and Stoic schools, their successors and their latest heirs. In his dialogue with Alexandre Kojève on tyranny and the politics of the philosophers, he commented in no uncertain terms in 1950 on the formation of sects and drew a sharp line between the philosopher and the sectarian.[20] Precisely because he had confronted the philosophical tradition so intensively, he was aware that the petrification of philosophy in the tradition can be cleared away again and again, he was aware that philosophical energy can be set free ever anew from its encapsulation in doctrines. And precisely because he was familiar with the history of the schools of the ancients, he was also aware that those schools helped essentially to make philosophy conspicuous as a way of life. In modernity, Rousseau and Nietzsche attempted to give the philosophical life a visible shape by emphatically drawing attention to their own lives.[21] The alternative was the founding of a school, which does not have to produce only members of a school. Aristotle was a member of Plato's school for twenty years, nearly twice as long as he was able to teach in his own school, the Lyceum. Aristotle left the Academy as a philosopher, and from his school emerged other philosophers in turn, just as from the school that Strauss founded philosophers have emerged – and by no means only "Straussians."

Since the end of the 1980s, I have had many conversations with my friends Seth Benardete and Christopher Bruell on the theme of this book and on the lectures by Strauss that are published in the Appendix. The same is true of Thomas L. Pangle, who has, in the meantime, published his confrontation with the biblical argument under the title *Political Philosophy and the God of Abraham,* to which I wish to refer the

---

20 *On Tyranny: Revised and Expanded Edition* (Chicago: University of Chicago Press, 2000), 194–96.

21 I hope in the not too distant future to publish two books that, with constant attention to the question of the philosophical life, confront Rousseau's *Rêveries* and Nietzsche's *Ecce Homo.* For the time being, I refer the reader to my essay *"Les rêveries du Promeneur Solitaire." Rousseau über das philosophische Leben* (Munich: Carl Friedrich von Siemens Foundation, 2005).

reader. Without Nathan Tarcov's friendly critique and thoughtful sug-
gestions on how to improve the American edition of my studies on the
theologico-political problem, this book would not be as close to the
German original as it is now.

H.M.
Munich, June 2005

THE THEOLOGICO-POLITICAL PROBLEM
On the Theme of Leo Strauss

Philosophieren ist: im Bewusstsein der schlechthinnigen Vergänglichkeit *alles* Menschlichen, aber gleich als ob einem die ganze Ewigkeit zur Verfügung stände, nach der Wahrheit suchen – mit vollkommener Ruhe, ohne jegliche Eile – stets dringlich, aber niemals eilig – mit dem Mut zum schönen Wagnis, und beständig bereit, ganz von vorn anzufangen.

(To philosophize is to be conscious of the absolute transitoriness of *all* that is human, but at the same time as if one had all eternity at one's disposal, to search for the truth – with complete calm, without any hurry – always with urgency, but never hurried – with the courage for a graceful venture, and constantly prepared to begin from the very beginning.)

– Leo Strauss, Note from April 1, 1937

THE THEOLOGICO-POLITICAL PROBLEM

Nothing is as controversial in the thought of Leo Strauss and nothing is as central to a proper understanding of it as the theologico-political problem. Not only is the position that Strauss takes on the theologico-political problem controversial. The controversy already concerns what position he in truth took. And since the theologico-political problem lies at the center of Strauss's political philosophy, the controversy shapes the confrontation with all the great themes of Strauss's oeuvre, ranging from the dialogue between the ancients and the moderns via philosophy as a way of life and the exoteric-esoteric art of writing to the critique of historicism.

In 1964, Strauss himself made clear beyond all doubt the centrality of the theologico-political problem in one of his not exactly numerous autobiographical remarks. The statement, which long received next to no attention, though it succinctly names the internal unity of his works in a single sentence, is prepared for by the opening of the "Preface to the English Translation" that he wrote in August 1962 for the American edition of his first work, *Die Religionskritik Spinozas*. The first paragraph reads: "This study on Spinoza's *Theologico-political Treatise* was written during the years 1925–28 in Germany. The author was a young Jew born and raised in Germany who found himself in the grip of the theologico-political predicament."[1] In October 1964, shortly after his sixty-fifth birthday, Strauss once again looked back at the beginnings of his path of thought in Germany, this time in the preface to Hobbes'

---

1 *Spinoza's Critique of Religion*, trans. E. M. Sinclair (New York: Schocken, 1965), 1. This is a translation of *Die Religionskritik Spinozas als Grundlage seiner Bibelwissenschaft. Untersuchungen zu Spinozas Theologisch-politischem Traktat* (Berlin: Akademie-Verlag, 1930), in *Gesammelte Schriften*, ed. Heinrich Meier, vol. 1 (Stuttgart/Weimar: Metzler, 1996; 2d, expanded ed., 2001), 55–361. Unless otherwise noted, all texts cited are by Leo Strauss.

politische Wissenschaft, the German edition of *The Political Philosophy of Hobbes.* Here he recalls his early study of the biblical criticism that began in the seventeenth century, particularly of Spinoza's *Tractatus theologico-politicus,* and the challenge that the theology of revelation has posed for him since the twenties: "The reawakening of theology, which for me is epitomized by the names Karl Barth and Franz Rosenzweig, seemed to make it necessary for one to study the extent to which the critique of orthodox – Jewish and Christian – theology deserved to be victorious." And then he adds: "The theologico-political problem has since remained *the* theme of my studies."[2]

This statement, which is as laconic as it is characteristic, appears in the first and, at the same time, last text with which Strauss, after an interruption of nearly three decades, addresses German-speaking readers. To understand correctly the perspective from which the preface to *Hobbes' politische Wissenschaft* was conceived, one must know that 1965, the year in which the volume would appear that comprised both the first publication of the German original of the Hobbes book he had finished thirty years earlier and the reprint of his "Anmerkungen zu Carl Schmitt, *Der Begriff des Politischen*" (first published in September 1932), was the same year for which Strauss had accepted an invitation to return as visiting professor to the University of Hamburg, where in 1921 he had received his doctorate, under the direction of Ernst Cassirer, with a dissertation on the problem of knowledge in Jacobi. At the last moment, health reasons ruined his plans to teach philosophy in Hamburg. A brief visit in 1954 – which took him to Freiburg im Breisgau, Heidelberg, Frankfurt am Main, and his birthplace, Kirchhain in Hessen – was thus to be Strauss's only stay in Germany after he had left Berlin in 1932 for Paris and later continued on to London and Cambridge.

When in 1964, with his return to Germany as both author and teacher in view, Strauss named the "theologico-political problem" as the unifying theme of his studies, he apparently assumed that the hint was more likely to be understood and taken up in Germany than anywhere else. However, this formulation of Strauss's for the urgent confrontation with the theological and the political alternative to philosophy could hardly find an echo among the German-speaking audience before a new access to political philosophy had been opened up. His formulation had to

2 *Hobbes' politische Wissenschaft* (Neuwied am Rhein/Berlin: Luchterhand, 1965), 7, in *Gesammelte Schriften,* vol. 3 (Stuttgart/Weimar: Metzler, 2001), 7–8.

meet with incomprehension so long as the confrontation with the theological and the political alternative was not grasped as the very heart of political philosophy. In view of the particular circumstances under which Strauss identified the theologico-political problem as *the* theme of his wide-ranging oeuvre, it may be appropriate that a German reader – one who came to know Strauss and engaged him just as he came to know and engaged other philosophers of the past, namely, solely by reading their writings and confronting their thought – makes the theologico-political problem his theme.

Why does Strauss – in the hint from October 1964 about the center and unity of his work, a hint that is unique in his publications – choose the concept "theologico-political problem"? Why does he not have recourse to the formula "Jerusalem and Athens," which he had employed time and again since the mid-forties? Why does he not speak of the conflict between philosophy and revelation? Why not of the tension between the commonwealth and philosophy? Why does he not appropriate the heading "ancients and moderns," under which friends and students had published a festschrift in his honor only a few weeks earlier? Clearly for him, the theologico-political problem designates the fundamental problem, the theme in which the other themes meet, through which they are bound together, and in whose light each is accorded its specific place.

Let us begin by considering the *querelle des anciens et des modernes,* which Strauss rekindled at the beginning of the thirties and which kept him in motion as it did no other philosopher of the twentieth century. For Strauss, the quarrel has its ultimate source in the different stance of the ancients and the moderns towards the theologico-political problem, a stance that in each case rests on different historical situations, is reflected in different political strategies, and, finally, is given expression in different philosophical assessments of the problem. In a lecture about "philosophy and revelation," which he gave in January 1948 at the Hartford Theological Seminary in Hartford, Connecticut, under the prescribed title "Reason and Revelation," Strauss brings the quarrel of the ancients and the moderns to a head in the thesis-like formula: "A philosophy which believes that it can refute the possibility of revelation – and a philosophy which does not believe that: this is the real meaning of la querelle des anciens et des modernes."[3] The

---

3 "Reason and Revelation," fol. N 5 recto. Leo Strauss Papers, Box 11, Folder 13. My transcription of the text may be found in the Appendix to this book.

theologico-political problem confronts us – we note first of all – with the difficulty of refuting the possibility of revelation.

The conflict between philosophy and revelation, from which arises the task of refuting the possibility of revelation, is articulated by Strauss more sharply in his lecture to the theologians at the Hartford Seminary than in any of his writings before or after. He works out the opposition in which the freedom of questioning and knowing that philosophy requires and the obedience to the sovereign authority that revelation commands stand to one another: "To the philosophic view that man's happiness consists in free investigation or insight, the Bible opposes the view that man's happiness consists in obedience to God." The opposition in principle between philosophy and revelation regarding man's happiness already proves in the next sentence to be the truly radical opposition regarding the right and the necessity of philosophy: "The Bible thus offers the only challenge to the claim of philosophy which can reasonably be made. One cannot seriously question the claim of philosophy in the name, e.g., of politics or poetry. To say nothing of other considerations, man's ultimate aim is what is really good and not what merely *seems* to be good, and only through *knowledge* of the good is he enabled to find the good." Strauss steers from the truly radical opposition directly towards the absolutely fundamental alternative, on which the conflict between philosophy and revelation is based and which concerns man as man: "But this is indeed the question: whether men can acquire the knowledge of the good, without which they cannot guide their lives individually and collectively, by the unaided efforts of their reason, or whether they are dependent for that knowledge on divine revelation. Only through the Bible is philosophy, or the quest for knowledge, challenged by *knowledge*, viz. by knowledge revealed by the omniscient God, or by knowledge identical with the self-communication of God. No alternative is more fundamental than the alternative: human guidance or divine guidance. *Tertium non datur.*"[4] That philosophy can seriously be called into question only in the name of revelation means two things: Revelation appears as *the* challenge to philosophy since it holds the prospect of the fulfillment of the deepest desire that moves philosophy, the knowledge of truth, and at the same time radically negates that desire itself as a free desire. The God of revelation claims to have at his disposal in perfection, without restriction, and without

4 "Reason and Revelation," fol. 4 recto/4 verso; cf. *Natural Right and History* (Chicago: University of Chicago Press, 1953), 74–75.

distortion, precisely that at which the eros of philosophy aims; but he makes access to it subject to his sovereign decision to reveal the truth he harbors within himself to whom he wishes, when he wishes, where he wishes, and how he wishes in the bounds that his will establishes and to the ends that his judgment determines. For philosophy, revelation represents both a theoretical and an existential challenge. Revelation challenges philosophy theoretically by confronting philosophy with the question of whether the truth, the all-important truth, is not missed when it is sought after freely by man, whether the sole possible access to truth does not instead consist in its devout acceptance of him who *is* *the* truth. Revelation challenges philosophy existentially by confronting philosophy with the commandment of obedience, which rejects the philosophical life in the name of the highest authority conceivable and imposes on that life the severest sanction imaginable. Politics or poetry are incapable of *seriously* calling philosophy into question since they – or so long as they – do not negate the philosophical life by appealing to the knowledge, truth, and power of the omniscient, the omnipotent, the unfathomable God and cannot add weight to their objection to philosophy with the prospect of eternal salvation or eternal damnation. The theologico-political problem draws our attention – we note secondly – to the requirement to defend the right and the necessity of philosophy against the double challenge that revelation and the life based on it, the life of the obedience of faith, represents for philosophy.

The tension between the political community and philosophy precedes the conflict between philosophy and revelation, and the same holds for the requirement to justify the right and the necessity of philosophy rationally and defend them politically. The philosophical life, which has its raison d'être in the fact that it is based on unreserved questioning and does not rest satisfied with any answer that owes its authentication to an authority, does not find itself in a precarious situation only with the appearance of revealed religions. As a distinct way of life that rests on a conscious choice and is held fast in the face of all resistance, philosophy is an answer to the question of what is right, an answer that is always already confronted with authoritative answers to the question of what is right and just for man. It meets the political obligations and moral demands that oppose it with the will to enforcement. It is subject to the law of the commonwealth, divine or human commandments and prohibitions. In the confrontation with the *theios* *nomos* of a given polis, it discovers *physis* and finds itself. So much for the situation of philosophy and the horizon in which the alternative of a life of human guidance or a life of divine guidance naturally arises. Has the tension between the commonwealth and philosophy been superseded by the conflict of philosophy with revelation? Does it, in view of the new, far more serious challenge lose any of its interest? Or how is the relationship of the truly radical opposition regarding the right and the necessity of philosophy to the absolutely fundamental alternative for man to be determined more precisely? In one of his latest and most important essays, his "Note on the Plan of Nietzsche's *Beyond Good and Evil*," Strauss says of Nietzsche in 1973: "Philosophy and religion, it seems, belong together – belong more closely together than philosophy and the city. . . . The fundamental alternative is that of the rule of philosophy over religion or the rule of religion over philosophy; it is not, as it was for Plato or Aristotle, that of the philosophic and the political life; for Nietzsche, as distinguished from the classics, politics belongs from the outset to a lower plane than either philosophy or religion."[5] When Nietzsche – in contrast to the political philosophers of antiquity, but in agreement with those of modernity – focuses on the question of whether religion should rule over philosophy or philosophy over religion, he takes account of the changed historical situation, which came about for philosophy through the rise of revealed religions and in particular through the ascent of Christianity. Strauss is far from placing in doubt the urgency or even the legitimacy of the question of rule. Rather than contesting that the vital interest of philosophy is to assert itself against a sovereign religion with a universal claim, which has the theological and the political means at its disposal to make philosophy subservient to it, Strauss instead subjects to an emphatic critique the more than millennium-long accommodation of a philosophy petrified in the tradition of its doctrinal contents to a powerful tradition of obedience or, in his words, the "perverse interweaving of a *nomos*-tradition with a philosophical tradition."[6] What objection does Strauss raise, then, against the alternative he attributes to Nietzsche? As we have seen, for Strauss, philosophy meets the decisive challenge in revelation. In the end, philosophy cannot be shaken in its ownmost claim by

---

5 "Note on the Plan of Nietzsche's *Beyond Good and Evil*" (1973), in *Studies in Platonic Political Philosophy* (Chicago: University of Chicago Press, 1983), 176.

6 Letter to Gerhard Krüger from November 17, 1932, in *Gesammelte Schriften* 3, 406; cf. "The Mutual Influence of Theology and Philosophy" (1952), *Independent Journal of Philosophy* 3 (1979), 113; *Persecution and the Art of Writing* (Glencoe, Ill.: Free Press, 1952), 19–21, 168, 179; *Thoughts on Machiavelli* (Glencoe, Ill.: Free Press, 1958), 184–85, 231; *Liberalism Ancient and Modern* (New York: Basic Books, 1968), 193.

politics, and its deepest desire is incapable of finding fulfillment in the political life. Yet if philosophy is to be in a position to respond appropriately to the challenge of revealed religion, it must seriously engage the expectations and demands that distinguish the political life, and it must confront the moral obligations, the notions of the common good and of the just rule of God or of men, that determine that life. What Strauss has in view when he accuses Nietzsche of regarding politics as belonging from the outset to a lower plane than philosophy and religion is the requirement that one start more radically with politics, with the commonwealth, with the foundations of its existence, with its vital element, the opinions and valuations of its citizens, in order to find the horizon in which philosophy and religion can begin their dispute with one another and carry it out.[7] The fundamental alternative – as we may put Strauss's objection – does not concern the question of whether philosophy or religion should rule. The fundamental alternative is opened up only by the question: *What is the right life?* And at stake in it is an eminently political question. The precise formulation with which Strauss chooses to characterize the unifying theme of his studies, namely, as a theologico-*political* problem – we note thirdly and finally – contains a hint about the path on which the right and the necessity of philosophy are capable of being justified and on which the confrontation with revelation is capable of being carried out successfully.

What is most conspicuous in Strauss's formulation I have yet to touch on. His mention of the "theologico-political problem" immediately calls to mind the theologico-political enterprise that drove modern philosophy forward. From Strauss's perspective, this enterprise was unsuccessful in at least one respect: it was unable to settle the theologico-political *problem*. The political success of the enterprise, the establishment of liberal society, gave the problem merely, but consequentially, a new twist: the old theological difficulty was left unresolved, whereas the new political challenge consisted henceforth in restoring the rank of the political and in making the dignity of the political life visible once again. The

---

7 An implication of his objection that Strauss did not spell out is the criticism that Nietzsche did not free himself to the extent necessary from the valuations of the political life because he did not take them seriously enough philosophically, and this holds first and foremost for the will to rule itself. Whether this criticism reaches the center of Nietzsche's philosophy or whether it bears only on his exoteric teaching, Nietzsche's project of rule by philosophers of the future, need not occupy us here. More important for us is the clue concerning the direction in which Strauss pursues a solution to the theologico-political problem.

historical process initiated by the theologico-political enterprise of modern philosophy led to the parceling of human life into a multiplicity of "autonomous provinces of culture." In the supposedly amicable cooperation and coexistence of the economy, politics, religion, art, science, and so on, philosophy loses the serious alternatives, and with them fades the awareness that philosophy is a special way of life. In the world of modern culture that it decisively helped to bring about, philosophy is less equipped than ever to carry out the confrontation with revelation successfully and to justify its right and its necessity rationally.

It is here that I come to the third or the first passage in which Strauss employs the epithet "theologico-political" in his own name to characterize his historical situation, his theme, and his endeavor. In 1935, in an enigmatic footnote to *Philosophie und Gesetz,* he raises in passing, as it were, the question of the appropriate philosophical treatment of the theologico-political problem. A radical critique of the modern concept of "culture" – as one crux of which he names the "fact of religion" and as its other crux the "fact of the political" – is possible, Strauss says, only in the form of a "theologico-political treatise." However, such a treatise would have to have, "if it is not to lead once again to the founding of culture, exactly the opposite tendency of the theologico-political treatises of the seventeenth century, especially those by Hobbes and Spinoza."[8] The thrust of the theologico-political treatises of the seventeenth century aimed at the recovery and the persistent safeguarding of the *libertas philosophandi* by means of an effective separation of politics from theology. Peace and security – thus read philosophy's conceptual offering in its secular alliance with the political sovereign – could be achieved on the path of the progressive domination of nature and the transformation enabled thereby of human living conditions in general. Philosophy would supply the reliable and manageable knowledge required for the methodical conquest of nature and the rational reorganization of society, while the sovereign would have to take care of political protection. With this comprehensive project, the battle of the theologico-political treatises against the "kingdom of darkness" and "superstition" took the lead. What begins with the emancipation of politics from theology results ultimately, after the successful unleashing of

---

8 *Philosophie und Gesetz. Beiträge zum Verständnis Maimunis und seiner Vorläufer* (Berlin: Schocken, 1935), 31, in *Gesammelte Schriften,* vol. 2 (Stuttgart/Weimar: Metzler, 1997), 30–31 n. 2; cf. "Jerusalem and Athens" (1967), in *Studies in Platonic Political Philosophy,* 147–49.

a world of increasing purposive rationality and growing prosperity, in a state of incomprehension of and indifference towards the original sense of the theologico-political critique, a state in which the demands of politics are rejected with the same matter-of-factness as those of religion. This state finds its conspicuous expression in the existence of the bourgeois, who closes himself to all claims that aim at the whole, and in a philosophy that no longer knows how to answer the question "Why philosophy?" A theologico-political treatise with "exactly the opposite tendency" of the treatises that founded the historical development of liberal "culture" – though their intention and achievement went beyond that founding[9] – would thus have to bring once again to awareness, in perfect clarity, the claims that the "original facts" of politics and of religion contain and reawaken the understanding of the connection that exists between the two.

When Strauss speaks of a theologico-political treatise, he is speaking of a philosophical writing that faces the theological and the political alternative and that leads, by way of the confrontation with the demands of politics and religion, to philosophy. The theologico-political treatise has, in other words, both an elenctic and a protreptic character. Yet where can the scrutiny begin, where does philosophy find its resistance and counterpoint, if the demanding alternative is no longer present or if its contours become blurred beyond recognition in the multiplicity of merely personal concerns, in which everything appears to be compatible with everything else? Must not the philosophical transgression be preceded under such conditions by a counterfounding whose author is the philosopher himself? As Rousseau, Hegel, and Nietzsche, for example, advanced political counterprojects in answer to the existence of the bourgeois and won over to philosophy the most gifted among their readers and listeners by giving their dissatisfaction with the prevailing situation a new orientation? Strauss neither attempted a founding that claimed the authority of revelation – of one of the competing traditions of revelation – after Alfarabi's or Maimonides' example, nor could bring himself to propose a political counterproject. All historical presuppositions were lacking for the former; the political experiences that the earlier counterprojects had brought about spoke against the latter. For Rousseau, Hegel, and Nietzsche had not stopped the process that led to the "philosophy of culture" or to "postmodernity," but on the contrary,

9 Cf. "The History of Philosophy and the Intention of the Philosopher: Reflections on Leo Strauss," 60, 66, and 72–73 below.

as far as the historical result is concerned, they had contributed to the intensification of that process. To say nothing of political reflections in the narrower sense. The decisive weakness of each and every political counterproject of excellence under the conditions of modernity was, incidentally, exposed by Rousseau in the penultimate chapter of *Du contrat social* in such a way that it can never be forgotten.

If a founding appeared to be ruled out for historical reasons, a historical founding could nevertheless be "repeated," that is, could be thought in its fundamental principles. That is precisely what Strauss undertook in *Philosophie und Gesetz*. Avicenna's statement that the treatment of prophecy and divine law is contained in Plato's *Laws* disclosed to Strauss a new access not only to the medieval philosophers Alfarabi, Avicenna, Averroes, and Maimonides but also to Plato. The sentence that Strauss came upon in 1929 or 1930 while reading Avicenna's *On the Divisions of the Rational Sciences,* and that more than four decades later he would use as the motto of his last book, his commentary on the *Laws* (the "most pious" and "most ironical of Plato's works"),[10] said nothing less than that long before the irruption of revealed religions in the world of philosophy, Plato had at his disposal the means that the philosophers of the Middle Ages needed and that the Platonic political philosophers used in order to meet the historical challenge with which they were confronted: that is to say, to understand it philosophically and to make the best of it politically for themselves and for their commonwealths. The Arabic philosophers and Maimonides followed Plato when they grasped the divine law, providence, and the prophet as objects of politics; they relied on the *Laws* when they treated the teaching of revelation, the doctrine of particular providence, and prophetology as parts of political science (and not at all of metaphysics); they moved in the politico-philosophical horizon of the *Republic* when they regarded the founding of the "perfect city" as the raison d'être of revelation. In this sense, Strauss can speak of our grasping in Plato the "unbelieving, philosophical grounding of faith in revelation in its origin." The endeavor to ground or to found faith in revelation distinguishes the rationalism of the Platonic political philosophers from modern rationalism, which was no less interested in a natural explanation, which endeavored no

10 *The Argument and the Action of Plato's "Laws"* (Chicago: University of Chicago Press, 1975), 1 and 2; "On Abravanel's Philosophical Tendency and Political Teaching" (1937), in *Gesammelte Schriften* 2, 198; cf. "The Spirit of Sparta or the Taste of Xenophon," *Social Research* 6 (1939), 530–32.

less to gain a philosophical understanding of faith in revelation, but which did not carry out the confrontation from the perspective of the founder.[11] In addition, unlike the theologico-political treatises of the seventeenth century, premodern rationalism begins the confrontation by focusing on the *nomos* or on the law in the original sense, on the comprehensive order of the commonwealth, an order that unites religion and politics and that, as religious, political, moral law, lays claim to the individual wholly, existentially. Premodern rationalism justifies the law so as to get beyond the law. If the philosophical justification of the law is the modus of understanding the law from the ground up as the politico-theological order of the commonwealth, then it is simultaneously the locus in which the question of the presuppositions and the right of the philosophical life is raised most acutely. For the Platonic political philosophers of the Middle Ages, justifying the law philosophically becomes the grounding of philosophy. In the guise of a historical recovery, *Philosophie und Gesetz* makes the theologico-political problem the object of a philosophical reflection that is focused completely on the matter at issue and thus tests the chances for knowledge that the turn away from "the premise, sanctioned by powerful prejudice, that a return to premodern philosophy is impossible,"[12] holds in store. The discovery of the sentence in Avicenna had opened a door for Strauss that was still firmly closed to him as he wrote his Spinoza book in 1925–28. It showed him a possibility of achieving a genuinely philosophical response to the challenge of historicism by returning to the history of philosophy.

Philosophie und Gesetz marks the beginning of a long series of theologico-political treatises with which Strauss pursues the opposite tendency of the treatises of the modern Enlightenment, and the "repetition" of the newly understood founding out of the spirit of the medieval Enlightenment is only one form that he chooses for his endeavor. Common to all the writings that follow upon *Philosophie und Gesetz*, however,

---

11 *Philosophie und Gesetz*, 65, in *Gesammelte Schriften* 2, 64; see also ibid., 49, 86, 118; *The Argument and the Action of Plato's "Laws,"* 7–11. Cf. *Thoughts on Machiavelli*, 288–90, 291–92; furthermore, my "The History of Philosophy and the Intention of the Philosopher," 60 below.

12 "Preface to Spinoza's Critique of Religion," in *Liberalism Ancient and Modern*, 257. I have elaborated the line of thought of this paragraph in the preface to the second volume of the *Gesammelte Schriften*, as well as in my "How Strauss Became Strauss," in Svetozar Minkov and Stéphane Douard, eds., *Enlightening Revolutions: Essays in Honor of Ralph Lerner* (Lanham, Md.: Lexington Books, 2005), chap. 21 (363–82). Additional references are provided in each.

is that in them, Strauss makes the theological and the political challenge theoretically as strong as he possibly can. Just as constant is the emphasis in them that he places on the insuperable opposition that exists between the philosophical life and its most powerful alternative, faith in revelation. Both – making the alternatives intellectually strong and the sharp emphasis on the most profound opposition – are intended to counteract the avoidance of the most important question. They are Strauss's answer to the "truly Napoleonic strategy" in which the Enlightenment strove for victory by marching past the seemingly impregnable fortress of orthodoxy in order to provide proof of its own power through the creation of a new world, trusting that the enemy's position would be historically "disposed of." For in Strauss's judgment, this strategy of evasion and bracketing made it possible, not coincidentally, for fantastic political hopes to arise and deep religious longings to take root in the midst of philosophy.[13] With his theologico-political enterprise, Strauss responds to a specific historical constellation: on the one hand, to the political danger that grew out of liberal culture; on the other, to the theoretical challenge that radical historicism represented. He writes his theologico-political treatises in direct confrontation with philosophy's oblivion of politics and of itself in the twentieth century. But he does not place those treatises at the service of a political project in the narrower sense. Unlike the theologico-political treatises of the seventeenth century, whose political intention was no longer adequately understood by the representatives of the moderate Enlightenment, Strauss's treatises, which pursue "exactly the opposite tendency" of those masterpieces of the radical Enlightenment of modernity, do not put philosophy to work for the purposes of politics; rather, they turn to politics for the sake of philosophy's self-reflection; their true addressees are neither the statesmen of the present nor the leaders of the revolution of the future; they make no attempt to draw persistently to themselves the attention of politically promising and ambitious readers by inspiring their political idealism or by feeding their will to rule; they do not elaborate a theory of politics, nor do they devise an image of the "perfect city" that would be capable of inducing identification and devotion; they do not promote, in a word, the political life as the writings of the

---

13 *Philosophie und Gesetz*, 21, in *Gesammelte Schriften* 2, 20; "Philosophy as Rigorous Science and Political Philosophy" (1971), in *Studies in Platonic Political Philosophy*, 33–34; "Note on the Plan of Nietzsche's *Beyond Good and Evil*," 181; "Existentialism" (1956), *Interpretation* 22 (1995), 315, 317–18.

political philosophers of the past did so emphatically at first glance. Having learned from historical experience, Strauss is not prepared to pay the price that Plato, Cicero, Marsilius of Padua, Machiavelli, Rousseau, Hegel, or Nietzsche were prepared to pay for their teachings of political founding and their projects of counterfounding.[14] Even Strauss's oft-cited "return" to Plato and Aristotle – alongside whom, not coincidentally, Xenophon and Aristophanes come to stand in his oeuvre – has nothing to do with the endeavor of a political restitution. To put it pointedly, the sole political endeavor, the sole political act of consequence, that Strauss brought himself to launch, after he had put the political activities and nationalistic aspirations of his early years behind him,[15] was to found a school, which the offer of a professorship in political philosophy at the University of Chicago in 1949 provided him the opportunity to do; and he was surely no less aware of the price he had to pay for making this political decision.[16]

Strauss's theologico-political enterprise is wholly in the service of self-examination and the justification of philosophy. His studies, his treatises, his commentaries, have as their preferred addressees readers who are able and willing to take upon themselves the effort of that self-examination and to make the task of that justification their own cause. The concentration on the question of the justification of the philosophical life is accompanied by the fact that other aspects of the theologico-political problem – the relationship between politics and religion in the well-ordered commonwealth, the protection and defense of philosophy, or the safeguarding of the bases for its future existence – fade into the background. And the preference for addressing philosophical readers, the turn to kindred natures, explains certain peculiarities of the emphasis and the rhetoric that are characteristic of Strauss's treatment of the theme. Two peculiarities will especially occupy us here: On the one hand, his persistent reference to the necessity of achieving a refutation of revelation, and his no less persistent reticence to spell out the possibilities of such a refutation. On the other hand, the predominant tendency, which grounds not only this conspicuous contrast, to

14 Cf. "Restatement on Xenophon's *Hiero*" (1954), in *On Tyranny: Revised and Enlarged Edition* (Glencoe, Ill.: Free Press, 1963), 220–21. See "The History of Philosophy and the Intention of the Philosopher," 60–61 below.
15 See the "Vorwort des Herausgebers zur zweiten Auflage," *Gesammelte Schriften* 1, xv–xx, as well as the "Vorwort des Herausgebers," *Gesammelte Schriften* 2, xxix, and "Why Political Philosophy?" 104–5 below.
16 Cf. his letter to Jacob Klein from July 12, 1949, in *Gesammelte Schriften* 3, 597.

heighten to the best of his ability the pressure for argumentation on the true addressees of his studies and to portray the intellectual situation of philosophy as extremely difficult and tense.

Let us begin with the second point. In order to counteract the avoidance of the most important question, the question of the right or the best life, Strauss not only makes the challenge posed by faith in revelation as strong as he possibly can. He also occasionally makes it stronger than it actually is, or (what amounts to the same thing) he allows the position of philosophy to appear weaker than it proves to be on closer examination. In a famous passage from the three famous paragraphs towards the end of the 1962 "Preface to Spinoza's Critique of Religion" in which he "summarizes" the results of the Spinoza book, a work he had finished in 1928, Strauss writes about the failure of the claim of Spinoza's *Ethica* to refute orthodoxy by means of a conclusive philosophical system: "Certain it is that Spinoza cannot legitimately deny the possibility of revelation." To this Strauss adds the general statement: "But to grant that revelation is possible means to grant that the philosophic account and the philosophic way of life are not necessarily, not evidently, the true account and the right way of life: philosophy, the quest for evident and necessary knowledge, rests itself on an unevident decision, on an act of the will, just as faith."[17] The three words "just as faith" seem to pass judgment on philosophy, to establish its inferiority to faith in revelation. For "just as faith" suggests – though Strauss explicitly does *not* say this – that what is at issue in the case of philosophy is a position of faith that, in comparison with the faith in revelation that philosophy opposes, has the weakness of not wanting to admit to itself that it, too, is faith. The faith of philosophy would thus distinguish itself from faith in revelation by a lack of probity. Let us set aside for a moment the question of what consequences it would have for philosophy if it were based on an act of the will and consider how the comparison looks from the perspective of the supposedly superior position of faith in revelation. Does faith rest for the believer on an unevident decision, or does he regard it as the work of him who is the truth? Can he be satisfied that faith in revelation originates from an act

---

17 "Preface to Spinoza's Critique of Religion," 255. In the original publication of the Preface, which organized the text in forty-two instead of fifty-four paragraphs, the "summary" of the earlier results is not found in the last three but in the last two paragraphs, which precede the concluding paragraph. There the passage reads somewhat differently: "an act of the will, just as faith does." *Spinoza's Critique of Religion*, 29. The definitive version strengthens the impression of the judgment that seems to be passed on philosophy.

of the will? Is he permitted to ascribe to himself faith as an achievement
of his own will? Or does he thereby fall prey to the temptation of pride?
Does the obedience to the God of revelation not require that one overcome the vice of pride and exercise the virtue of humility? Yet humility,
which finds its completion as the virtue of obedience in its not knowing
itself to be virtue, proves itself in attributing faith to the grace of God. If
humility commands the believer to believe that faith rests on an act of
the unfathomable will of God, the certainty of his faith must already be
a sign of pride. A faith that cannot know itself and a virtue whose true
mark of distinction is ignorance necessarily lead to a *circulus vitiosus*.
Its course is predelineated by the task of being obliged to distinguish
between faith and justice, humility and pride, one's own will and the will
of God, in order to preserve the purity of the heart or the good conscience. The problem around which the vicious circle revolves again
and again is the problem of probity and self-deception.

Strauss continues the cited statement after the three words "just as
faith" as follows: "Hence the antagonism between Spinoza and Judaism,
between unbelief and belief, is ultimately not theoretical, but moral."
What "ultimately" means is stated more precisely at the end of the third
paragraph of the "summary": "The last word and the ultimate justification of Spinoza's critique," we read there, "is the atheism from intellectual probity which overcomes orthodoxy radically by understanding it
radically, that is, without the polemical bitterness of the Enlightenment
and the equivocal reverence of romanticism." To this conclusion of the
"summary," translated by Strauss word for word from the introduction
to *Philosophie und Gesetz* from 1935, he adds a single new sentence in
1962 in which he culminates his critique of "atheism from intellectual
probity," and thus his critique of the ultimate result of the historical
development that the treatment of the theologico-political problem in
modern philosophy has brought about: "Yet this claim, however eloquently raised, cannot deceive one about the fact that its basis is an act
of will, of belief, and that being based on belief is fatal to any philosophy."[18] The antagonism between unbelief and belief has now turned
into an opposition in which belief confronts belief. Of Spinoza's philosophy, which had failed in its attempt to refute the possibility of revelation by means of a comprehensive system that would leave no room for
an unfathomable God, Strauss had said that it rests "on an unevident

18 "Preface to Spinoza's Critique of Religion," 256. See also *Philosophie und Gesetz,* 28, in
    Gesammelte Schriften 2, 26.

decision, an act of the will, just as faith," yet regarding that philosophy, he had also expressly spoken afterwards of "unbelief." By contrast, of the philosophy following Nietzsche, which no longer makes any serious effort to refute the possibility of revelation but instead rests satisfied with its cruelty towards itself and, out of probity, forbids itself belief,[19] he says that "its basis is an act of will, of belief." Whence the difference originates between the former philosophy, which rests on an "act of the will," and the latter philosophy, which is based on an "act of belief," Strauss makes quite clear in the final paragraph of the "summary": "A new kind of fortitude which forbids itself every flight from the horror of life into comforting delusion, which accepts the eloquent descriptions of 'the misery of man without God' as an additional proof of the goodness of its cause, reveals itself eventually as the ultimate and purest ground for the rebellion against revelation.... This final atheism with a good conscience, or with a bad conscience, is distinguished from the atheism at which the past shuddered by its conscientiousness. Compared not only with Epicureanism but with the unbelief of the age of Spinoza, it reveals itself as a descendant of biblical morality."[20] What distinguishes the philosophy of the age of Heidegger from the philosophy of earlier ages is its morality. What allows it to be based on belief are its unquestioned moral presuppositions. What constitutes its weakness in the face of faith in revelation is the insufficient confrontation with moral and political opinions not only that are determinative for its opponent but also by which it allows itself to be determined.[21]

---

19 Cf. "Preface to Spinoza's Critique of Religion," 235: "The controversy can easily degenerate into a race in which he wins who offers the smallest security and the greatest terror and regarding which it would not be difficult to guess who will be the winner. But just as an assertion does not become true because it is shown to be comforting, it does not become true because it is shown to be terrifying." See Friedrich Nietzsche, *Zur Genealogie der Moral*, in *Werke Kritische Gesamtausgabe* [= *KGW*], VI.2 (Berlin/New York: de Gruyter, 1967 ff.), III, aph. 27.

20 "Preface to Spinoza's Critique of Religion," 256. Compare *Philosophie und Gesetz*, 26–28, in *Gesammelte Schriften* 2, 25–26. On this point consider the preceding remarks: "And is not being based on belief, which is the pride of religion, a calamity for philosophy? Can the new thinking consistently reject or (what is the same thing) pass by revelation?" "The efforts of the new thinking to escape from the evidence of the biblical understanding of man, that is, from biblical morality, have failed. And, as we have learned from Nietzsche, biblical morality demands the biblical God." "Preface to Spinoza's Critique of Religion," 236 and 237.

21 Cf. "Preface to Spinoza's Critique of Religion," 236–37. Consider Martin Heidegger, "Phänomenologische Interpretationen zu Aristoteles" (1922), ed. Hans-Ulrich Lessing, *Dilthey-Jahrbuch* 6 (1989), 246 n. 2.

Let us return to our argument and consider another example of Strauss's tendency to heighten the pressure on philosophy by means of the contrasting strengthening of faith in revelation. "If philosophy cannot justify itself as a rational *necessity*" – we read in the lecture "Reason and Revelation," in which Strauss addresses the theologians from the Hartford Seminary and Karl Löwith in 1948, here with a formulation that goes farther than the previously cited passage from the 1962 Preface – "a life devoted to the quest for evident knowledge rests *itself* on an unevident assumption – but this confirms the thesis of faith that there is no possibility of *consistency*, of a *consistent life* without faith or belief in revelation."[22] What makes the life of faith in revelation a consistent life? Can it be regarded as consistent insofar as it surrenders itself without exception to divine guidance and obtains its inner unity from obedience to the One Sovereign Authority, by which it allows itself to be ruled completely? Yet, like every human life, the life that believes itself to be based on revelation necessarily requires human judgment, human insight, and human decision. It must therefore rely on human guidance, which would be interrupted or surmounted by the call or the invocation of God so that at best it could be regarded as a *mixtum compositum* of human and divine guidance. And obedience to God is, from the start, dependent upon the interpretation of his commandments and the reading of his will, such that the life of obedience remains a life in conflict, in discord over the right and the wrong interpretation, in the disunity between the speculations that one's own subjectivity and the demands that the different human authorities in their particular subjectivity seek to get out of the commandment and the will of God. Is the life of faith in revelation consistent, since it wants to be based only on faith and believes itself to be nothing but faith? Yet the life that would like to understand itself out of the truth of revelation and live up to this truth must claim for itself that it rests not on just any, but on true, faith. It cannot but distinguish true faith from frivolous arbitrariness or obstinate self-deception, on the one hand, from mere opinion or simple conjecture, on the other hand, and finally and above all, from the diverse temptations of false belief. The believer cannot be satisfied with only believing that he believes. Everything depends for him on his believing truly and his believing the truth. Or should the life of faith in revelation be called consistent solely because its incoherence is thoroughgoing and its irrationality is endemic to it? Because all objections

22 "Reason and Revelation," fol. N 4 recto.

of reason are only so many grounds for belief? Because for it, no abyss can be too deep to prove one's resolve to leap and no dogma too absurd to test the strength of faith against it? "For the absurd is precisely the object of faith and the only thing that can be believed."[23] The life of faith in revelation would find its true coherence and its ultimate security therefore in the *credo quia absurdum*, in a faith for which everything appears possible because it knows nothing to be necessary.[24]

When Strauss speaks of the thesis of faith that there is no possibility of leading a consistent life without faith in revelation, at issue for him is solely the consistency of philosophy. He considers faith insofar as it can be a challenge to the philosophical life. Revelation is of interest to him insofar as it is able to call him himself, his cause and his existence, into question. That explains the seeming "indifference towards the content of revelation" that struck a critic about Strauss early on. Whereas for the believer *everything* depends on the material determinations of revelation, for Strauss they, to cite our critic once more, "*do not much matter. Whether Jewish or Christian revelation is of concern makes no difference whatsoever.*"[25] In view of the fact that Judaism, Christianity, and Islam agree in their negation of the philosophical life, the dispute that the competing traditions of revelation carry out with one another over the truth of faith and that can, of course, be carried out only regarding content, only on the doctrinal plane, is of subordinate significance for Strauss. It is of no concern to him as a philosopher.[26]

The demand for consistency that Strauss makes on philosophy does not arise from a general ideal of a consistent life, whatever its unity,

23 Søren Kierkegaard, *Concluding Unscientific Postscript to "Philosophical Fragments"* (Princeton, N.J.: Princeton University Press, 1992), 211.
24 Cf. Tertullian, *De carne Christi*, V, Opera omnia (Paris: Migne, 1866), II, 805B–807B; also Leo Schestow, *Athen und Jerusalem* (Graz: Schmidt-Dengler, 1938), 38, 272–73, and 496.
25 Julius Guttmann, *Philosophie der Religion oder Philosophie des Gesetzes?* in *Proceedings of the Israel Academy of Sciences and Humanities* V, 6 (Jerusalem 1974), 27 (172); my emphasis. Guttmann's critique of *Philosophie und Gesetz* was written between 1940 and 1945 and was published more than two decades after his death. Cf. *Gesammelte Schriften* 3, 726, 727–28, 764, 765. What appears to the believer to be "indifference" proves on closer inspection to be a conscious dissociation and ultimately a rejection. The structural correspondences among the various traditions of revelation stand in the foreground regarding the challenge they mean for philosophy. An in-depth analysis of the content of revelation is imperative, however, if the philosopher is going to refute revelation.
26 Concerning Spinoza, Strauss asks: "Why does he take the side of Christianity in the conflict between Judaism and Christianity, *in a conflict of no concern to him as a philosopher?*" "Preface to Spinoza's Critique of Religion," 244 (my emphasis). Cf. "Eine Erinnerung an Lessing," *Gesammelte Schriften* 2, 607.

wholeness, and happiness might consist in. It aims at the rational justification of philosophy, or, in Strauss's words, at the justification of
philosophy as a rational necessity. What consequences would it have for
philosophy if it were to rest on an unevident assumption, an unevident
decision, or an act of the will? The answer to this question, to which
the two passages cited from "Reason and Revelation" and the "autobiographical preface" give rise, depends on what *to rest* means and *which
will* is under discussion. Is philosophy not sustained by the will that is
actualized again and again to follow the "natural desire for truth"[27] and
to give it a concrete form in time? Could the philosophical life ever gain
consistency were it not determined by the will to follow the path that
the philosophical eros grasps as its natural and necessary path, to follow
that path in spite of all oppositions, obstacles, and distractions, to follow
it farther, to follow it to the end? Can philosophy be thought at all as a
distinct, conscious way of life without an act of the will or decision that
makes a difference in the whole and makes one aware of this difference,
such that it can never be lost from view again? The act of decision or of
the will, on which philosophy may by no means rest if it is to justify its
necessity, does not concern that beginning or deep break to which the
philosophical life owes its conscious peculiarity. Rather, it designates
a starting point or resolve that is not obtained argumentatively, whose
rationality is never demonstrated, and that therefore remains groundless. As for the specific will that is in question in the confrontation with
revelation, two options especially concern us: the will to probity, on the
one hand, and the will to security, on the other.[28] Strauss showed in his
critique of "atheism from probity" that probity, or the self-satisfaction at
the moral merit that derives from renunciation, sacrifice, and the cruelty towards oneself, does not suffice for the justification of philosophy.
However important probity may otherwise be as a *means* for the successful execution of the philosophical investigation, however helpful it
may be as a driving and regulating *force* in the philosopher's uncom-
promising self-questioning, a philosophy that would want to base itself
on probity as "*the ultimate and purest ground*" would rest not only on an
act of the will but also on belief in the precise sense insofar as it is
based on biblical morality. And biblical morality demands, "as we have

27 *Philosophie und Gesetz*, 15, in *Gesammelte Schriften* 2, 14.
28 On the distinction of the will to probity and the will to security from the natural desire for
      truth or from the love of truth, cf. *Philosophie und Gesetz*, 15, 22–24, 26–27, in *Gesammelte
      Schriften* 2, 14, 21–23, 25.

learned from Nietzsche," the biblical God. But how about the will to security? Is it not beyond the moral biases of the will to probity and free of all biblical presuppositions? Does it not arise from the orientation towards the good, one's own good? The philosophers have good reason to keep their security in view when they are confronted with the claim of an unfathomable God, thus of a God who, unlike the God of natural theology, cannot be thought in analogy to the knowledge, insight, and magnanimity of the philosophers and imagined as their perfection, the claim of an inaccessible God who may damn error as sin and proscribe the natural quest for knowledge as disobedience and threaten it with eternal punishment. They pursue a legitimate interest when they develop conceptions and take precautions with the aim that "man be protected from the grip of the omnipotent God."[29] Yet they cannot achieve this aim if the protection consists merely of artifacts of their will. A world skillfully fabricated in the interest of security only feeds the illusion of security. By contrast, security can be attained in no other way than on the basis of truth. The will to security points, when properly understood, beyond itself. Like the will to probity, it must be governed by the desire for truth, by the quest for the truth. Philosophy must rule both, the will to security and the will to probity. It can rest neither on the one nor on the other.

Strauss sharpens the situation for philosophy still more not only by contesting the consistency of philosophy insofar as it rests on belief (the good conscience of probity), on an act of the will (the interest in security), or on an unevident assumption (such as Spinoza's postulates in the system of his *Ethica*), but also by ultimately calling into question whether the very quest for evident knowledge is an evident necessity in view of revelation. For faith in revelation denies precisely this: that *the* truth is accessible to the quest for evident knowledge, that it can be made visible to an impartial observer. The truth that decides the salvation of man is held to be bound not to the insight of reason and to sense perceptions but to piety, to the obedience of faith. Revelation negates the truth-criterion of philosophy. It challenges philosophy as radically as philosophy can be challenged. "If there is revelation," Strauss says in "Reason and Revelation," "philosophy becomes something infinitely unimportant – the *possibility* of revelation implies the *possible meaninglessness* of philosophy. If the possibility of revelation remains an open

---

29 "Preface to Spinoza's Critique of Religion," 237; *Philosophie und Gesetz*, 23, 26, in *Gesammelte Schriften* 2, 22, 25.

question, the *significance of philosophy* remains an open question. Therefore, philosophy stands and falls by the contention that philosophy is
the One Thing Needful, or the highest possibility of man. Philosophy
cannot claim less: it cannot afford being modest."[30] One can hardly
put it more clearly: If the choice of philosophy is not to rest on an
unevident decision, if its right and its necessity is to be rationally justified, the refutation of faith in revelation becomes the indispensable
task.

The restraint that Strauss imposed on himself in the public treatment
of the question of how this *officium* of philosophy is to be fulfilled has
resulted in the position being widely attributed to him that, in the face of
revelation, philosophy finds itself in a blind alley from which it can free
itself only by means of a decisionistic act. This attribution has to appear
all the more paradoxical as no philosopher denied with greater clarity
that a blind, unproven decision can ever be a sound foundation for the
philosophical life. Strauss not only allowed for the misleading impression that he holds a decisionistic position, but he even helped to nourish
it with a number of remarks that suggested a stalemate between philosophy and faith in revelation.[31] His rhetorical strategy can be characterized as follows: Political considerations[32] induce him if not to rouse then

---

30 "Reason and Revelation," fol. N 4 recto. Cf. *Persecution and the Art of Writing*, 107; "The
    Mutual Influence of Theology and Philosophy," 118.
31 *Inter multa alia:* "Philosophy is victorious as long as it limits itself to repelling the attack
    which theologians make on philosophy with the weapons of philosophy. But philoso-
    phy in its turn suffers a defeat as soon as it starts an offensive of its own, as soon as it
    tries to refute, not the necessarily inadequate proofs of revelation, but revelation itself."
    "Generally stated, I would say that all alleged refutations of revelation presuppose unbe-
    lief in revelation, and all alleged refutations of philosophy presuppose already faith in
    revelation. There seems to be no ground common to both, and therefore superior to
    both." "The Mutual Influence of Theology and Philosophy," 116, 117.
32 The political considerations need no further explanation so long as the central con-
    cerns of political philosophy are at stake: protection and defense of philosophy, on
    the one hand, the role ascribed to religion in a well-ordered commonwealth, on the
    other. That Strauss had the possible political consequences of his – seemingly merely
    historical – studies clearly in view is attested by his correspondence. Thus, he writes
    on February 16, 1938, in a letter to Jacob Klein of the discoveries that he made while
    studying Maimonides' *More Newuchim:* "If I let this bomb blow in a few years (should I
    live that long), a huge battle will flare up. Glatzer, who is now here, said to me that for
    Judaism Maimonides is more important than the Bible – thus if one deprives Judaism of
    Maimonides, one deprives it of its basis. (You understand Glatzer's remark: in a certain
    way, after all, Thomas Aquinas is more important to the Catholics than the N. T.) Thus,
    it will yield the interesting result that a merely historical observation – the observation
    that Maim. was *absolutely* not a Jew in his belief – is of extremely timely significance:
    the incompatibility in principle of philosophy and Judaism ('clearly' expressed in the

at least to support the opinion in the great majority of his readers that in the confrontation with faith in revelation, he takes a decisionistic stance, whereas he gives the philosophical addressees to understand through his insistence on the requirement of a rational justification that they may not rest satisfied with a decisionistic position. The notion of a blind alley or stalemate, the support of which prudence in political matters demands, is at the same time welcome to Strauss in view of the philosophical readers of his theologico-political treatises. For them, the stalemate harbors the demand to question further and to think for themselves; the blind alley contains the appeal to seek after paths that lead out of it. Strauss's oeuvre shows such paths, or it points to them, as we have seen, from afar and not infrequently by arguing *e contrario*. Although they interlock and interpenetrate variously, four approaches may be distinguished and characterized in an extremely abbreviated form.

The confrontation with the claim to knowledge by faith in revelation or the concentration on morality. Philosophy seeks to gain a common ground on which the confrontation with faith in revelation can be carried out concerning assertions that are accessible to examination. It finds that ground above all in the opinions that the believer expresses on morality and the central significance of morality, and it subjects to thorough scrutiny the knowledge that faith asserts in matters of morality and, in connection with them, about the voice of conscience or the call and presence of God. The means of Socratic dialectics, which proved successful in the scrutiny of the opinions about justice by exposing the internal contradictions and necessary presuppositions of those opinions, are

2d verse of Genesis) will be demonstrated *ad oculos*." *Gesammelte Schriften* 3, 549–50; cf. Strauss's letter from July 23, 1938, to Klein, ibid., 554. On May 20, 1949, Strauss writes in a letter to Julius Guttmann in Jerusalem: "But as far as Maimonides is concerned, there is a still more profound difficulty here. If my hunch is right, then Maimonides was a 'philosopher' in a far more radical sense than is usually assumed today and really was almost always assumed, or at least was said. Here the question arises immediately of the extent to which one may responsibly expound this possibility publicly – a question that certainly makes the problem of esotericism immediately a timely or, as one says these days, an 'existential' one. This was one of the reasons why I wanted to present the problem in principle of esotericism – or the problem of the relationship between thought and society – *in corpore vili*, thus with respect to some strategically favorable, non-Jewish object. I chose Xenophon, partly due to the connection with the problem of Socrates, partly because the assumption is that if *even* Xenophon, this seemingly harmless writer, then all the more.... The little writing [*On Tyranny*] is a preliminary study. At some point I should like to finish the interpretation of Xenophon's four Socratic writings." Leo Strauss Papers, Box 4, Folder 8.

crucial to this approach. Thus, it should be no surprise that Strauss's two late books, *Xenophon's Socratic Discourse* and *Xenophon's Socrates*,[33] are of particular significance to the confrontation in question.[34] He already provides a precise formulation of the starting point and the guiding thought, however, in the notes to "Reason and Revelation": "Faith as faith *must* make assertions which can be *checked* by unbelievers – it *must* be based at *some* point on alleged or real *knowledge* – but that 'knowledge' is *necessarily* only *alleged* knowledge, owing to the *basic* fallacy, of faith, the attribution of *absolute* importance to *morality* (the pure heart)."[35]

The determination of the limits of what is possible or the concentration on security. Philosophy shows on which assumptions the articles of faith in revelation – the creation of the world, an omnipotent God as lawgiver, lord of history, and guarantor of justice, the power of miracles and providence – are possible. It demonstrates *what* must be presupposed in order to defend the possibility of revelation, therefore what the security of faith in revelation depends on, the security with respect to which all human security is said to shatter and to pale. It provides faith in revelation with the concepts faith needs in order to attain its theoretical strength: the *creatio ex nihilo*, without which the omnipotence of God cannot be thought, and the unfathomability of God's will, without which the omnipotence and omniscience, the goodness and justice of God, are not compatible with one another. Philosophy determines the price that must be paid if unfathomability is to reconcile all the contradictions in the divine attributes, if God is not to be bound to any intelligible necessity, if he is to be the lord of everything. The multiplicity of the questions in which the whole is articulated for us collapses into one question, and we see ourselves faced with one single question mark.[36]

The explanation of revelation or the concentration on politics. Philosophy grasps revelation as a work of reason, as an attempt to solve the problem of human life, or, more precisely, as a possibility of answering the

---

33 *Xenophon's Socratic Discourse: An Interpretation of the "Oeconomicus"* (Ithaca, N.Y.: Cornell University Press, 1970); *Xenophon's Socrates* (Ithaca, N.Y.: Cornell University Press, 1972); cf. Strauss's letters to Gershom Scholem from September 6, 1972, and November 17, 1972, in *Gesammelte Schriften* 3, 762, 764–65.

34 See the pathbreaking essay by Christopher Bruell, "Strauss on Xenophon's Socrates," *Political Science Reviewer* 14 (1984), 263–318.

35 "Reason and Revelation," fol. N 5 recto. Cf. *Natural Right and History*, 75–78; "Jerusalem and Athens," 154, 155, 161–62.

36 "Jerusalem and Athens," 162. Cf. my *The Lesson of Carl Schmitt: Four Chapters on the Distinction between Political Theology and Political Philosophy*, trans. Marcus Brainard (Chicago: University of Chicago Press, 1998), 11, 86–95.

political question of social life in the commonwealth. It explains revelation by founding it philosophically, or by reconstructing the development of faith in revelation historically. The starting point for the philosophical founding, as well as for the historical reconstruction, is the concept of divine law. Strauss, who dealt first in *Philosophie und Gesetz* and finally in *The Argument and the Action of Plato's "Laws"* with the philosophical founding of revelation, outlines in "Reason and Revelation" a genealogy of revelation. "The task of the philosopher," we read there concerning the explanation of revelation, "is to understand how the original (mythical) idea of the *theios nomos* is modified by the radical understanding of the moral implication and thus transformed into the idea of revelation." Strauss then goes on to develop the logic of this transformation in eleven steps, from man's need for laws to the incarnation of God.[37]

The concentration on the question: quid sit deus? Philosophy reflects – in view of the demands, assertions, hopes, expectations of revealed religions – on the question that is coeval with philosophy: *quid sit deus?* It asks what kind of god the God of faith in revelation is, the God who is held to safeguard steadfast justice, to guarantee unshakable security, the God who is held to be owed unlimited obedience, to whom one is to turn with undivided love, the God who gives and receives this love, as well as that obedience, as a gift of his grace. In asking its question about kind or species, philosophy is led by the knowledge that it gains in the analysis of the political life and that it can test ever anew by the experiences of political life: in the study of the different forms of government, the qualities and interests of the lawgivers, their virtues and their passions, the connection between protection and obedience, the relationship between mastery and servitude, and so on. And in the end it will, due to the more precise determination of the *quid* its question is asking after, make clear to itself *what* it is able to grasp and to recognize as God.[38]

In Strauss's theologico-political oeuvre, the interpretation of Aristophanes' comedies that appeared in 1966 under the title *Socrates and*

---

37 "Reason and Revelation," fol. 9 verso–fol. 10 verso; cf. "The Mutual Influence of Theology and Philosophy," 116.
38 "Jerusalem and Athens," 162; "The Mutual Influence of Theology and Philosophy," 113; *The City and Man* (Chicago: Rand McNally, 1964), 241; *Thoughts on Machiavelli*, 148, 152, 186–89, 198–99, 207–8, 209–11, 214–15, 218–19, 244; "Progress or Return?" (1952), *Modern Judaism* 1 (1981), 43; *The Argument and the Action of Plato's "Laws,"* 27–31; *Natural Right and History*, 122–24.

THE THEOLOGICO-POLITICAL PROBLEM

Aristophanes occupies a special place. Next to *Thoughts on Machiavelli,* the most carefully written treatise on revealed religion, *Socrates and Aristophanes* is the longest and most astonishing of his books.[39] In it, Strauss makes audible the theologico-political critique that Aristophanes brings to bear against the pre-Socratic Socrates. In this way, he shows with a clarity achieved nowhere else the extent to which the Socratic turn to political philosophy, on which the writings of Plato and Xenophon focus, is a response to that critique.[40] The book as a whole revolves around the question *quid sit deus?* that the comic poet does not voice but nevertheless raises and treats with his means.[41] Strauss toyed with the idea of using as the motto for *Socrates and Aristophanes* a passage from Calvin's *Institutio christianae religionis,* whose interdict against the question *quid sit deus?* Strauss had paraphrased more than three decades earlier in *Die Religionskritik Spinozas,* and in fact, as he judged in retrospect in a letter to Seth Benardete, "en pleine ignorance de la chose."[42] I do not know what moved Strauss not to use the motto in the end. Nor do I know how he himself would have determined the specific

39 On May 29, 1962, Strauss writes to Alexandre Kojève: "I am preparing for publication three lectures on the city and man, dealing with the *Politics,* the *Republic* and Thucydides. Only after these things have been finished will I be able to begin with *my real work, an interpretation of Aristophanes.*" *On Tyranny: Revised and Expanded Edition, Including the Strauss–Kojève Correspondence,* ed. Victor Gourevitch and Michael S. Roth (Chicago: University of Chicago Press, 2000), 309 (my emphasis).

40 *Socrates and Aristophanes* (New York: Basic Books, 1966), 4–5, 8, 16, 19, 22–23, 32, 46, 48, 49, 51, 64, 67, 77, 102, 173, 311, 313–14.

41 *Socrates and Aristophanes,* 18, 21, 23, 25, 33, 44, 53, 83, 143, 234, 245, 296, 313.

42 "I believe that I should introduce an observation which is apparently very trivial by a broader reflection. Many years ago I was struck by the fact that Glaucon while wholly unprepared for the doctrine of ideas, accepted it almost immediately. A clue is offered by his reference to Momos. In brief, he is prepared for the ideas by the gods (a certain kind of gods, the gods who have no proper name proper). Everyone knows that Nike was present at Marathon, Salamis etc., that she is the same whether sculptured by x or y, worshipped in a or b etc. (cf. the reference in the Republic to the statue they are making of the just man). In other words the ideas replace the gods. In order to do that the gods must be a prefiguration of the ideas. But since the doctrine of ideas is not simply a myth, that doctrine must contain an answer to the question 'what is a god'. From this I jump to the further conclusion that the primary and most important application of the question 'what is' is the question 'what is a god'. Needless to say this question is equipollent to the question 'what is man'. This conceit supplies the key to Aristophanes and to many more things. There is a very clear remark on this subject in Calvin's Institutio which I have summarized en pleine ignorance de la chose in the first two pages of my chapter on Calvin in my German book on Spinoza: I plan to use the key sentence of Calvin as a motto to my book on Aristophanes." Letter to Seth Benardete from May 17, 1961, in my possession. See *Die Religionskritik Spinozas,* in *Gesammelte Schriften* 1, 248–50. Cf. *The Lesson of Carl Schmitt,* 87 n. 54.

ignorance on which his early writing was based. Yet does not everything speak for Strauss's having been enabled by his lifelong confrontation with the theologico-political problem to understand better what philosophy owes its enemies, or what the "good in the evil" is?[43] Does philosophy not become a special and conscious way of life solely insofar as it must assert itself against an authoritative objection? Does Calvin's or Luther's *No* to the *quid sit deus?* not draw our attention to the central question? Does it not hit the right target?[44] And, speaking in view of the present, are there not more important things to learn at the frontiers where philosophy is negated than within the new *juste milieu* in which, for the time being, the slogan holds: "Anything goes"? Calvin's critique of curiosity in the name of the obedience of faith and the critique of the disregard of the political and religious conditions of the commonwealth with which Aristophanes confronts his friend Socrates converge – this much can be said with certainty – insofar as they give the philosopher reason to engage in self-examination and consequently to seek self-knowledge. Yet nothing gives him more reason to engage in self-examination, nothing is a greater challenge to his self-knowledge, than the God of revelation.

43 Cf. Plato, *Republic* 373e, 379e.
44 Consider Luther's treatment of the *quid sit deus?* according to which raising this question inevitably sets one on a path that must end in nothingness. For the details on this, see *The Lesson of Carl Schmitt,* 86–88. Cf. Strauss's letter to Gershom Scholem from November 22, 1960, in *Gesammelte Schriften* 3, 743.

ON THE GENEALOGY OF FAITH
IN REVELATION

In the middle of his philosophical life, at the height of a renewed and deepened confrontation with the theologico-political problem, one conducted more penetratingly than ever before, Strauss sketched a genealogy of faith in revelation. The sketch is unique in his oeuvre. It is part of the fruits of a "shipwreck" as a result of which Strauss saw himself compelled in the summer of 1946 "to begin once more from the beginning."[1] His renewed reflections found lucid expression in a manuscript that he wrote around the end of 1947 for the lecture "Reason and Revelation" and in notes from the same year on which he drew for the lecture, presented at the Hartford Theological Seminary. The manuscript,

---

1 On August 15, 1946, Strauss writes in a letter to Karl Löwith that he has "once again suffered shipwreck" and sees himself compelled "to begin once more from the beginning." *Gesammelte Schriften* 3, 660. That the "shipwreck" concerned the confrontation with faith in revelation becomes clear from notes that Strauss wrote – before and after the letter to Löwith – likewise in August 1946. (See the beginning of the letter to Löwith from August 20, 1946, ibid., 666.) The earliest document of the "shipwreck" is dated August 11, 1946. The note, which Strauss writes in German, provides an important clue as to what gave rise to the crisis. Since it sheds sudden light on the attitude and the spirit in which he began his renewed reflections, we cite the beginning of the note here in full in English translation: "8–11–46 / I herewith strike out everything I have done so far – I must *really* begin from the *very* beginning. / I must once again get clear on what the real question is – and I have to change my working plans accordingly (to the extent that I am not bound by promises – courses). / Thus far I have assumed that the account of the original concept of philosophy (including the critique sketched of the modern concept of philosophy) could suffice, since for me the right and the necessity of philosophy was certain. Impressed by Kierkegaard and recalling my earlier doubts, I must raise the question once again and as sharply as possible whether the right and the necessity of philosophy are completely evident. / Since this is the case, much more important than the topic 'Socrates' and 'Introduction to pol[itical] philos[ophy]' becomes – *Philosophy and The Law* or (perhaps) *Philosophy or The divine guidance.*" Leo Strauss Papers, Box 11, Folder 11.

insofar as it is completed, culminates in the genealogical sketch. This sketch concludes an astonishingly open dialogue to which Strauss has the lecture lead: In the eighth and final section entitled "Revelation cannot refute philosophy," in an immediate clash of argument and counterargument, Strauss subjects philosophy to the objections of theology, which he answers for philosophy. Altogether he voices seven theological arguments, whereby arguments 3, 4–5, and 6 are dealt with in an explicit dialogue between "the theologian" and "the philosopher." At the center of the dialogue stands the laconically formulated double objection:

> *The theologian:* philosophy is self-deification; philosophy has its root in *pride.*
> *The philosopher:* if we understand by God the most perfect being that is a *person,* there are no gods but the philosophers (Sophist in princ: θεός τις ἐλεγκτικός). Poor gods? Indeed, measured by imaginary standards. – As to "pride," who is more proud, he who says that *his* personal fate is of concern to *the* cause of the universe, or he who humbly admits that his fate is of no concern whatever to anyone but to himself and his few friends.[2]

The dialogical discussion concerns six theological arguments: (1) The life of man without God, without the God of revelation, is miserable. (2) The philosophers are blind to the fact, and the power, of sin. (3) It is inconsistent of the philosopher not to admit the validity and indispensability of the strictest moral demands, since the love of truth to which he lays claim requires radical self-denial and thus a strict morality. (4) Philosophy is self-deification. (5) Philosophy has its root in pride. (6) The understanding that philosophers have of man is superficial: they are not able to fathom his depths, his despair, what is hidden in his craving for distraction and in the mood of boredom, which discloses more of man's reality than all his rational activities.

---

2 "Reason and Revelation," fol. 9 recto. The most laconic objection in the dialogue actually contains, as the crosswise articulation of the retort makes clear, two objections. For the theologian they coincide because for him, the question of God is essentially a morally determined question, the relationship to God being ultimately a relationship of obedience or disobedience. The philosopher divides what the theologian combines in one objection (merely interrupted by a semicolon) into two arguments (separated by a period and a dash). The philosopher distinguishes between person and cause, the political-moral from the cosmological aspect, which the theologian combines in the one creator- and lawgiver-God.

Under the subheading "Philosophy cannot explain revelation – ?"[3] Strauss begins anew in order to present the seventh and concluding argument: "Perhaps the most impressive theological argument is taken from the insufficiency of the philosophic *explanation* of the belief in revelation." From the theologian's perspective, the decisive deficiency of the philosophical explanation consists in its inability to do justice to the uniqueness or the radical historicity of revelation: "Philosophy *must* interpret revelation as a *myth*. I.e. it must overlook the essential *difference* between myth and revelation." The difference between myth and revelation that Strauss elucidates by means of four comparisons can, on closer inspection, be traced back to the fact that revelation, in contrast to myth, does not seem to have any connection to nature: Unlike myth, it knows no species of gods but only the one omnipotent God, no impersonal fate that controls the gods but only the actions of God, no recurring phenomena but only absolutely unique, unrepeatable events, and, in contrast to myth, which has no distinct relation to historical events, revelation has an essential relation to historical events (the role of history in the Old Testament, "Crucified under Pontius Pilate"). If willfulness, decision, and historicity take the place of regularity, necessity, and intelligibility – where would philosophical explanation find its starting point? And what would that explanation achieve?

Yet the four points of comparison that Strauss brings into play in taking up the theological objection neither exhaust the difference between myth and revelation nor sufficiently determine the points of contrast and those held in common within the myth–revelation–philosophy triangle: "the philosopher would admit the essential difference between the Bible and myth: the Bible presupposes, just as philosophy itself, the realization of the *problem* of myth." Philosophy and revelation are connected by the fact that each in its own way insists on truth contrary to myth. On the other hand, myth and revelation belong together insofar as the critical-skeptical spirit has no predominance for them. Whereas what is common to myth and philosophy is that morality possesses no predominance for them. These delimitations and classifications, which are made in only a few strokes, are enough for Strauss to show that the

3 "Reason and Revelation," fol. 9 verso. All the quotations that follow without more precise reference are taken from the section entitled "Philosophy cannot explain revelation – ?" and may be found on pages fol. 9 verso, 10 recto, and 10 verso. The subtitle of this section initially read: "Philosophy cannot refute revelation – ?" Later Strauss replaces *refute* with *explain*. Is the *explanation* of revelation a necessary prerequisite for the *refutation* of revelation? Or can the *explanation* take the place of the *refutation*?

philosophical explanation of revelation is by no means forced to pass over the "essential difference between myth and revelation," but, on the contrary, is able to take account of the difference if it knows how to begin correctly. The success of the attempt at explanation depends, on the one hand, on philosophy's directing its attention to the distinction that separates revelation from both myth and philosophy: "The starting-point of philosophic explanation of *revelation* would therefore be the fact that the foundation of belief in revelation is the belief in the central importance of morality." On the other hand, the success of the undertaking requires that precisely that difference between myth and revelation on which the theological objection focuses, that the uniqueness of revelation, its radical historicity, the negated bond with nature, be made the object of the explanation. The philosophical explanation of revelation requires, in other words, that the gulf separating myth and revelation be closed by means of a genealogical reconstruction that is oriented towards morality, or that the transition from nature to historicity, the derivation of the asserted singularity from intelligible necessity, be achieved.

The position of the genealogy of revelation in the dialogue of "Reason and Revelation" is thus specified. That Strauss treats what is "perhaps the most impressive theological argument" in a special part and more thoroughly than the six preceding arguments taken together, that in this case he does not leave the answer to "the philosopher," that, as we shall soon see, he instead first formulates as "the task of the philosopher" what a philosophical explanation would have to achieve and outlines an attempt of his own to fulfill this task – all of this underscores the weight that he accords the explanation of faith in revelation within the confrontation between philosophy and revelation. If the explanation were sufficient, philosophy would demonstrate its superiority not only in the determination of the limits of what is possible. Philosophy would prove at the same time to be the judge of the articulation of revelation in human reality. The genealogical sketch reads as follows:

> The task of the philosopher is to understand how the original (mythical) idea of the θεῖος νόμος is modified by the radical understanding of the moral implication and thus transformed into the idea of revelation.
>
> 1) Need of man → society, or else sociability was irreducible: need for *law.*
> 2) [need] for *good* law: original criterion for goodness: ancestral.
>   Rational basis: a) tested things, b) concern with stability.

3) the law depends on the ancestors = the *father* or fathers, *the* source of one's being, loving (beneficent) and demanding obedience (cf. Fustel de Coulanges).

4) absolute superiority of the ancestors: superhuman[4] beings, *divine* beings – *divine law*: the first things, the sources of our being are *gods*.

5) contradiction between various divine laws: only *one* divine law.

6) *full* obedience to the law: the law must be the source of *all* blessings → the god must be *omnipotent* → there can be only *one* God – Maker, Creator ≠ Generator.

7) *full* obedience to the law: obedience not merely a duty to be fulfilled in order to get something *else* as reward: full obedience is *love* of the one God with all one's heart, all one's soul and all one's power.

8) *full* obedience to the law: no human relation is left to irresponsible arbitrariness → love of *all* men. God is the father of all men, and all men are brothers. בצלם אלהים [in the image of God – Gen. 1:27].

9) *full* obedience to the law: not only external actions, but the right *intention*: purity of the heart (loving God with *all* one's heart) – impossibility for man of achieving this: *sin*: need for *mercy*: the loving God forgiving sin more important than God as Judge.

10) full obedience to the law: rejection of ὕβρις, self-assertion in *any* sense: critique of cities, arts, kings – *especially* of science which is *the* vehicle of human self-assertion.
A unique final revelation which has taken place in the past is *the* correlative of absolute obedience, absolute surrender.
No science: no universals – goodness a derivative from a *particular, individual* phenomenon (goodness = being Christian, Jew . . .). *The* guidance is not knowledge of universals, but the record of the deeds of the mysterious God.

11) full obedience to the law: the *required* law must be the *gift* of God: *God* must purify our heart, if our heart is to be pure – *God* must open our lips if our mouth is to proclaim His praise. God must communicate *Himself* to man → He must come *close* to him: Incarnation.[5]

The label "genealogical sketch" is merely a rough characterization of what Strauss tackles at the end of "Reason and Revelation." It gives a first approximation of the thrust and the form of the text that will occupy us. It therefore must be stated more precisely. The task that he puts to the philosopher goes beyond a genealogical reconstruction. It consists in

---

4 Strauss first wrote *divine*, then changed it to *superhuman*.

5 "Reason and Revelation," fol. 10 recto/10 verso. Strauss grouped points 5 and 6 by means of a brace written alongside them. Either he wanted to emphasize their intimate connection or he intended to reduce the eleven steps of his genealogy to ten.

combining two ideas, two *eidê*, two kinds – the species of divine laws and
the species of divine revelations – with one another in such a way that
the sequence of their historical appearance can be not only followed
but also (through the demonstration of the logic on which the transformation of both ideas is based) *understood.* The programmatic statement
with which Strauss prefaces the outline makes it clear that the attempt
to achieve a true understanding goes in both directions, is aimed at
both species, moves between both ideas, illuminating, scrutinizing, and
clarifying the one in the light of the other. As we have seen, the philosophical explanation requires that the stretch of road that lies between
myth and revelation be traversed or bridged. But the explanation of revelation is not all there is to it, and when Strauss makes divine law one
focal point of his elliptical reflections, he does so not only with regard
to the other focal point. Divine revelation remains incomprehensible
if it is not linked with divine law. It remains a *factum brutum,* dumb and
in itself a matter of indifference, so long as no demand is derived from
it, so long as no claim is made to it as the authoritative source of commandments and prohibitions. The *theios nomos* is neither dumb nor in
any sense a matter of indifference, but is all demand. Wherever it finds
an ear, wherever obedience to its commandments and prohibitions is
enforced, it determines the order of the commonwealth and stamps
the life of the individual. The law, which combines politics and religion
within itself, requires and deserves the attention of the philosopher
not only in view of revelation. Before anyone and anything else, the law
claims to have knowledge of being.[6] The law answers the question of
what is right before philosophy is able to raise it, and at the same time it
answers the question of what something is: God or man, life and death,
war and peace, justice or wisdom. When the polytheistic idea of divine
law is modified – as a consequence of "the radical understanding of the
moral implication" (which urges one beyond that idea) – in such a way
that it is transformed into the monotheistic idea of revelation, then the
understanding of the genealogical results – or, put more precisely, of
the underlying logic of transformation – will serve the clarification of
the divine law in its original form no less than it will the explanation
of revelation.

6 See "On the Minos," in *Liberalism Ancient and Modern,* 67, 68, 73, as well as Seth Benardete,
  Plato's "Laws": The Discovery of Being (Chicago: University of Chicago Press, 2000), esp.
  the opening chapter, "The Eidetic and the Genetic."

The natural beginning of a genealogical reconstruction is the needi-ness of man. His neediness refers him to other men. Being in need of others accounts for the requirement that one live in society, and living with others in society requires a law. The derivation of the law from the neediness of man does not presuppose that the need be anchored in the sociable nature of man. The derivation loses none of its conclusiveness if the genealogical undertaking digs back to an unsociable, solitary state of nature, such as Lucretius attempted in *De rerum natura* or Rousseau in the *Discours sur l'inégalité*. For even a genealogy that negates natural sociability reaches the point at which the neediness of man – however it may be explicated in detail given changed historical circumstances – makes the transition to the social state necessary and at which the need for law therefore becomes undeniable.

The first step of the sketch indicates that the fundamental principle from which the logic of the transformation of the two ideas starts out is the orientation towards the good. For their own good, men need a law, they need commandments and prohibitions, they cannot be without a limit having been set. For their own good, they need a good law and they strive for it, since, despite all the conflict over the question of what is good, men agree that they want the good for themselves. They find a foothold in the ancestral, in that with which they are most familiar and which is dearest to them. The primordial identification of the good as the ancestral has a rational core, "rational" in the sense of an orienta-tion towards the good. On the one hand, that which has been passed down by the ancestors has withstood the test of time and accumulated and absorbed the collective experiences of the commonwealth in which it proved itself. On the other hand, it promises stability, an interest that can be analyzed into two moments, an external and an internal aspect: The commonwealth preserves its identity by virtue of the special order and way of life prescribed by the ancestral law; it develops its own char-acter, it distinguishes and dissociates itself from others; in this way it perseveres in its being. Every alteration of the law, every instance of dis-regard for and every divergence from the ancestral, harbors the danger that the authority of the law will be undermined, that its contingency, its irrationality regarding its particulars, its arbitrariness will become apparent; doubt about its inviolability and the loss of its steadfastness, however, impair the efficacy of the law.

If the law depends on the ancestors, if it is traced back to the father or fathers, then it goes back to the source of one's own being. By way of the origin, which it has in common with my own being, it is bound up with my vital interest in my own good, for the father shares this interest as my generator. So long as the ancestral is taken into account as the criterion for the goodness of the law and the law is derived from the ancestors, the reference to one's own good continues to be preserved in principle in the foundational context of the law itself – no matter how relaxed or distantly imparted it may be. The linking of the law and my being in one cause or one author gives rise – insofar as it establishes the authority that answers the question in advance – to the question of the purpose or goal of my being. What am I made for? To whom do I owe thanks? What requirements must I fulfill? I encounter the father as the one who gave me being and is turned towards me in love, and who at the same time gives me the law and demands obedience from me.[7] But he does not give me the law in the same way that he gave me being. The lawgiver is maker, not generator. The one author is split into generator and maker. His conventional unity proves to be a natural duality.

So long as the authority of the ancestors can be placed in question, the authority of the law remains questionable. If the father is to be both generator and maker at the same time, on what would his superiority as lawgiver be based so that it would be able to justify his claim to obedience? And if he does not give the law but merely passes it on, wherein would the superiority be grounded of those from whom he received it in obedience? The question of the superiority of the ancestors that the recourse to the ancestral entails finds its answer in the postulate of superhuman ancestors. Only superhuman beings can give the law an inviolable and steadfast authority, one that binds men absolutely: the divine law requires divine beings. Not our first forefathers but rather the authors of our first forefathers are the authors of the law and our being. With the divine law, the fourth step gives us the gods.

The gods are an answer to the question of the superiority of the lawgiver, the first lawgiver, the lawgiver in the emphatic sense. But not even the gods are capable of giving the divine law inviolable and steadfast authority if the divine law is not one law. Striving for the good law, for the absolutely binding law, does not reach its end in the *theios nomos* so long as the *theios nomos* appears in the plural, so long as the commandments

---

7 Cf. Numa Denis Fustel de Coulanges, *La Cité antique. Étude sur le culte, le droit, les institutions de la Grèce et de Rome* (Paris: Hachette, 1864; 19th ed., 1905), "La religion domestique," 31–38, esp. 35; "L'autorité dans la famille," 92–103, esp. 93, 96–97; "La loi," 218–26, esp. 220–22.

of one divine law contradict those of another divine law and their prohibitions cannot be made to agree. If the divine laws are in conflict with one another, then so too are apparently their authors. If the authority of the divine law remains doubtful, the authority of the gods can be placed in doubt. Do the gods accord with the divine laws because the being of the gods is the cause of the laws, or do the divine laws accord with the gods because the laws are the cause of the being of the gods? Does the conflict of the divine laws and among the gods make a new ascent necessary on the model of the ascent from the human ancestors to the divine authors of the ancestors, to the gods as the cause of the law and our being? The ascent from the divine authors of the laws to the first things, which underlie the authors of the laws but give no laws? So that the cause of the laws and the cause of our being would no longer be one cause? Rather, laws and being become separated? The alternative is: There is only one divine law. The divine law has absolute authority, and it demands absolute obedience. Strauss always begins the subsequent steps of the reconstruction with the words "full obedience to the law." Each of the steps contributes to the development of what the demand of the one divine law involves. The one divine law tolerates no opposition and knows no counterpart, no other divine law that could contradict it, and no political, religious, or moral instance that would be fundamentally exempt from its rule. As a law by virtue of divine authority, it lays claim to full obedience – first of all, regarding its scope and its reach, or extensively: obedience that does not omit any sphere of life (otherwise man would remain the judge of the jurisdiction of the law) and that does not distinguish between center and periphery, between dispensable and indispensable commandments of the law (otherwise man would remain the judge of the binding force of the commandments of the law and of the importance or valence of its parts in view of his own good). For the sake of the good, man strives for a law that demands unqualified obedience, to which he must submit his particular interest in each individual case, to which he must cede the final decision about what is good for him. The law can demand obedience in all respects, however, only if the law is the source of all that is good for man. So that the law can become one law and the source of all blessings, the lawgiver must be an omnipotent God; a God to whom nothing is denied and to whom nothing remains concealed, who in the life to come and in this life is able to bind and absolve, who can work miracles, who is subject to no necessity; a God who tolerates no gods beside him; one God who is attentive to the works of his creation out

of the fullness of his sovereign power and not out of neediness, who
is not bound to them in love, who is maker and not generator. Once
again generator and maker are divided. Yet unlike in the case of the
father, the division does not result from placing the superiority of God
as maker in question. Rather, it is precisely his superiority as maker that
is not compatible with his neediness as generator. If he is not bound to
his creatures through a common being, the question arises as to why
he as the omnipotent lawgiver should be the source of all that is good
for them. Does he face his work as a poet faces his poetry? Is everything
that he creates through his word, that he commands to come into and
pass out of being, the expression of the wish to reveal his magnificence?
Is he bound to his creatures through the desire for glory? Is he in need
of glory from needy men?

The obedience that the divine law demands is full obedience in the
extensive and intensive sense: obedience in all respects, without exception and without distinction, and, in addition, complete obedience without reservation and without ulterior motive, obedience that does not
stop with the fulfillment of the law but that is devoted completely to
the divine lawgiver. The author of the law is not to be respected merely
for the sake of the good that comes from him; he must be loved for
his own sake. Eros, which can never be completely bound by the law,
never entirely subdued – it is the rival of the law as the source of all
that is good – must undergo a reorientation, the reorientation towards
the perfect being of the one God. As the love of God, full obedience
is self-forgetting devotion to the eternally beautiful. The orientation
towards the good, which determines the first six steps of the genealogy,
is outbid in the seventh step; that is, it is abandoned and superseded
by the orientation towards the beautiful, which satisfies itself, bears its
reward within itself, and is beyond all calculation and weighing. The
authority of the omnipotent God, which is demanded regarding the
good of man at the vertex of the sketch (6.2), becomes independent
the instant it is demanded, and in the splendor of its magnificence it
causes the good of man to appear paltry. That full obedience is the love
of God, and in fact, love with all one's heart, all one's soul, and all one's
power can be read in two ways: Obedience would be completed by being
able to command even love and in that way would manifest itself in the
unqualified love of God. Or: Perfect obedience would be possible only
if it were realized as absolute love. Only he who would unqualifiedly
love him who demands obedience could obey him completely, in a self-
forgetting way, "without remainder." And is not absolute obedience in

the form of absolute love the sole stance towards the omnipotent God that holds the hope of "requited love"?

Full obedience in the extensive sense, which encompasses every sphere and every relationship in human life, leads to the commandment to love all men. The duty of the universal love of mankind or the demand for universal justice corresponds to the one divine law that is valid for all men, and it corresponds to the one God who has created all men in like manner. The eighth step is immediately connected to points 6.1 and 5. Yet 7 is also taken up: If the omnipotent God is to be bound to man, if God is to be induced to "requite love," he must return as the father. The father as generator, however, founds a relationship of succession; he involves transformation and replacement, becoming in time. Hence, the father's love of his own in the generated can be demanded or courted only by appeal for that which is created by God as maker, which remains extrinsic to the perfect being of God. The transmission of the love of one's own in the generated to the made would bring together in God both determinations of the father from the third step – to be simultaneously loving (beneficent) and demanding obedience. But they are successfully brought together only by means of and in a metaphor. Neither *are* all men brothers nor *is* God their father.

Full obedience in the intensive sense, which demands that man love the omnipotent lawgiver with all his heart, reaches into man's innermost, most concealed, least fathomable being. External actions cannot satisfy it. It calls for the right intention. It insists on the purity of the heart. Man's incapability of such obedience and the inevitability of sin find expression in the believer's consciousness of sin. The judgment of faith that all men are sinners alludes to human nature as the obstacle to the fulfillment of obedience. If man is to disregard his own good and orient himself solely towards the beautiful, if he wants to abandon himself in order to allow himself to be determined completely by the commandment of the sovereign authority and to become perfectly aware of God, then he gets caught up in the circle of self-negation and the consciousness of sin, the circle in which for the sake of the purity of the heart humility must be secured against pride, virtue conceived of as grace, and obedience transformed into love. Sin calls for mercy. The God who has mercy on men and forgives them their sins becomes more important than the God who gives them the law and passes judgment on them. What in point 9.2 is presented as the necessary consequence of the paradoxical turn in point 7 can be gathered from the course of the reconstruction itself. Up to point 6.2, the authority of God as lawgiver and judge was the topic. From point 6.2 on, God's love is the problem. All lines lead up to, go back to, and meet in omnipotence.

The moral implications of the *theios nomos* come to light when the obedience that the one divine law, the *theios nomos* in its most powerful form, requires is more closely examined. Points 6 to 9 – the exactly worded openings "*full* obedience to the law:" underscore that they are intimately connected – explicate obedience in the most extensive (points 6 and 8) and the most intensive (points 7 and 9) forms thinkable. After the analysis of the obedience that corresponds to the divine law and of the consequences that this obedience brings about, the tenth step returns to the divine law itself. To the absolute obedience that the omnipotent God demands corresponds a divine law that is one not only synchronically but also diachronically, that excludes the plural not merely at the same time but also over time; one divine law for which there is no becoming, that knows no openness to new prophets as future lawgivers, that consequently is not subject to any relativization regarding its provisionality or outstrippability; one divine law that rests on a unique event, that owes its claim to validity solely to the authority of the divine lawgiver who decreed it historically, that remains inaccessible to knowledge, knowledge that is oriented towards the universally valid and is grounded in what is of necessity. For if obedience could be met or even replaced by a knowledge that serves the self-assertion of man, since it gives him his own footing and support, absolute obedience would no longer – or not yet – be at issue. To absolute obedience corresponds a unique, final revelation that took place in the past and in which the unfathomable God proclaimed his will as binding law or compelling commandment. Historical revelation is the perfect correlate of absolute obedience, the absolute surrender of the human will and of human reason (a surrender that is accompanied by the empowerment of the representatives, the interpreters, the administrators of the revelation of the past), since it is equivalent to the most radical negation of the ground of human self-assertion in knowledge. It denies that knowledge of the good is possible for man as man. The tenth step, which introduces historical revelation, and the fifth step, which introduces the one divine law – the two steps for which Strauss provides the longest and the shortest elucidations in the sketch – are bound together by the fact that they both, at first *ex silentio*, then *e contrario*, point to the fundamental alternative, which nowhere is called by its name: philosophy.

The need of man that stood at the beginning of the reconstruction also stands at its end. The insight that men need a law for their own good returns, is transformed, and is subsumed in the belief that the one divine law or the commandment that demands absolute obedience is a gift of God or a work of his grace. Once the demand for universal justice and unqualified love of God or self-forgetting devotion to the beautiful has brought about an ever greater distance from the good, once sin has shifted the mercy and forgiveness of God into the foreground, and once the historical revelation in its particularity and individuality has drawn all attention to the sovereign deed of God, faith in revelation shifts action completely to the side of God. Obedience is now fulfilled by transferring the burden of the obedience of man to the power of God. Not only the law must be his gift. Universal justice and unqualified love must flow from his grace. Purity of the heart must be caused by him. And even that men bestow on him the praise and honor they owe him must be thanks to his deed. The maker must take everything on himself through the free devotion to his creatures; he must take all their hardships upon himself; he must redeem the vessels of his glory. The infinite gulf that the omnipotence of God has torn open in the center of the reconstruction can be closed again only by virtue of the unfathomability of God. Only God can bridge the distance to man. Only he can find the way back to the neediness of man. God must love man. He must be maker and generator. He must reveal himself as lawgiver and as father. God must become man.

The philosopher knows how to explain faith in revelation insofar as he knows how to link revelation to the *theios nomos* and think both ideas himself, that is, insofar as he is able to trace them back to their underlying necessities and to grasp them in light of their developmental possibilities. That the philosopher is able to grasp the idea of the *theios nomos* and the idea of revelation in light of their developmental possibilities means, in other words, that he can determine their limits and understand their logic. His understanding is furthered by the fact that both the *theios nomos* and revelation point to philosophy. Philosophy is for both *the* alternative. It is inscribed in both as the way of life that they negate in themselves or in whose negation their contours become most sharply visible. But how, if we look back once again, do matters stand regarding the particular implementation of revelation, regarding its individual translation into the divine law by the human lawgiver? Is the philosopher able to explain that as well? Put more precisely: Are experiences of the kind the lawgiver claims for himself in order to justify his divine task not utterly inaccessible to the philosopher? So that he must assign the establishment of the divine law, insofar as he does not grasp it as the work of superior reason – as a rational act of wise lawgivers who saw themselves compelled to support the law by "having recourse to the intervention of heaven and honoring the gods with their own wisdom"[8] – to an entirely different human type? A type of which he could at best say "as the man so also his God,"[9] and regarding whose special, extraordinary experience he can only ascertain that it is denied to him or that he does not understand the divine wisdom that it reveals? There are, however, extraordinary experiences of *beatitudo* that are no less accessible to the philosopher than to that other human type – let us call him the prophet: The beautiful is suddenly disclosed and visible, the whole that was perceived only piecemeal and disparately lights up in a flash, insights converge and gain an undreamt of, unforeseeable, overwhelming radiance in whose light things are no longer as they seemed, and life can no longer remain as it was. The prophet will be absorbed in the devotion to the beautiful. He is remolded, transformed, and newly minted in his individuality. He knows himself to be a vessel of God and nothing more. He will trace the happiness of transcending his own limitedness, the subsumption of the particular in the universal, his losing himself in the whole; he will trace his experience of the "practice of dying and being dead" in awe and reverence back to the author of the whole. In his felicity he will become aware of his mission. He will place himself completely in the service of the sovereign authority and, with all the resources available to him, defend the order that it guarantees him and that he craves. The philosopher turns his gaze in the opposite direction. He relates the beautiful back to the good. In his felicity he becomes aware of his own activity. In his erotic nature he recognizes the strength that carries him beyond himself and the power that enables him to find himself again in the whole. The experience of the *beatitudo* confirms for him that the highest *eudaimonia* is bound up with the dialectic that determines and moves the highest activity. It encourages him to live the dialectical tension between the "practice of dying and being dead," on the one hand, and eros, on the other,[10] between

---

8 Jean-Jacques Rousseau, *Du contrat social* II, 7, *Oeuvres complètes* (Pléiade) [=*OCP*] (Paris: Gallimard, 1959 ff.), III, 383.

9 Johann Wolfgang von Goethe, *West-östlicher Divan. Besserem Verständniss. Israel in der Wüste*, ed. Hendrik Birus (Frankfurt a. M.: Deutscher Klassiker Verlag, 1994), 246.

10 Cf. Seth Benardete, *On Plato's "Symposium" – Über Platons "Symposion"* (Munich: Carl Friedrich von Siemens Foundation, 1994; 2d, rev. ed., 1999), 29–31. Reprinted in *The Argument of the Action: Essays on Greek Poetry and Philosophy*, ed. Ronna Burger and Michael Davis (Chicago: University of Chicago Press, 2000), 167.

the necessarily anonymous truth and its individual understanding,[11] between the devotion to the beautiful and the knowledge of our needy nature, which allows this devotion to be good for us. The "overlapping experience" of the prophet and the philosopher bifurcates and leads in opposite directions. But the wonder that is consummated in obedience is not closed from the start to the wonder that continues in questioning. It need not be denied to the philosopher to understand what is at stake when the prophet asserts for himself the experience of the call. Even this experience, even that to which Moses, Paul, or Mohammed lay claim, he can integrate in the comprehensive movement of reflection in which he takes up what he is not, what is opposed to him and is able to call him into question. The movement of reflection deepens the insight into the conditions of his existence and the presuppositions of his happiness, and this insight in turn drives the movement of reflection onward in such a way that he is in a position to think and to affirm in its necessity the fundamental alternative that negates the philosophical life without succumbing to or falling prey to that alternative in his thinking.

11 On this, see "The History of Philosophy and the Intention of the Philosopher," 71–73 below.

3

DEATH AS GOD
A Note on Martin Heidegger

At the end of his lecture "Reason and Revelation," immediately following the eleven steps of the genealogy of faith in revelation, Strauss considers three possible objections to his sketch. The first concerns the problem of the presence of God or the experience of the call. In that context, Heidegger's name comes into play in an unusual way. The problem of the presence and the call is not characteristic of the Bible, Strauss remarks succinctly. The phenomenon under consideration is not confined to the monotheistic faith in revelation. What is at issue, in other words, is not the experiences or the interpretations of experiences for which historical uniqueness is claimed – as it is for the revelation that took place in the past, for the divine law or the commandment that requires absolute obedience. Regarding the asserted presence of God or the call that people believe themselves to hear, what is at issue is not unique events that – if a link to nature is to be shown – first require a genealogical reconstruction or whose explanation makes necessary the demonstration of a logic of historical transformation. What, Strauss asks, was the presence of the god Asclepius in Athens, for example? Hallucination. Then he notes: "Cf. also C. F., Heidegger: God is death." Even if we add the surname to the initials "C. F." that was inadvertently left out and read the reference that Strauss wrote down for himself in the way we must read it: "Cf. also C. F. Meyer, Heidegger: God is death," it remains enigmatic at first. The mention of Heidegger in the same breath with the Swiss writer and the linking of both names in and with a statement that is meant to be authorized by both or to bear on both is surprising: God = death. If both indeed agree that death takes the place of God or that death becomes God, does Heidegger's thought give information about a remark made by Conrad Ferdinand Meyer, or does a remark of Meyer's shed light on the thought

45

of Martin Heidegger? What precisely does Strauss have his eye on with his note from the concluding objections and responses of "Reason and Revelation"?[1]

The matter at issue for Strauss becomes clearer if we turn to an obscure footnote he wrote fifteen years later for the preface to the English translation of his Spinoza book and published in 1965. The footnote looks far less obscure once we bring it together with the note from "Reason and Revelation." Like the line from 1947, footnote 23 of the famous "autobiographical preface" from 1962 mentions Heidegger and C. F. Meyer in one breath, but now in reverse order and with textual references; by contrast, the common denominator is not named: "Heidegger, *Sein und Zeit*, sect. 57. Consider C. F. Meyer's *Die Versuchung des Pescara.*" Conrad Ferdinand Meyer is meant to elucidate Heidegger. We are invited to consider § 57 of *Sein und Zeit* in light of the novella *Die Versuchung des Pescara.* Before we follow this invitation, let us pause for a moment to examine the text to which the footnote refers. The footnote comes at the end of a weighty paragraph, which – like the objection at the conclusion of "Reason and Revelation" – has the presence or the call of God as its theme. Strauss discusses the problem of the experience of God or the "absolute experience" on the example of Martin Buber's theses. Yet the confrontation leads far beyond Buber. Nor is it limited to the "absolute experience" that faith in revelation claims for itself.[2] In the latter half of the paragraph, Heidegger becomes the real interlocutor. Footnote 23 bears on the entire paragraph. In particular, however, it refers to the latter half or the last three sentences of the paragraph. The first of them reads: "Every assertion about the absolute experience which says more than that what is experienced is the Presence or the Call, is not the experiencer, is not flesh and blood, is the wholly other, is death or nothingness, is an 'image' or interpretation; that any one interpretation is the simply true interpretation is not known, but 'merely believed.' "[3] That Strauss not only brings Heidegger's analysis of the "call of conscience" to bear here against Buber's interpretation of the "absolute experience" but also introduces it into the confrontation with a critical intention towards Heidegger becomes clear from the careful choice of the individual terms and the arrangement

1 For the complete text that follows the genealogy and with which the lecture ends, see "Reason and Revelation," fol. 11 recto.
2 Cf. Strauss's letters to Gershom Scholem from November 22, 1960, February 26, 1973, and March 19, 1973, in *Gesammelte Schriften* 3, 743, 767, and 769.
3 "Preface to Spinoza's Critique of Religion," 235–36.

of the complex syntax: it is not without reason that "death or nothing-ness" appears as the *finis ultimus* in the series of assertions about the "absolute experience." But if death or nothingness, the vanishing point in Heidegger's analysis, is to be counted among the interpretations of the presence or the call, then the critique of Buber, or of an interpreta-tion based on faith in revelation of the "absolute experience," advanced in the last sentence of the paragraph, so it seems, with recourse to Hei-degger, is also to be applied to Heidegger's interpretation: "The very emphasis on the absolute experience as experience compels one to demand that it be made as clear as possible what the experience by itself conveys, that it not be tampered with, that it be carefully distin-guished from every interpretation of the experience, for the interpreta-tions may be suspected of being attempts to render bearable and harm-less the experienced which admittedly comes from without down upon man and is undesired, or to cover over man's radical unprotectedness, loneliness, and exposedness."[4] At this point, Strauss adds footnote 23: "Heidegger, *Sein und Zeit*, sect. 57. Cf. C. F. Meyer's *Die Versuchung des Pescara.*"

The section from *Sein und Zeit* that Strauss associates in 1962 with Conrad Ferdinand Meyer's novella had impressed the young Strauss. "Conscience as the Call of Care" received his special attention and appreciation, since Heidegger's analysis, as Strauss said in 1930, pro-mised to give access for the first time to an adequate understanding of the conscience and thus to an adequate interpretation of religion.[5] Three decades later, Strauss regarded the clarification of the conscience within the horizon of the natural possibilities of man as no less neces-sary or weighty.[6] But the will to probity, the new fortitude, the heroic resoluteness to subject oneself to what is most painful, the will that came to be determinative for the modern critique of religion and of which Strauss had still said approvingly in 1930 that with the interpretation of the call in *Sein und Zeit* he sees that will "reach its completion," this will had been subjected in the meantime to a far-reaching critique as the expression of a new belief, a belief in which philosophy relinquishes its ownmost strength and superiority. The critique of "atheism from probity" regarding its morality, in view of its devoutness, that Strauss

---

4 "Preface to Spinoza's Critique of Religion," 236.
5 See Strauss's letter to Gerhard Krüger from January 7, 1930, in *Gesammelte Schriften* 3, 380.
6 Cf. *Thoughts on Machiavelli*, 148–49, 193–96, 203–4.

brought in 1935 in the introduction to *Philosophie und Gesetz*, is taken up again, clarified, sharpened, and further developed in 1962 in the "autobiographical preface."[7]

In the development of the critique of the character of belief proper to atheism out of conscientiousness, the paragraph that footnote 23 concludes is accorded a key role. It starts with a concise diagnosis of the self-destructive logic that underlies the will to probity, understood as the cruelty towards oneself, when it takes charge and is to provide thinking with its ultimate orientation. Each step that, in obeying the commandment of cruelty towards oneself, leads one to deny oneself a wish, to take one's leave of a longing, to leave behind a security, results in a further step that calls for one to give up a new wish, to track down and negate a deeper longing, to attack a new security. So long as something continues to exist that is capable of being negated, the cruelty was presumably not cruel enough; the greatest terror apparently has still failed to materialize: "The controversy can easily degenerate into a race in which he wins who offers the smallest security and the greatest terror and regarding which it would not be difficult to guess who will be the winner. But just as an assertion does not become true because it is shown to be comforting, it does not become true because it is shown to be terrifying."[8] Once intellectual probity is emancipated from the love of truth, the good – or bad – conscience becomes the unappealable instance. The comfort taken in one's own resoluteness, fortitude, conscientiousness takes the place of binding knowledge. The point of the paragraph is that its end combines with its beginning and places before our eyes the most extreme possibility in which the logic of the absolutely posited commandment of cruelty towards oneself, "our last virtue," can be suspended, in which the "race" that obeys that commandment can be cut short or brought to a standstill. For that is precisely the result of the application of the critique of the interpretation based on faith in revelation of the "absolute experience" to Heidegger's interpretation of the call to which the latter half of the paragraph invites us: Heidegger's orientation towards "death or nothingness" as the unoutstrippable, all-decisive possibility of Being that each *Dasein* "enters into" is no less suited than the religious claim by the "wholly other" "to cover over

---

7 *Philosophie und Gesetz*, 22–28, in *Gesammelte Schriften* 2, 21–26; "Preface to Spinoza's Critique of Religion," 255–56 and 234–37. See "The Theologico-Political Problem," 14, 17–18, and 21–22, above.
8 "Preface to Spinoza's Critique of Religion," 235.

man's radical unprotectedness, loneliness, and exposedness," to whose defense, after all, that orientation seems to have devoted itself. How? Insofar as it provides an ultimate footing, gives a final meaning. Only man can die. Death as his "ownmost ability-to-be" is his indestructible distinction. In his resolute orientation towards death, man becomes aware of his uniqueness. In the anticipation of death his fortitude is tested, his life attains its seriousness, the weight of the "thou shalt" that wrests his life from comfort, taking things lightly, and shirking. The authority of death brings *Dasein* "into the simplicity of its fate." It thrusts *Dasein* into its "guilt," the guilt of man with respect to Being, which is not without him. Death claims man wholly; it commands him, fills him with angst, and elevates him; it makes him receptive to the call like a God.[9]

Strauss's critique of the character of belief proper to Heidegger's position does not concern a mere attunement (*Gestimmtheit*) – although this attunement by no means remains extrinsic to the character of belief. And it exceeds the critique of the belief rooted in groundlessness that is proper to a philosophy incapable of rationally demonstrating its right and necessity – though it is no coincidence that with that belief, a devoutness of another kind enters into philosophy that gives rise to new irrational expectations.[10] The reading of Meyer's *Die Versuchung des Pescara* to which footnote 23 invites us confirms and sheds light on the specific point that Strauss has his eye on in his confrontation with Heidegger's interpretation of the call. The hero of the novella that is set in Renaissance Italy during Charles V's reign, the emperor's supreme commander Pescara, voices what Strauss himself calls by name in none of his publications and nowhere makes the express object of critique. Pescara, who is held to be "godless," confesses: "I believe in a divinity, and truly not any imaginary one." His divinity is death: "A dark but wise divinity." The supreme commander, "who avoided setting foot on Christian ground," becomes so dominated and fulfilled by his god, once he has heard the call, that his face ultimately shows and says nothing but "piety and obedience." The piety and obedience to his god make Pescara inaccessible to the temptation to change sides, to cease being the emperor's supreme commander and the head of his Spanish

---

9 Martin Heidegger, *Sein und Zeit* (Halle a. d. S.: Niemeyer, 1927), § 49, pp. 247–48; § 50, pp. 250–51; § 51, pp. 252, 254; § 53, pp. 263, 264; § 57, pp. 275, 276; § 62, pp. 308, 310; § 63, p. 313; § 74, pp. 384, 386; § 75, p. 391.
10 Cf. "Why Political Philosophy?" 102 and 105.

troops and to join a league for the liberation of Italy from Spanish domination. Neither the emissary from the league, which the Duke of Milan forged with Venice, the Vatican, and France, nor Pescara's wife, the poet Victoria Colonna who is enthusiastic about Italy, are able to win the supreme commander over for their political objective, for the fight against tyranny, and for the independence of the Italian states (among which the kingdom of Naples was to be awarded to Pescara), an undertaking that would presuppose Pescara's betrayal of his worldly lord. "Italy talks in vain, it wastes its energy," Pescara replies to Victoria's patriotic appeal. "I have long known the temptation, I saw it coming and peak like an oncoming wave, and did not waver, not for a moment, not with the slightest thought. For I was not confronted with any choice, I did not belong to myself, I stood outside of things." And he adds the reason why he does not allow political considerations to touch him, what keeps him from at all pondering a decision that bears on his own good, why he keeps to the path he had once set out on, the moral stance that he has adopted, with unconditional resoluteness: "My divinity has quieted the storm all around my oars."[11]

Meyer is mentioned by Strauss once more. The name occurs again in a letter to Seth Benardete from January 1965, specifically in the context of a brief discussion of the question *ti esti theos:* "If one starts from the experience, one finds the Presence or the Call – the Wholly Other which is both terrible and gracious-graceful – one might say that wholly other is death (cf. C. F. Meyer, *Die Versuchung des Pescara*) or nothingness – but *experienced* not as such but as a being, preferably as a human being or rather as ἀνθρωποειδής. 'Timor fecit deos': fear belongs to the irascible – θυμός ($\neq$ ἐπιθυμία) necessarily 'personifies.' Yet one must add immediately: Amor (ἔρως τοῦ καλοῦ) fecit deos – a love which is not satisfied (rightly) with any actual καλόν because of its essential caducity."[12] In light of the double answer that Strauss outlines in a few strokes, one can say that the repeated reference to Heidegger/Meyer aims at an elementary experience to which each of the authors gives apt expression in his own way. The longing for security and justice on the one hand, for the beautiful on the other, makes the gods. In his genealogical reconstruction from 1947, Strauss had taken into account

11 Conrad Ferdinand Meyer, *Die Versuchung des Pescara. Novelle* (Leipzig: Haessel, 1887), 110, 122, 127, 163, 167, 169, 176, 182, 184 (towards the end of the third chapter, fourth chapter, and first half of fifth chapter).
12 Letter to Seth Benardete from January 22, 1965, in my possession.

both of the anthropological roots to which he has recourse in the letter to Benardete: *thymos* from the first step of the genealogy on and in the context of the explication of obedience to the omnipotent God of revelation in the eighth point with the demand for universal justice; *eros* in the seventh point with the devotion to the eternally beautiful.

Heidegger's interpretation of the call retains its importance and interest for the middle and later Strauss. But unlike for the early Strauss, what now stands in the foreground is not the potential of the interpretation insofar as it opens up a perspective on an adequate understanding of the phenomenon of belief so much as the potential of the phenomenon insofar as it emerges in Heidegger's interpretation and gains influence on his thought. The authority that Heidegger accords death has its counterpart in the primacy that his philosophy gives to praxis, in the call to authenticity and in the insistence on an ultimate certainty that is unshakeable. After the death of God, death takes the place of unchangeable Being or of that unfathomable power in the face of which all that is vain perishes, before which all that is groundless, all that is fragile breaks, against which all that is inauthentic wrecks. The kind of authority that Heidegger grants death is shown by a glance at Socrates, whose life in the unabated tension between eros and death Plato and Xenophon placed before our eyes as the philosophical life simply. Montaigne says of him that he regarded dying as a natural and morally indifferent event.[13] Nevertheless, or precisely for that reason, the death that Socrates died in Athens became the historical event that founded political philosophy.

---

13 "Il appartient à un seul Socrates d'accointer la mort d'un visage ordinaire, s'en apri-
    voiser et s'en jouer. Il ne cherche point de consolation hors de la chose; le mourir
    luy semble accident naturel et indifferent; il fiche là justement sa veuë, et s'y resoult,
    sans regarder ailleurs." Michel de Montaigne, *Essais* III, 4, *Œuvres complètes,* ed. Albert
    Thibaudet and Maurice Rat (Paris: Gallimard, 1962), 810.

II

THE HISTORY OF PHILOSOPHY AND THE INTENTION OF THE PHILOSOPHER

Reflections on Leo Strauss

Philosophy is the highest form of the mating of courage and moderation. In spite of its highness and nobility, it could appear as Sisyphean or ugly, when one contrasts its achievement with its goal. Yet it is necessarily accompanied, sustained and elevated by *eros*. It is graced with nature's grace.

– Leo Strauss, What Is Political Philosophy?

Leo Strauss occupies an exceptional position in the history of philosophy. No philosopher before him has made the history of philosophy the object of his study with a similar penetration and urgency, not to say exclusiveness, nor has anyone among those who have demonstrated a comparable power in confronting the thought of other philosophers engaged in this confrontation with Strauss's constant consideration of political philosophy. The question that Strauss seeks to answer with his historical interpretations explicitly reads "What is political philosophy?" and not "What is metaphysics?" But why does Strauss engage in a massive, wide-ranging historical research project, which extends from Heidegger via Machiavelli and Alfarabi to the pre-Socratics, in order to answer a question that in itself is by no means a historical one? For a reflection that stays on the surface of his oeuvre even for only a few moments, the central issue becomes the intention that the philosopher Strauss pursues when he turns his – so it seems – serious and undivided attention to the history of philosophy.

The historical starting point of Strauss's project of historical research and revision is the thesis held by radical historicism that all thinking, understanding, and action is historical, namely, that it has no other ground than groundless human decision or a dispensation of fate, and consequently the assertion that any possibility of understanding philosophers of the past exactly as they understood themselves has to remain denied to us. The position of radical historicism, which found its deepest expression in Heidegger's thought, became a continuing and decisive challenge for Strauss in two ways: On the one hand, as the keenest philosophical critique of the time that placed the idea of philosophy itself in question insofar as it denied the possibility of leaving the historical cave; on the other hand, as the most powerful prejudice of the time, which gained its pointed expression in the formula that everything that is essential is essentially historical. If, according to its original sense, philosophy is the ascent from opinion to knowledge, and if this ascent has to begin with the weightiest, the most influential, the least doubted opinions of the present, then the necessity of a thorough confrontation with historicism arose naturally for Strauss. Historicism had to be placed in question for the sake of philosophy; it had to be scrutinized unreservedly for the sake of the philosopher's knowledge of himself. In order to subject historicism to an appropriate scrutiny, however, historical investigations were indispensable. The demand for more precise historical studies is obvious if one wants to scrutinize the assertion that in the most important respect a philosopher's thought remains bound to the historical horizon to which it owes its genesis and that it therefore can always be understood only differently than it was by the philosophers of the past; and the demand for such studies is just as obvious in the case of the critical application of the historicist thesis to historicism itself, that is, the attempt to elucidate the historical presuppositions to which the so-called historical consciousness was tied in turn. The clarification of these presuppositions appeared to Strauss to be a task all the more urgent as the power of the "historical consciousness" showed in a particularly striking way the influence philosophy had gained, in the course of its history, on the perception of reality, the formation of the dominant weltanschauung, and the strengthening of prevailing opinion. In the case of radical historicism, it turned out that the thinking that considered itself able or obliged to exclude the possibility of leaving any historical cave on philosophical grounds decisively contributed to the hindrance of the ascent out of the contemporary cave, insofar as it made itself the mouthpiece for the most powerful conviction of the time.[1]

Historicism was the newest and a particularly important example, but nevertheless only *one* example, of the extent to which the teachings of philosophy or of modern science had in the meantime impregnated opinions and found their way into the beliefs of many. To give expression to the altered situation, in contrast to the initial conditions of the Platonic figure of the cave, Strauss in 1930–32 began speaking of a "second cave," which had to be imagined as lying below the Platonic cave.

---

1 *Natural Right and History,* 12 and 18–34; "Philosophy as Rigorous Science and Political Philosophy," 30–34; "Political Philosophy and History" (1949), in *What Is Political Philosophy?* (Glencoe, Ill.: Free Press, 1959), 57, 63–64, 67–68, 70, 72–73, 75, and 77.

The men of the present are said to find themselves in that lower-lying cave of increased mediation and artificiality and have first of all to work their way forward from this point to that other cave in which the ascent of the philosophers originally took place. Far from having come nearer to the light of the sun or having an advantage over the inhabitants of the ancient cave, the inhabitants of the new shaft, which has been driven into the depths with diligence and method, have to travel a stretch of road that has become considerably longer and more arduous if they are to come out into the open.[2] Accordingly, the equipment for the expedition, the tools and resources, and not least the provisions for the journey, had to be chosen. With the image of the second cave, Strauss illustrated the fact that the ascent required preparation, that philosophy required an altered introduction. The philosopher had to become a good historian if he wanted to become a true philosopher.

In this sense Strauss became a good historian. His historical investigations served the reconstruction of the process that had as its result the current situation of philosophers as well as nonphilosophers in the second cave. That is the context of Strauss's well-known studies on the

---

2 Strauss employs the figure of the "second cave" for the first time in print in his review of Julius Ebbinghaus's booklet *Über die Fortschritte der Metaphysik* (*Deutsche Literaturzeitung* 52 [December 27, 1931], col. 2453, in *Gesammelte Schriften* 2, 438–39): "The turn from admitted ignorance to book learning is not natural, as the position on book learning held by the classical teacher in the knowledge of ignorance proves; it is only to be understood on the basis of the peculiarity of the *presently* possible and necessary knowledge of ignorance. If it is true that 'those springing into the sea are themselves pulled into the abyss by the ballast of the rescue vessels which they picked up from the shore of the present' (p. 8), then the present has no possibility at all of engaging in natural, or as it is often called, 'systematic' philosophizing; then the actual ignorance in the present is not at all the natural ignorance with which philosophizing has to begin; then a long detour, a great effort, is first required in order to return at all to the state of natural ignorance. Taking up the classical account of the natural difficulties of philosophizing, the Platonic figure of the cave, one may say: we find ourselves today in a second, much deeper cave than those happy ignorant ones with whom Socrates was concerned; we therefore need history first of all in order to climb *up* into the cave from out of which Socrates can lead us into the light; we need a propaedeutic which the Greeks did not need, precisely that of book learning." In an autobiographical note stemming from the first half of the thirties, which can be found in Strauss's literary estate and in which he stresses five insights arising from the development of his thinking, the following is given as the fifth point: "The historical consciousness is linked to a certain historical situation; today we have to be historians because we do not have the means at our disposal to answer the real question properly: 'second cave.' 1930–1932." Leo Strauss Papers, Box 10, Folder 2. Cf. *Philosophie und Gesetz*, 14, in *Gesammelte Schriften* 2, 14; "Die geistige Lage der Gegenwart" (1932), in *Gesammelte Schriften* 2, 451–52 and 461; and "How to Study Spinoza's *Theologico-Political Treatise*" (1948), in *Persecution and the Art of Writing*, 155–56.

development of modern philosophy and on the break with classical philosophy brought about by the founding fathers of modernity. Two aspects of the modern project should be mentioned: the will to philosophy's becoming practical or to the transformation of nature and of human living conditions in general by means of philosophy and at the risk of it; then, the endeavor to establish philosophy as a new edifice from the ground up on a solid foundation that nothing and no one can shake, an edifice that by virtue of the specialization and cooperation of many in their work over the centuries permitted a continuous extension and perfection. It was not difficult to see that both impulses would mutually support and strengthen one another. The systematic conquest of nature and the rational reorganization of society required a type of knowledge that is reliable, is manageable, and keeps step with change. The progress of knowledge – were it to occur along a broad front by means of method, experiment, and public instruction – was in turn dependent upon the social conditions favorable for research, but particularly upon effective political protection. Both impulses seemed to point in the same direction: that of a prospering undertaking named "philosophy" or "science," which would find itself in harmony with the increasing prosperity of the commonwealth on the basis of an unprecedented development of technology and a growing control over nature. It is not necessary to retrace the lines in detail which led, for instance, from the concentration on the *verità effettuale della cosa*[3] to the demand *Hâtons-nous de rendre la philosophie populaire*,[4] or from the promise of *rendre nous comme maîtres et possesseurs de la nature*[5] to the vision of the *last men*, who say "we have invented happiness" and blink.[6] From these two aspects of the modern project – philosophy's becoming practical and its becoming progressive – the significance history had to have for philosophy becomes sufficiently clear. If philosophy pushes ahead the transformation of living conditions in general, if it becomes a public power that attempts to exert, and actually does exert, a sustained influence on politics, morality, and religion, then it places itself in a position of dependence upon the powers it desires to influence. It becomes a part of the process that it wants to control and thus, if it wants to become cognizant of its own situation, can no longer abstain

3 Niccolò Machiavelli, *Il Principe*, XV, ed. Bertelli, 65.
4 Denis Diderot, *Pensées sur l'interpretation de la nature*, XL; *Œuvres complètes* IX, 69.
5 René Descartes, *Discours de la méthode*, VI, ed. Gilson, 62; cf. 61, 63, 65, and 67.
6 Friedrich Nietzsche, *Also sprach Zarathustra*, Vorrede 5, *KGW* VI.1, 14.

from a historical reflection, a critical examination of the path traveled thus far.

Strauss's historical introduction to philosophy could not stop with the reconstruction of the modern development. Since the modern project had been conceived in a nonmodern horizon, the latter had to be regained in order to grasp modern philosophy's turn to becoming practical on the basis of its *principium* – its beginning and persistently effective principle. Besides, philosophy's becoming practical was not the sole path that led to the second cave outlined by Strauss. Another consisted in subordinating philosophy to the rule of an authority and using it for the greater glory of this authority. Thus in the Christian Middle Ages, it became an instrument in the service of faith: a path that all the more surely had to end in that cave below the Platonic one, since the faith that used philosophy for its own purposes and that adopted concepts, arguments, and insights from philosophy in order to strengthen its own doctrine made a universal claim, that is, proclaimed for its part an ascent that was supposed to transcend the particular opinions and the limitations of political communities. Philosophy's intimate association with a powerful tradition of obedience for more than a millennium decisively contributed to its being forgotten that philosophy, by its natural sense, is neither a tool nor a weapon but a way of life – and, in fact, a way of life whose raison d'être excludes its subordination to any authority.[7]

7 "The Mutual Influence of Theology and Philosophy," 113; *Persecution and the Art of Writing*, 21. In a letter to Gerhard Krüger dated November 17, 1932, Strauss writes: "That *we today* cannot do without history, that is a fact extrinsic to philosophizing; connected with this is the fact that (1) through the perverse interweaving of a *nomos*-tradition with a philosophical tradition, that is, of Biblical revelation with Greek philosophy, of a tradition of obedience with a 'tradition' of questioning that, insofar as it is traditional, is no longer a questioning, and (2) through the fight, to a certain extent led in the dark, against the tradition of revelation, we have been maneuvered into the second cave and today no longer have the *means* for natural philosophizing. We, too, are natural beings – but we live in an entirely unnatural situation." *Gesammelte Schriften* 3, 406. Near the end of a lecture, which he gave on February 6, 1932, on "The Spiritual Situation of the Present" ("Die geistige Lage der Gegenwart"), Strauss explains in reference to a statement made by Maimonides on the altered situation that is caused for philosophy by the tradition of revealed religions, hence prior to the politico-theological demands specific to the *Christian* tradition: "Thus it is not being accustomed to texts in general, not having grown up in a tradition in general [that increases the natural difficulties of philosophizing and that prevents man from recognizing the truth], but rather being accustomed to *completely specific* texts, having grown up in a tradition of a *completely specific* character: namely, in a tradition possessing *authority* as *absolute* as that of the *tradition of revealed religions*. The fact that a tradition based on revelation has come into the world of philosophy has

If one wants to understand sufficiently how philosophy became practical, one has to recognize the political decision in favor of the worldly sovereign that gave rise to the modern turn, and if one wants to understand what moved the founding fathers of modern philosophy to seek out an alliance with state authority, one has to take into account the enemy with whom they found themselves confronted. The instruments of power and the benevolent deeds they promised their allies through the modern project were the price they had to pay for the realization of their own purpose in the theologico-political confrontation: for the restoration and lasting protection of the *libertas philosophandi*. Only later, in historical retrospect, would it turn out that this was just the lesser part of the actual price. For the newly initiated process had grave repercussions for philosophy itself, and what was finally in question was, as we have seen, no longer its mere safety but its very possibility. Nor can the second aspect of the modern project be properly understood so long as one does not take account of that *against which* it was directed. The quest for absolute certainty was a response to the challenge of revealed religion; the plan to erect a solid, firmly constructed, ever more comprehensive edifice of knowledge on an indubitable foundation was conceived in direct confrontation with the teaching concerning particular Providence and the irruption – possible at any time and in any place – of miracles into the world of natural events. In short, one could say that modern philosophy was the attempt to make philosophy safe in a twofold sense. Yet it thereby remained dependent upon its Christian counterpart in a twofold way. Strauss's propaedeutic analysis showed why the attempt to make philosophy safe ended in the second cave of the present instead of leading out into the open.

Before we return to the historical point of departure of Strauss's philosophical undertaking, it may be appropriate to pursue another consideration briefly. If through the political action of philosophers from the beginning of modernity on, history obtained a significance for philosophy hitherto unknown, if for the comprehension of modern philosophy the patient study of its development became indispensable, this does not mean that history had no importance for premodern

increased the *natural* difficulties of philosophizing by adding the *historical* difficulty. In other words, the classical account of the natural difficulties of philosophizing are found in Plato's figure of the cave. The historical difficulty can be illustrated by saying: there is *now* yet another cave *beneath* the Platonic cave." *Gesammelte Schriften* 2, 456. Cf. "Religiöse Lage der Gegenwart" (1930), *Gesammelte Schriften* 2, 386–87, and *Philosophie und Gesetz*, 46, in *Gesammelte Schriften* 2, 45.

philosophy or that it became an obstacle only through the break that the moderns brought about. The philosophical tradition with which the moderns broke testifies in itself to the extraordinary historical efficacy of the political action of ancient and medieval philosophers. Thus, in view of what Plato did for philosophy in the Greek polis, Cicero in Rome, Alfarabi in the Islamic world, and Maimonides in Judaism, Strauss can say: "the political action of the philosophers on behalf of philosophy has achieved full success." Discreetly drawing attention to the problem that historical success harbors within itself for philosophy, Strauss adds: "One sometimes wonders whether it has not been too successful."[8] Not only does such success make it all too easy to overlook the precarious status of what has been achieved politically, in particular it lets the questionableness of the beginning fall into oblivion and, along with it, the principal philosophical reflection, the arguments for and against philosophy that form the basis of the successful tradition. In every tradition, the answers gain the upper hand over the questions, and in fact to such an extent that the answers come to be taken for granted and are no longer questioned; thus, considerable effort is ultimately required in order once again to become conscious of which questions they answered and how the alternatives looked. Whatever may be a given for any other tradition, whose pros and cons deserve to be prudently weighed against one another, such oblivion in the case of the philosophical tradition is a problem of absolutely vital significance for philosophy. For if philosophy is a way of life, the answers to the constitutive questions "How should I live?" and "Why philosophy?" can never be left to the tradition, can never in reliance on the reason of one's predecessors be transferred to the history of philosophy, if philosophy is not to be based on belief. And no philosopher has recalled with greater urgency than Strauss "that being based on belief is fatal to any philosophy."[9]

Does the danger of the descent into a second cave therefore begin as soon as there is success in making philosophy politically respectable and in institutionalizing it in schools in order to carry it further in instruction with the aid of a growing body of doctrines? Be that as it may, Strauss's confrontation with the tradition is not limited to the tradition

8 "Restatement on Xenophon's *Hiero*" (1954), in *On Tyranny*, 220–21.
9 "Preface to Spinoza's Critique of Religion," 256. Cf. "Niccolò Machiavelli," in *History of Political Philosophy* (Chicago: University of Chicago Press, 2d ed., 1972), 271–72 [= (Chicago: University of Chicago Press, 3d ed., 1987), 296–97], and *Natural Right and History*, 167.

of modernity and is not carried out as a historical return to premodernity. In order to fight one's way out of the horizon of the "certainties" of the present and those "things that are taken for granted" by the tradition and into the openness of a *skepsis* in the original sense of the term, Strauss inaugurates a retrial of philosophy that advances in a direction contrary to that of "historical progress." The retrial of philosophy goes hand in hand with Strauss's historical propaedeutic without coinciding with it. The new trial is entirely devoted to the *issue* that was controversial between the two parties. Beginning with traditional judgments, it inquires unreservedly into both the grounds that have entered into the decisions and the missed questions that are contained in the historical answers. It no longer serves merely to prepare an ascent. In its core, it *is* the ascent. The conflict between enlightenment and orthodoxy is newly tried by Strauss just as much as is the *querelle des anciens et des modernes,* which through him again has found a place in the philosophical debate. In his own way, Strauss once again sets into motion the attempts at refutation and at refutation of the refutation that reason and faith undertook in the Middle Ages. And the "problem of Socrates" that had been on the agenda since the critique that Nietzsche had brought to bear on that "one turning point and vortex of so-called world history" virtually becomes the vanishing point of Strauss's revival of supposedly obsolete, "historically decided" controversies.

The active search for fundamental confrontations and the renewal of the conflict are Strauss's answer to the petrification of philosophy in the history of its teachings and systems. The attempt at meeting the predominance of the answers with radical questioning links him to the "destruction of the tradition" undertaken by the early Heidegger, whose example decisively inspired Strauss, if it did not allow him for the first time to find his way to his own distinctive undertaking.[10] There are, however, above all three points that separate Strauss's destruction of the history of philosophy from radical historicism. *First:* hermeneutic openness, or the maxim that the greatest effort must be made to

---

10 In an unpublished version of what later became his Hobbes book, Strauss writes: "Hobbes *misses* the question that has to be answered for political science to be science. He does not begin with the question: which, then, is the right order of human social relations? or with the equivalent question: τί ἐστιν ἀρετή." To the word emphasized with italics, 'misses' (*versäumt*), Strauss adds the note: "We have Heidegger to thank for this expression; see *Being and Time,* I, 24 and 89 ff. Heidegger's idea of the 'destruction of the tradition' is what first made possible the investigation carried out in this and in the previous sections." Cf. *Gesammelte Schriften* 3, xviii–xix.

understand the philosophers of the past exactly as they understood themselves. Such an effort will be made only by one who remains open to the possibility of learning something of the greatest importance from those whom he attempts to understand. Whoever allows himself to be led by the hermeneutic premise that the thinkers of the past can always be understood only *differently* than they understood themselves, because he believes himself to have recognized, in contradistinction to his predecessors, that all thought is radically conditioned by history, and who therefore, supported by a sense of superiority based on some kind of philosophy of history, thinks he can understand all of his predecessors *better* than they understood themselves, thereby excludes from the very start the possibility that is crucial for him. *Second:* the rediscovery of the art of exoteric-esoteric writing, or the insight into the difference that exists between the generally accessible *teachings* and the *thought* of the philosophers of the past. In light of the "art of careful writing," the "destruction of the tradition" proves to be a still more demanding task – since it is one much more complex – than Heidegger had assumed. On the other hand, on the basis of the rediscovery of a historical fact that largely fell into oblivion for one and a half centuries, but which earlier was well known among philosophers, the assertion that all thought is essentially conditioned by history had to appear to be very much in need of revision. If the art of careful writing consists in addressing different addressees in different ways, on different levels of presentation, and with different arguments, in short, if there is an essential difference between the double-faced, exoteric-esoterically presented teaching and the thought of the philosophers, then it cannot be concluded from the "historically bound" writing and speaking of philosophers – which takes the expectations, opinions, and prejudices of their contemporaries into consideration in order to find an audience and to fulfill its political purpose – that in their thinking the authors were subject to the same expectations, opinions, and prejudices. The historical dependence of their philosophy is no longer a self-evident presupposition but an open question for the destruction of the history of philosophy. *Third:* the primacy of political philosophy, or the concentration on that part of philosophy in which the whole of philosophy is in question, in which its political defense and its rational foundation are of concern, in which the self-knowledge of the philosophers has its place. If the removal of the sediments of the tradition and the examination of its omissions are carried out following the guiding thread of political philosophy, the confrontation with the objects "politics,"

"morality," "religion" cannot be put off – until they demand that trib-
ute be paid to them in the form of a "historical dispensation of fate."
If one concentrates on political philosophy, the alternatives to philosophy themselves come into view. One does not let the actual or supposed
"mortal enemy" be without continuing to pay serious attention to him –
only to fall thereafter increasingly under his influence.[11]

Hermeneutic openness, the beginning with the exoteric-esoteric
double-face, the concentration on political philosophy – taken together,
all three elements make possible and sustain Leo Strauss's deepest
response to the challenge of radical historicism by making possible
and sustaining a movement that distinguishes him not only among the
philosophers of the twentieth century: the movement from the history
of philosophy to the intention of the philosopher. For to want to understand a philosopher of the past in all seriousness as he understood himself requires that one return *from* the philosopher's transmitted "contribution" to the "history of philosophy" *to* his intention. It requires
that one seek to understand his oeuvre as an articulated whole out of
the unifying center of his thought. And giving political philosophy primacy means seeking out the stratum in which this thought had to make
certain of its presuppositions, the medium in which it had to account
to itself for its own fundamental position, and the activity in which, if
ever, it achieved clarity concerning itself. A key role is thereby accorded
to the rediscovery of the exoteric-esoteric way of writing. The recovery
of the art of careful writing not only recalls the historical conditions
under which the works arose whose authors employed this art. It leads
at the same time to the principal political and philosophical reflections that form the basis of the art of careful writing on the part of the
philosophers. It yields, in a word, the connection between hermeneu-
tics and political philosophy. That a proper understanding of texts that
were written under conditions of censorship and in view of the danger of persecution is impossible so long as the historical circumstances
relevant to the interpretation are not taken into account requires no
further discussion. The grounds that induced the philosophers to write
exoteric-esoterically, however, go far beyond political considerations
of censorship and persecution. They arise from the insight into the
insuperable tension that exists between the political community and

---

11 Cf. Martin Heidegger, *Phänomenologie und Theologie* (Frankfurt a. M.: Klostermann,
   1970), 32; *Wegmarken, Gesamtausgabe* 9 (Frankfurt a. M.: Klostermann, 1976), 66. The
   lecture was held in 1927 in Tübingen and in 1928 in Marburg.

philosophy. The exoteric-esoteric double-face is the attempt to protect philosophers from society and nonphilosophers from philosophy. It is destined to take account of the necessities of politics on the one hand and of the requirements of the philosophical life on the other. The art of careful writing is therefore the expression of an equally fundamental and comprehensive reflection on politics, philosophy, and the nature of the philosopher.

One aspect is due special mention in this context. The recovery of the art of careful writing contributes essentially to the "liquefaction," as it were, of the traditional philosophical teachings in the medium of interpretation and to the release of the philosophical energies bound up in them. The insight into the different ways of addressing different addressees, into the interconnection of rhetorical presentation and philosophical argument, into the conscious inclusion of contradictions and ambiguities, is synonymous with the insight that the author expects those readers for whom an actual understanding of the issue under discussion is important to participate actively in the discussion he leads. In this way, the art of careful writing places the question concerning the intention of the philosopher in the center for the interpreter. If he wants to answer it, he has to get completely involved in the author's movement of thought. To be able to consummate the author's movement of thought, however, the interpreter himself has to think through the issue towards which this movement is directed. The hermeneutic effort turns smoothly into philosophical activity in the proper sense of the term.

The movement that Strauss achieves with his philosophical undertaking is one from history to nature. It becomes recognizable when one follows the hermeneutic movement from the history of philosophy to the intention of the philosopher. Strauss proved the fruitfulness of his procedure in numerous interpretations, each of which bears witness as much to the art of careful reading as to that of careful writing. For anyone who has eyes to see, Strauss shows that the natural potential of philosophy can be unfolded through the course of the epochs of its history and athwart them. He demonstrates the possibility of a philosophical dialogue beyond all historical barriers to understanding, in that he as an interpreter actually leads such a dialogue with medieval and ancient as well as modern philosophers. On closer inspection, it turns out that this dialogue ultimately rests not on the fusion of historical horizons but on the meeting of kindred natures. The dialogue becomes possible by virtue of the similarity of the problems that are discussed in it and by virtue of the correspondence of faculties that are actualized in it. The questions that open up the whole have a transhistorical scope, and this holds true first and foremost for the fundamental questions that have to be raised about the philosophical life itself: Why philosophy? What is the Good? *Quid sit deus*? A transhistorical common ground, however, is no less inherent in the experiences that the confrontation with these questions has in store for one, provided that all one's strength is employed to think the issue through or to understand another properly who had likewise thought it through. Strauss draws our attention to the experiences that are common to philosophers, because what most deeply binds them to one another comes to bear in those experiences. In light of what unifies philosophers, of what causes them to agree regarding what is most important, it becomes clear that what separates them, what distinguishes them in their teachings and systems, is of subordinate significance.[12]

As for the difference it makes whether the interpreter's presentation places the philosopher's intention or his contribution to the history of philosophy in the center, Strauss has shown this in the case of Rousseau, to whom he devoted two studies in rapid succession, which significantly differ from each other. The first bears the title "On the Intention of Rousseau" and appeared in December 1947 in essay form. The second is the chapter on Rousseau in *Natural Right and History*, which Strauss read in October 1949 as part of the Walgreen Lectures in Chicago and published in 1953 in book form.[13] "On the Intention of Rousseau" is an intensive confrontation with the *Premier Discours* that brings Rousseau's discourse to speech philosophically as no interpreter had done before. The Rousseau chapter from *Natural Right and History* occupies itself primarily with the *Second Discours*, which Strauss rightly calls "Rousseau's most philosophic work," but Rousseau's philosophy is here considered from a historical point of view. The opening sentence reads: "The first crisis of modernity occurred in the thought of Jean-Jacques Rousseau." The concluding sentence of the first paragraph links the foregoing to Nietzsche, who would repeat Rousseau's "attack on modernity" just over a century later and "who thus ushered in the second crisis of

12 Cf. Leo Strauss, "What Is Political Philosophy?" (1954), in *What Is Political Philosophy?* 40; *On Tyranny*, 105; further, *Die Religionskritik Spinozas*, 183, in *Gesammelte Schriften* 1, 249; *On Tyranny*, 109; *The City and Man*, 241; *Socrates and Aristophanes*, 33, 45, 49, and 52–53; *Xenophon's Socrates*, 29–30, 115, 118, 119–20, 122, and 125.

13 "On the Intention of Rousseau," *Social Research* 14, no. 4 (December 1947), 455–87; *Natural Right and History*, 252–94.

modernity – the crisis of our time." In this way, the perspective in which Rousseau will be illuminated is identified right at the beginning, and the historical movement is indicated in which he will be situated and described as one of its moments. In the foreground stands the archaeological view, which always already sees what will emerge from Rousseau's philosophy, what will be based on it, what will transform it and cover it over. The interest in the reconstruction of the development that stretches from Rousseau up to the crisis of the present takes the lead. Kant and Hegel, Marx and Nietzsche, romanticism and historicism not only are always considered in the interpretation of Rousseau's thought but also are included in the presentation. Shifts in emphasis, obfuscations, and reductions result from this abbreviation. The Rousseau chapter in *Natural Right and History* shows in its own way that the endeavor to situate a philosophy in the narrative logic of a comprehensive course of history has its price. Since one of the most significant interpretations we possess of Rousseau in general and of the *Discours sur l'inégalité* in particular is of concern here, it may be appropriate to give four examples of how Rousseau's position undergoes a weakening or a blurring by being viewed in light of the history of its reception. (1) On the nature of man we read on page 271: "Man is by nature almost infinitely perfectible. There are no natural obstacles to man's almost unlimited progress or to his power of liberating himself from evil. For the same reason, there are no natural obstacles to man's almost unlimited degradation. Man is by nature almost infinitely malleable. In the words of the Abbé Raynal, the human race is what we wish to make it. Man has no nature in the precise sense which would set a limit to what he can make out of himself." Obviously, Strauss *knows* that the last two sentences cited have, in fact, validity for several of those "disciples" of Rousseau who "clarified his views" – and distorted them at the same time – but certainly not for Rousseau himself. Strauss *knows* just as obviously that the validity of the four preceding sentences is assured for Rousseau solely by the "almost" expressed four times, in which case we are not dealing with a trivial qualification. Rather, almost the entire interpretation of Rousseau's thought depends on a more detailed determination and a precise unfolding of this quadruple qualification "almost." (2) Of "Rousseau's moment," of where Rousseau situates himself in history, if not in a philosophy of history, Strauss says on page 273 what one could say more fittingly of "Hegel's," or "Marx's," or "Nietzsche's moment": "man will no longer be molded by fortuitous circumstances but rather by his reason. Man, the product of blind fate, eventually becomes the seeing master of his fate." (3) On page 278, Rousseau is acknowledged as the predecessor of German idealism: "Above all, he suggests that the traditional definition of man be replaced by a new definition according to which not rationality but freedom is the specific distinction of man. Rousseau may be said to have originated 'the philosophy of freedom.'" As correct as it is to work out the "connection between the developed form of 'the philosophy of freedom,' i.e., German idealism, and Rousseau" from a historical standpoint, it is just as important to stress on philosophical grounds that *perfectibility* as the specific difference of man is worlds apart from the *freedom* of German idealism, and that freedom in the systems of German idealism occupies quite a different position than does perfectibility in the "*système Rousseau.*" (4) The last three paragraphs of the chapter emphasize in constant consideration of later developments that the solitary existence towards which Rousseau oriented himself beyond his political project was not sufficiently determined to be a philosophical existence and that the solitary individual was not identified with the philosopher. "The type of man foreshadowed by Rousseau, which justifies civil society by transcending it, is no longer the philosopher but what later came to be called the 'artist.'" However, the keen-sighted description of the consequences provides no substitute for the understanding of the philosophical and political grounds that led Rousseau to his theoretical conception of the solitary existence and to its literary presentation. Much the same holds for the famous portrayal of solitary contemplation, of which Strauss says: "By 'solitary contemplation' he does not understand philosophy or the culmination of philosophy. Solitary contemplation, as he understands it, is altogether different from, not to say hostile to, thinking or observation. It consists of, or it leads up to, 'the feeling of existence,' i.e., the pleasant feeling of one's own existence." For the "glowing terms" in which Rousseau "has spoken of the charms and raptures of solitary contemplation" are in any case not to be separated from his own philosophical existence and from the experiences that his *thought* inaugurated and opened up for him.

Whereas Strauss, in his interpretation of the *Discours sur l'inégalité,* recognizably pursues the intention to situate Rousseau's most philosophical work in the historical movement of modern thought, in his essay on the *Discours sur les sciences et les arts,* to which most interpreters ascribe merely a historical interest, he gets completely involved in the movement of the author's thought in order to reach the fundamental position of the text. As becomes apparent, Rousseau is so far from adopting an infinitely malleable human nature that, on the contrary, he makes the natural inequality of men the starting point of his entire oeuvre and of his public activity in general. Not only the prize-winning text of 1750 but also his political philosophy as a whole, which is unfolded in Rousseau's subsequent books, presuppose the continued existence of the difference between philosophers and nonphilosophers. No other philosopher of modernity confronted more intensely the conflict between the good or well-ordered commonwealth and philosophy, and none was more convinced than Rousseau that the tension on which this conflict is based is insuperable. The essay "On the Intention of Rousseau" shows us Rousseau as a master in the art of careful writing. It shows us an author who is conscious of the fact that society has its vital element in opinions and belief, whereas philosophy cannot do without unreserved questioning and doubt. It shows us a political philosopher who draws the conclusion that the problem that political philosophy recognizes must be forgotten if the political "solution" that political philosophy suggests is to be realized. Strauss sketches the physiognomy of a zetetic philosopher who gives primacy to "theoretical" and not "practical" reason, who does not adjust *mania* in matters of philosophy beforehand in accordance with the requirements that *sophrosyne* holds to be expedient with regard to morality, religion, or politics, and who, unlike his successors, is able to maintain and endure in his thought the conflict between politics and philosophy. For Rousseau "had the 'well-contrived head for which doubt is a good cushion.' "[14] He was the right man who not only was able to subject philosophy in the form of Enlightenment to a cutting critique in the name of virtue and freedom or from the citizen's point of view and for the sake of the good commonwealth, but also was skilled first and foremost in the seeming paradox of attacking philosophy in order to defend its enterprise. To defend it he had to orient his rhetoric and his strategy to the conditions of his historical moment: "The classical statements about science and society, especially those of Plato, still had to serve the purpose of combating a prejudice against philosophy, whereas Rousseau had to fight perhaps an even more dangerous prejudice in favor of philosophy: by his time, philosophy had become not merely a generally revered tradition, but a fashion."[15] In this passage we find a variation on the theme of the second cave. Of far greater importance for us, however, is that the intention of Strauss coincides with the intention of Rousseau

14 "On the Intention of Rousseau," 482; cf. 472.   15 Ibid., 485.

precisely at the point – and at least at the point – where at issue is the defense of philosophy's cause against the danger of its petrification in the tradition and against all attempts to make it *populaire*. This common feature is expressed quite nicely in a question raised by Rousseau that Strauss takes from the *Discours sur l'inégalité*, communicating it in the central note of "On the Intention of Rousseau": "Shall we never see reborn those happy times when people did not dabble in philosophizing, but when a Plato, a Thales, a Pythagoras, seized by an ardent desire to know, undertook the greatest voyages *solely* in order to instruct themselves?"[16]

In view of the interpretation that Strauss gave of the *Discours sur les sciences et les arts*, the contours become discernible that an interpretation of the *Discours sur l'inégalité* or the *Rêveries* might take on if it concentrated on the intention of the author in just as sustained a manner and followed the movement of his thought without reservation. Were one to apply the principles of the essay "On the Intention of Rousseau" to "Rousseau's most philosophic work," then our special interest would be directed to the conceptual consequences and to the material results to which the "primacy of theoretical reason" leads. Rousseau's return to the solitary state of nature, for instance, would be grasped not on the basis of the quest for an ideal vehicle for laying claim to individual freedom, but rather on the basis of the break with the teleological presuppositions of the tradition and on the basis of the denial of the postulate of a historically privileged moment. Perfectibility, in turn, would prove to be conceived in order to situate man as a part in the comprehensive whole of nature without underestimating his eccentricity in this whole – on the contrary, in order to be able to determine more precisely his turn against the whole, his readiness for depravity, the radically problematic character of his position within and over against nature. Above all, we could not avoid seeing that Rousseau turned against the biases in favor of philosophy not only in his public teaching but most of

16 Jean-Jacques Rousseau, *Discours sur l'origine et les fondements de l'inégalité parmi les hommes*, Note X, in *Discours sur l'inégalité*, ed. Heinrich Meier (Paderborn: Schöningh, 1984; 5th ed., 2001), 342. Strauss cites the passage in the French in n. 38, p. 467, of his text and there emphasizes the word *uniquement* by placing it in italics. In his personal copy, he adds a reference to Cicero, *De finibus*, V, 19, 50. Furthermore, he quotes the following statement made by Rousseau in *Dernière Réponse:* "La Gréce fut redevable de ses mœurs et de ses loix à des Philosophes, et à des Législateurs. Je le veux. J'ai déjà dit cent fois qu'il est bon qu'il y ait des Philosophes, pourvû que le Peuple ne se mêle pas de l'être." *Œuvres complètes* III, 78. Cf. "Einführender Essay über die Rhetorik und die Intention des Werkes," which precedes my critical edition of the *Discours sur l'inégalité*, lvi.

all in his thought, and by no means only because these positive biases had become fashionable but also because they come naturally to and suggest themselves to philosophers.[17] The philosopher can know himself to the extent that he gains distance from what most suggests itself to him. Rousseau knew that he had to occupy an eccentric position if he wanted to succeed in finally being himself in a self-centered whole.[18]

Strauss's deepest response to the challenge of historicism, his answer to the question of whether philosophy is at all possible in the original meaning of the term, is contained in the movement from the history of philosophy to the intention of the philosopher. It is not the subject of Strauss's teaching in the sense in which, for instance, his reconstruction of the "three waves of modernity," historically inaugurated by Machiavelli, Rousseau, and Nietzsche, respectively, can be the subject of teaching and learning.[19] It is disclosed solely in consciously and independently carrying out the hermeneutic venture itself that Strauss exemplified in his penetrating interpretations. Whoever is wholly devoted to understanding a philosopher exactly as he understood himself, and whoever allows himself to be led in the study of that philosopher by the maxim that the greatest effort and care is to be employed in order to discover whether his oeuvre contains truth, may reach the point at which it no longer makes any difference to him whether he thinks the thoughts of the philosopher or his own, because he moves on a plane on which the arguments take the lead and the alternatives visibly emerge that, beyond the "historical embeddedness" of both the author and the interpreter, determine the issue towards which the thought of both is directed. Strauss's interpretations show that this point can be reached in the study of Nietzsche or Rousseau as well as in the study of Plato or Maimonides. And it is no less reachable in the confrontation with Strauss, who clothes his philosophy almost exclusively in the garb of commentary. "It may be added" – as Strauss asserted of Alfarabi in an essay full of self-explicative statements – "that by transmitting the most precious knowledge, not in 'systematic' works, but in the guise of a historical account," Strauss "indicates his view

17 On this point, cf. "On the Intention of Rousseau," 464.
18 The lines of the interpretation indicated here are further elaborated in my "Einführender Essay" and in my essay "The *Discourse on the Origin and the Foundations of Inequality among Men:* On the Intention of Rousseau's Most Philosophical Work," trans. J. Harvey Lomax, *Interpretation* 16, no. 2 (Winter 1988–89), 211–27.
19 *What Is Political Philosophy?* 40–55; "The Three Waves of Modernity," in *Political Philosophy: Six Essays,* ed. Hilail Gildin (Indianapolis: Pegasus/Bobbs-Merrill, 1975), 81–98.

concerning 'originality' and 'individuality' in philosophy: what comes
into sight as the 'original' or the 'personal' 'contribution' of a philosopher is infinitely less significant than his private, and truly original and
individual understanding of the necessarily anonymous truth."[20]

If it is possible to return from the history of philosophy to the intention of the philosopher, and if the individual "contribution" of a philosopher can direct our attention to the truly individual understanding of
the necessarily anonymous truth, then the contributions to the history
of philosophy themselves appear in a different light. Do they not allow
us to come to the insight that "leaving the cave" was always possible at
those times for which the traditional contributions give testimony?[21]
And do they not at the same time provide us with the opportunity
to undergo, in turn, the liberating experience that accompanies the
ascent from opinion to knowledge? The contributions to philosophy
would thereby gain a justification that reaches deeper than their history and carries more weight than the danger of their petrification in
the tradition. For despite their material or doctrinal content in the
more restricted sense, those contributions have in common that they
introduce and lead some of us to the philosophical life. Consequently,
they refer to a reflection that precedes the individual contributions and
convinces the most diverse philosophers that the philosophical life is

20 "Farabi's 'Plato,'" in *Louis Ginzberg Jubilee Volume* (New York: American Academy for
Jewish Research, 1945), 377. Preceding this passage, we read in the same paragraph:
"Only because public speech demands a mixture of seriousness and playfulness, can
a true Platonist present the serious teaching, the philosophic teaching, in a historical,
and hence playful, garb." Cf. 375–76.
21 "...there were always people who were not merely exponents of the society to which
they belonged, or of any society, but who successfully endeavored to leave 'the cave.'
It is those people, and those people only, whom we still call philosophers, lovers of
the truth about 'the whole' and not merely about 'the whole historical process.' The
independence of the philosopher, as far as he is a philosopher, is only one aspect of a
more fundamental independence, which was recognized equally by those who spoke
of a presocial 'state of nature' and by those who emphasized so strongly the fact that
'man is generated by man and the sun,' not by society. It sometimes happens that a
genuine philosopher agrees with the political views of his family, or sect, or class, and
that therefore the political (and moral) opinions which he expounds in his writings
are merely more impressive and imaginative expressions of what his father or uncle
or brother also said. But if one wants to understand the hidden reason why he chose
these political views and not those of another class – for he was, as a philosopher, free to
choose – one must look beneath the surface of his teaching by disinterring his esoteric
teaching which is indicated between the lines, and which is usually not very flattering to
father, uncle, or brother." "Persecution and the Art of Writing," *Social Research* 8, no. 4
(November 1941), 503 n. 21; in the reprint of his essay in the volume bearing the same
title, Strauss deleted this note. Cf. *On Tyranny*, 223.

good – that it will be good for kindred natures even if they are to reach answers that considerably deviate from their own.[22] Precisely the same reflection is the ultimate ground of the art of careful writing. Thus, Strauss can say of the works to which the philosophically inspired art of writing gives rise that they are "written speeches caused by love."[23]

22 Cf. *What Is Political Philosophy?* 40; *Thoughts on Machiavelli,* 299; *Liberalism Ancient and Modern,* 8; "Farabi's 'Plato,' " 392–93.
23 "Persecution and the Art of Writing" (1941), 504; *Persecution and the Art of Writing,* 36.

III

WHAT IS POLITICAL THEOLOGY?

The concept of political theology is most intimately connected with the name of Carl Schmitt. Not only was it "introduced in the literature" by Schmitt, as Erik Peterson wrote in 1935.[1] Today, nearly seventy years later, one has to say that Schmitt has helped the concept "political theology" to gain prominence throughout the world, across disciplinary and national boundaries, as well as across political and theological fronts. Above all, however, Schmitt's own position is determined by the concept. Political theology names the core of Schmitt's theoretical enterprise. It characterizes the unifying center of an oeuvre rich in historical turns and political convolutions, in deliberate deceptions and involuntary obscurities. The intimate connection with this oeuvre, which has sowed enmity and reaped enmity as only few have, would alone be enough to make political theology a controversial concept.

Neither is the issue of political theology, of course, to be equated with the concept's gain in prominence nor did it enter into the world with the articulation of Schmitt's theory. Political theology is as old as faith in revelation, and it will continue to exist, as far as human beings can tell, as long as faith in a God who demands obedience continues to exist. The question "What is political theology?" thus leads and points far beyond the confrontation with, or reflection on, Schmitt's position. It is of far more fundamental significance. Yet whoever poses the question today asks it within the horizon of the debate that Schmitt inaugurated. The questioner runs up against opinions, expectations, and prejudices that have emerged from this debate. That is precisely why he would be prudent to begin at the beginning of the present quarrel. Furthermore,

---

1 Erik Peterson, *Der Monotheismus als politisches Problem. Ein Beitrag zur Geschichte der politischen Theologie im Imperium Romanum* (Leipzig: Jakob Hegner, 1935), 158.

the consideration of the first theoretician in the history of political
theology to make that concept his own and to use it for the purpose
of self-characterization sheds light on the issue of political theology
itself.

On no less than three occasions, during three quite different phases
of his career, and in three very different historical moments, Schmitt
raises the flag of *Political Theology* for all to see. In 1922 he publishes the
first book with this title. The subtitle reads: *Four Chapters on the Doctrine
of Sovereignty*. In 1934, one year after joining the National Socialist Party,
he publishes an abridged and revised edition, which he now opens with
a most instructive introduction. Nearly forty years later, he presents his
final book-length publication under the title *Political Theology II*. Its subtitle, *The Legend of the Disposal of Every Political Theology*, already signals to
the reader on the cover that he is faced with a disputed concept and that
in reading the book he will be dealing with a case surrounded by legends. But the legend Schmitt refers to here – the legend promulgated
by Erik Peterson and his followers of the final disposal of all political
theology – is only one among many legends that surround political
theology. Another rather widespread legend reduces the concept to a
simple and narrow technical term to be used by historians interested in
the secularization of theological concepts during the different phases
of modernity, or it detoxifies and renders political theology a thesis in
the fields of "philosophy of science" or "conceptual history," which is
concerned with certain "correspondences," "analogies," or "structural
affinities" between theology and jurisprudence. Yet it was precisely this
legend that Schmitt tried to support in his last work when, in retrospect, he styled his *Political Theology* of 1922 as a "purely juridical text"
and asserted that all of his remarks on that topic were "statements of a
jurist" who moved in the "sphere of inquiry in the history of law and in
sociology."[2]

---

2 Carl Schmitt, *Politische Theologie II. Die Legende von der Erledigung jeder Politischen Theologie*
   (Berlin: Duncker & Humblot, 1970), 30, 101 n. 1; cf. 22, 98, 110. Schmitt does not
   hesitate to slip into the same passage the statement: "My writing *Politische Theologie* of
   1922 bears the subtitle *Vier Kapitel zur Soziologie des Souveränitätsbegriffes* [*Four Chapters on
   the Sociology of the Concept of Sovereignty*]." The *most obvious* reason for self-stylizations of
   this kind – the indefensibility of which any careful reader of *Political Theology* and *Political
   Theology II*, to say nothing of Schmitt's other writings, will readily discern – is alluded
   to towards the end of the cited note. Concerning the *most profound* reason for Schmitt's
   defensive strategy, see my *Carl Schmitt and Leo Strauss: The Hidden Dialogue*, trans. J. Harvey
   Lomax (Chicago: University of Chicago Press, 1995), 57–60; notice the especially blatant
   instance documented on 77 n. 92.

In order to grasp what kind of flag Schmitt raises when, without any explanation whatsoever, he chooses the title *Political Theology* for a book on the doctrine of sovereignty, one has to know – in keeping with Schmitt's own explicitly stated principles of understanding – which enemy it is raised against, which "concrete opposition" he has "in view" when using the concept.[3] Schmitt does not take the expression from the Stoics[4] or from Varro,[5] as did Augustine and his followers – and as all of Schmitt's predecessors had done – with the intention of criticizing political theology. Instead, he takes it from Bakunin. He does not follow the long tradition of the *theologia tripertita*,[6] but responds to the challenge of the Russian anarchist. Bakunin had hurled the concept against Mazzini, attacking what he called *"la théologie politique de Mazzini."*[7] He used it as a weapon in a war in which two irreconcilable armies face one another, one under the banner of Satan, the other under the sign of God.[8] Schmitt uses the weapon in the same war. But he wants to help the opposite camp to victory – and whereas everything said about the struggle between God and the Devil was nothing but a man-made fiction for the atheistic anarchist, the very same thing is a God-given reality for the political theologian. Bakunin attacks the truth of revelation and disavows the existence of God; he wants to do away with the state; and he negates the universal claim of Roman Catholicism. Under the slogan *Ni Dieu ni maître*, he revolts "with Scythian fury" against all dominion, all order, all hierarchy, against divine as well as human authority.[9] In Bakunin Schmitt sees the "true enemy of all traditional concepts of Western European culture" enter the arena. In Bakunin he believes he discerns, generations ahead of the "barbarians in the Russian republic of soviets," the most persistent adversary of morality and religion,

3 Carl Schmitt, *Der Begriff des Politischen* (Munich/Leipzig: Duncker & Humblot, 1932; new ed. 1963), 31.

4 Cf. Karl Reinhardt, *Poseidonios* (Munich: Beck, 1921), 408 ff.

5 M. Terentius Varro, *Antiquitates Rerum Divinarum*, ed. Burkhart Cardauns (Wiesbaden: Steiner, 1976), vol. I, fr. 6, 7, 9, 10, pp. 18–20 and 37; cf. commentary, vol. II, pp. 139–44, and see Ernest L. Fortin, "Augustine and Roman Civil Religion: Some Critical Reflections," *Études Augustiennes* 26 (1980), 238–56.

6 Cf. Godo Lieberg, "Die 'theologia tripertita' in Forschung und Bezeugung," *Aufstieg und Niedergang der römischen Welt* I, 4 (Berlin/New York: de Gruyter, 1973), 63–115.

7 Mikhail Bakunin, *La Théologie politique de Mazzini et l'Internationale* (1871), in *Œuvres complètes* I (Paris: Champ Libre, 1973).

8 Ibid., 43–44; cf. 45 and 72.

9 "Toute autorité temporelle ou humaine procède directement de l'autorité spirituelle ou divine." Mikhail Bakunin, *Dieu et l'Etat* (1871), in *Œuvres complètes* VIII (Paris: Champ Libre, 1982), 173.

of the pope and God, of idea and spirit.[10] Whereas Bakunin used the
term "political theology" to brand and mortally wound the opponent
against whom the anarchist is waging his war, Schmitt makes the polemical concept his own so as to answer with the most decisive affirmation
what seems to him in 1922 to be the most extreme assault on theology
and politics.[11]

The "concrete opposition" in view of which Schmitt makes the concept "political theology" his own is thus the opposition between authority and anarchy, faith in revelation and atheism, obedience to and
rebellion against the supreme sovereign. But *authority, revelation,* and
obedience are the decisive determinations of *the substance* of political
theology – independent of the particular actualization of it advanced
by Schmitt. Precisely because with his indictment, Bakunin negated the
"right" thing (*das Richtige*) in the twofold sense of the word,[12] Schmitt
can transform political theology into a positive concept without its
remaining – neither for Schmitt himself nor for any other political
theologian – polemically dependent on Bakunin or the opposition to

---

10 Carl Schmitt, *Politische Theologie. Vier Kapitel zur Lehre von der Souveränität* (Munich/
    Leipzig: Duncker & Humblot, 1922), 45, 49, 50, 55, 56 (2d ed., 1934: 64–65, 69, 71,
    81, 83–84); *Römischer Katholizismus und politische Form* (Hellerau: Jakob Hegner, 1923),
    74–78 and 80 ([Munich/Rome: Theatiner, 2d, slightly rev. ed., 1925], 49–51 and 53);
    Die geistesgeschichtliche Lage des heutigen Parlamentarismus (Munich/Leipzig: Duncker &
    Humblot, 2d ed., 1926), 79, 83, 87; cf. *Der Begriff des Politischen*, 60, 64, and esp. the
    third version (Hamburg: Hanseatische Verlagsanstalt, 1933), 45.
11 Schmitt makes no mention of *La Théologie politique de Mazzini.* Yet he does say of Bakunin:
    "His battle against the Italian Mazzini is like the symbolic border skirmish of a vast world-
    historical upheaval that has greater proportions than the migration of the Germanic
    peoples [in the late Roman Empire]. For Bakunin, the Free Mason Mazzini's *faith
    in God* was, *just as all faith in God,* only proof of slavery and the *true root* of all evil,
    of all governmental and political authority; it was metaphysical centralism" (*Römischer
    Katholizismus*, 75 [49]; my emphasis). Furthermore, cf. the contrast drawn between
    Bakunin and Mazzini in the last sentence of that book, which, according to Schmitt's
    report in his *Politische Theologie*, was written "at the same time" as this "in March 1922." His
    Politische Theologie itself culminates in an attack on the enemy, on whom Schmitt trains his
    sights in choosing his title: the concluding sentence figures Bakunin as "the theologian
    of the anti-theological" and "the dictator of an anti-dictatorship." That Schmitt, precisely
    as far as the key terms and sentences of his work are concerned, quite consciously
    abstains from giving "references" can be shown by a number of examples. On this, see
    The Hidden Dialogue, 46, 82 nn. 103 and 104; cf. 61–62.
12 The two senses of *das Richtige* (the right thing) are, on the one hand, that which is
    in itself right – for Schmitt, that is the authority of God and the state, which Bakunin
    negates. On the other hand, it is the thing whose negation enables Schmitt to transform
    "political theology" into a positive concept and thereby to reverse the value of a concept,
    which in Bakunin's parlance is thoroughly negative. It is the "right thing" because its
    negation is just what Schmitt needs in order to appropriate it for his own purposes.

anarchism.[13] Political theology, understood as a political theory or a political doctrine that claims to be founded on faith in divine revelation, now becomes for the first time a concept of self-identification and self-characterization. Not only political theologians who take up Schmitt's teaching or refer approvingly to it will use the concept in the future in this new, affirmative sense.[14] This is also and ever more frequently true of those who sharply reject Schmitt's political options or do not share *his* faith: political theologians whose basic attitude is conservative or liberal, who have revolutionary or counterrevolutionary convictions, whose creeds may be Catholicism or Protestantism, who may belong to Judaism or Islam. One is tempted to say that the concept of political theology – via Bakunin's challenge and Schmitt's response – finally found its way to its true substance.

We must return, however, to Schmitt for a moment. "Political theology" is the apt and solely appropriate characterization of Schmitt's *doctrine*.[15] But at the same time, the concept serves Schmitt as a universally deployable *weapon* within the framework, and for the promotion of the aims, of his political theology. The concept thus marks,

13 Consider the determination of the enemy and of his own identity at the end of the "Afterword" (124–26), which Schmitt wrote for his *Politische Theologie II* and which is by far the most important part of the entire book. Cf. Carl Schmitt, *Donoso Cortés in gesamteuropäischer Interpretation* (Cologne: Greven, 1950), 9–10.

14 Early examples are the book by the Protestant theologian Alfred de Quervain, *Die theologischen Voraussetzungen der Politik. Grundlinien einer politischen Theologie* (Berlin: Furche-Verlag, 1931), and the essay "Politische Theologie" by the Catholic theologian Karl Eschweiler in *Religiöse Besinnung* 1931–32, no. 2: 72–88. In the meantime, the flood of books and essays that include the concept "political theology" in their titles has become vast. It is noteworthy that the first essay ever written about Schmitt was entitled "Carl Schmitts Politische Theologie" (in *Hochland* [June 1924], 263–86). However, its author – the writer Hugo Ball, who was first strongly influenced by anarchism and was then adamantly Catholic – was not yet familiar with the conceptual heart of Schmitt's political theology, the new version of the concept of the political, which was worked out between 1927 and 1933.

15 In *The Hidden Dialogue*, which was first published in 1988, I sought to develop this point at greater length and to argue it with greater precision. In the same work, I have subjected Schmitt's position to an in-depth critique (see esp. 41 ff. and 79 ff.). This interpretation was unexpectedly and quite clearly confirmed by the publication of *Glossarium. Aufzeichnungen der Jahre 1947–1951*, ed. E. Freiherr von Medem (Berlin: Duncker & Humblot, 1991) from Schmitt's literary estate (cf., e.g., 28, 63, 89, 95, 139, 165, 203, 212, 213, 269, 283). By the same token, I regard this work as having confirmed my critique in all points. After a reading of the postwar notes, it should now be difficult to play down Schmitt's anti-Semitic attacks from the period before 1945 as "opportunism" or as acts of "camouflage" and to deny their connection with his political theology. Cf. *The Hidden Dialogue*, 6–7 n. 5, 43 n. 40, 61–62 n. 64, and 81, as well as *The Lesson of Carl Schmitt*, 151–59.

on the one hand, Schmitt's locus within the political battle of faith. On the other hand, it is the instrument he uses with the greatest skill in order to force his adversary to join in this battle. For he does not use the term "political theology" only for political theories that, like his own, claim to be anchored in theology. Rather, he knows how to detect "political theologies" even where all theology is expressly repudiated, where the political is negated, and where all political theology is declared to have been "disposed of."[16] Either the adversaries' positions are based on "transfers" and "recastings," or they prove to be forms and products of "secularization," or they are passed off as metaphysics *malgré lui.* Schmitt's political theology, its "pure and whole knowledge" about the "metaphysical core of all politics," provides the theoretical foundation for a battle in which only faith meets faith – in which the right faith counters the thousand varieties of heretical faith. On the plane of political theology, there can be no "neutral parties," but always only "political theologians," even if they be "theologians of the antitheological" – as Schmitt likes to refer to Bakunin. Neither indifference nor ignorance offers a way out. The truth of revelation calls for and brings about the distinction between friend and enemy. Whoever denies that truth is a liar. Whoever places it in question obeys the Old Enemy. Whoever does not side with it sides against it. The truth to which political theology lays claim proves its power to seize everything and to permeate everything precisely by forcing everyone to make a decision, by confronting everyone with an Either-Or that cannot be evaded.

One reason why political theology is a controversial concept is that political theologians themselves prefer to use it as a weapon in their battles. Schmitt excelled in this game *à deux mains,* his peculiarity being that he used the concept of political theology even after its "positive recasting" as a weapon to force his enemy to fight on Schmitt's own battleground. But whereas Schmitt seeks to make his enemies, as it were, "akin" to himself with the concept, it is frequently used by other political theologians with quite the opposite intention: in order to distance themselves from political theologians whose political doctrines they

---

16 On this and what follows, see the references in *The Hidden Dialogue,* 68–79. In the text of his *Politische Theologie,* Schmitt uses the concept "political theology" exactly three times: on 40, 44, 45 (56, 63, 64). The first and third employments refer to the "writers of the Restoration," the political theologians Maistre, Bonald, Donoso Cortés, Stahl; the second, by contrast, has the concept appear in the context of Kelsen's view of democracy as the "expression of relativistic, impersonal scientificity."

disapprove of and to attack any political theology that is not grounded in their own faith.

In the twentieth century, the most famous example of this rather common practice is Erik Peterson's 1935 treatise on monotheism, which culminates in his oft-cited thesis of the "theological impossibility of a 'political theology.'" In the guise of a learned book in the center of which stands the critique of the political theology of Eusebius, bishop of Caesarea, Schmitt's friend from the 1920s attacks all those political applications of theological notions that he considers to be misuses of Christian theology. The Christian theologian reaches the conclusion that "in principle," the Trinitarian dogma marks "the break with every 'political theology' that *misuses* the Christian Proclamation for the justification of a political situation."[17] Whatever one may think about the persuasiveness of this assertion from a theological or historical point of view, there can be no doubt that Peterson's book attacks a *particular* kind of political theology. His verdict is aimed at the theological legitimation of a political rule or regime – at least to the extent that the author disapproves of that rule or regime for political-theological reasons – for example, the legitimation expressed in the formula "One God, one ruler of the world." Peterson's theological treatise is an attempt to exert influence in a purposive manner both politically and within the church.[18] It contains a clear admonition addressed to his old friend, who in the meantime had made himself an advocate of the National Socialist regime. And last but not least, the book contains a barely hidden attack on Judaism.[19] Thus, it is a highly political treatise, written by an extraordinarily gifted political theologian, as any unbiased reader of his works can see.[20]

17 Peterson, *Der Monotheismus als politisches Problem,* 99 (my emphasis).
18 On this point, see the informative and illuminating dissertation by Barbara Nichtweiss, *Erik Peterson. Neue Sicht auf Leben und Werk* (Freiburg: Herder, 1992), 764–79.
19 "There can be something like a 'political theology' only on the ground of Judaism and paganism." *Der Monotheismus als politisches Problem,* 99–100. Cf. Karl Löwith, *Mein Leben in Deutschland vor und nach 1933* (Stuttgart: Metzler, 1986), 94.
20 Peterson, *Der Monotheismus als politisches Problem,* 70, 95–97, and "Kaiser Augustus im Urteil des antiken Christentums. Ein Beitrag zur Geschichte der politischen Theologie," in *Hochland* 30, no. 2 (Aug.–Sept. 1933), 289–99, esp. 289 and 298–99, but also *Die Kirche aus Juden und Heiden* (Salzburg: Anton Pustet, 1933), 24–26, 31, 34, 40, 42, 56, 62, 64, 71 n. 28, as well as the book that immediately followed *Der Monotheismus als politisches Problem,* namely, *Zeuge der Wahrheit* (Leipzig: Jakob Hegner, 1937), 14–15, 20, 22, 39–45, 58, 60, 68. Nichtweiss has presented a wealth of additional material from Peterson's unpublished papers that shows just how much he was a political theologian; cf. 789–90, 797–98, 805, 807, and esp. 820–26.

That the concept of political theology is used in many different ways as a weapon does not render hopeless the attempt to clarify the substance of political theology. Of far greater weight is the incontestable fact that the number of political theologies that avail themselves of the concept in characterizing their *own* positions is growing. Thus, it has become possible to employ the concept in such a way that it, firstly, names the cause aimed at in the question "What is political theology?" without attacking it; secondly, includes the most important representatives of this cause without doing violence to them; and, thirdly, remains a concept of distinction without fostering discrimination in a pejorative sense. I have already defined the cause: a political theory, political doctrine, or a political position for which, on the self-understanding of the political theologian, divine revelation is the supreme authority and the ultimate ground. Among the most important representatives of political theology in the history of Christianity, Paul[21] may be named, as well as Tertullian and Augustine, Luther and Calvin. Finally, political theology remains a concept of distinction insofar as it is separated by an ineradicable difference from *political philosophy*.

Political theology and political philosophy are bound together by the critique of the self-forgetful obfuscation or of the intentional bracketing of what is most important. Both agree that the quarrel over what is right – over what is just rule, the best order, real peace – is the fundamental quarrel and that the question "How should I live?" is the first question for man. However, with the answer that each gives to this question, they stand in insuperable opposition to one another.[22] Whereas political theology builds unreservedly on the *unum est necessarium* of faith and finds security in the truth of revelation, political philosophy raises the question of what is right entirely on the ground of "human wisdom"[23] so as to develop the question in the most fundamental reflection and the most comprehensive way available to man. In the most comprehensive way, insofar as all known answers are examined, all conceivable

21 Arguing from the standpoint of political theology, Jacob Taubes himself made "Paul's political theology" the object of a series of lectures held on the *Epistle to the Romans* at the Forschungsstätte der evangelischen Studiengemeinschaft in Heidelberg just a few weeks before his death (*Die politische Theologie des Paulus* [Munich: Fink, 1993]).

22 For a discussion of this, see my *The Hidden Dialogue*, as well as *The Lesson of Carl Schmitt*. Compare the distinction between political theology and political philosophy that Ralph Lerner and Mushin Mahdi draw in the world of medieval Judaism and Islam: *Medieval Political Philosophy: A Sourcebook* (Glencoe, Ill.: Free Press, 1963; Ithaca, N.Y.: Cornell University Press, 1978), 7–20.

23 Plato, *Apology* 20d–e.

arguments are taken up, and all demands and objections that claim to be authoritative are included in the philosophical confrontation – in particular, those that political theology advances or could advance. In the most fundamental reflection, because the level on which the confrontation takes place cannot be surpassed or outbid by any argument, and because the way of life that enables the most comprehensive confrontation with the question "What is right?" is itself made the central object of that confrontation, or thorough reflection.

From the very beginning, political theology denies the possibility of a rational justification of one's own way of life. Political theology knows that it is grounded in faith and wants to be so grounded because it believes in the *truth of faith*. Political theology subordinates everything to this truth; it traces everything back to this truth. Insofar as political theology champions the binding force of revelation, it places itself in the service of obedience. To obey revelation or be consistent with itself, political theology has to want to be "theory" out of obedience, in support of obedience, and for the sake of obedience. The *obedience of faith*[24] is the raison d'être of political theology in the best sense. The fact that the doctrines and demands that the believing obedience is able to derive from revelation can deviate from and even massively contradict one another does not contradict the principle that rules political theology. Political theology may support worldly authority or revolution. In a concrete historical situation, it may also abstain from taking up any *political* option – in the *narrower* sense of the word "political."

The answer briefly sketched here to the question "What is political theology?" is aimed, on the one hand, at restoring to a diffusely employed concept the sharpness that alone enables one to make distinctions regarding the matter at issue.[25] On the other hand, our answer attempts to take political theology's own claim to truth radically seriously in order to enter the horizon of its strength. For only when political philosophy engages political theology in the horizon of its strength, or,

---

24 Cf. Calvin's commentary on Romans 1:5, in *Commentarius in Epistolam Pauli ad Romanos*, ed. T. H. L. Parker (Leiden: Brill, 1981), 16.

25 It helps one to keep apart what does not belong together and yet, disregarding what is most important, is often mixed together. Thus, e.g., Rousseau's *religion civile*, which long played a prominent role in the discussion surrounding political theology, is a conception informed by political philosophy. The "articles of faith" that Rousseau postulates in *Du contrat social* IV, 8 *"comme sentiments de sociabilité"* are proposed by a political theoretician who was most definitely not a political theologian and who subjected the presuppositions of political theology to a far-reaching critique. Cf. Rousseau, *Discours sur l'inégalité*, ed. Meier, xxxii ff., 70 ff., 104, 150, 168, 270, 318 ff., 386 ff.

equivalently, when political philosophy thinks political theology itself, can political philosophy – in its confrontation with political theology – gain clarity on its own cause and know what it itself is not, what it cannot be, and what it does not want to be.[26]

If the question "What is political theology?" first obtains its philosophical significance with respect to the self-knowledge of the political philosopher, then its political relevance arises from the increasing interest political theology has met with in recent years. It gains its sustenance from quite different sources and can be observed in quarters that are separated by great differences. I would like to mention four aspects of this interest. (1) The collapse of the Soviet empire and the worldwide erosion of Marxist hopes that preceded it have in many places inspired the search for a new certainty of faith. (2) Not only do revealed religions promise a security that none of the faded ideologies approach. They also seem to offer an effective foothold for resisting the global triumph of the union of liberalism and capitalism, or rather to present an alternative to the secularism of modernity in its entirety. The weight that both moments have in the anti-Western type of political-religious radicalism is obvious. Such radicalism is, however, just one, even if at present the most spectacular, variety of the revival of Islamic, Jewish, and Christian orthodoxies. (3) Both the disenchantment of political-antireligious utopias and the expectations of salvation that are bound up with the establishment of a theocracy have restored an urgency to the question of the relationship between politics and religion that few granted it for a long time. (4) Compared with the three viewpoints just sketched – the free-floating yearnings for a new absolutely binding commitment, the return of orthodoxies, and the reflection on the question of the theologico-political foundations of the community – the fourth aspect seems to be of lesser significance. Still, it should not be underestimated, given the intellectual climate in which a political theory that claims to be grounded in faith in divine revelation is gaining appeal and an audience. I am thinking of those diffuse expectations that in the broad stream of "postmodernity" revolve around the *Ereignis* (appropriating event), which, should it occur, will put an end to the "wandering

---

26 The lines of argumentation that I elaborated in *The Lesson of Carl Schmitt* have been extended and continued in my epilogue "Eine theologische oder eine philosophische Politik der Freundschaft?" to *Carl Schmitt, Leo Strauss und "Der Begriff des Politischen."* *Zu einem Dialog unter Abwesenden* (Stuttgart/Weimar: Metzler, 1988; 2d, expanded ed., 1998), 153–90. Part II of the epilogue confronts Jacques Derrida's *Politiques de l'amitié* in light of the distinction between political theology and political philosophy.

in the deserts," and yet must not, if it is to show itself openly in its otherness, if it is to occur precisely as the *Ereignis,* be made the object of a thinking that conceives, distinguishes, and therefore aims at dominance. Jean-François Lyotard has recalled the divine commandment given to Abraham to sacrifice Isaac and Abraham's faithful obedience as the paradigm of the *Ereignis* – of the unforeseeable call as well as the attitude in which one must answer it. The proximity of some "postmodern" authors not only to Kierkegaard, the famous religious writer from Copenhagen, but also to Schmitt, the political theologian from Plettenberg in Westphalia, is greater than it may at first seem. In an intricate way – *dans un état de latence ou dans un état de langueur* – they are turned towards the decisive determinations of the political theologian's cause: authority, revelation, and obedience.

IV

WHY POLITICAL PHILOSOPHY?

We all know the picture of the philosopher that Aristophanes drew in the *Clouds* for both philosophers and nonphilosophers. As he is shown to us in this most famous and thought-worthy of comedies, the philosopher, consumed by a burning thirst for knowledge, lives for inquiry alone. In choosing his objects, he allows himself neither to be led by patriotic motives or social interests nor to be determined by the distinctions between good and evil, beautiful and ugly, useful and harmful. Religious prohibitions frighten him as little as do the power of the majority or the ridicule of the uncomprehending. His attention is fixed on questions of the philosophy of nature and of language, in particular, on those of cosmology, biology, and logic. By the keenness of his mental powers, the intransigence of his scientific manner, and the superiority of his power of discourse, he casts a spell on his pupils and gains co-workers, who assist him in his zoological experiments, astronomical and meteorological observations, or geometrical measurements. His self-control and endurance enable him to withstand every deprivation that results from carrying out his scientific projects. By contrast, he lacks moderation. Piety and justice do not count among the qualities on which his reputation is based. Authority and tradition mean nothing to him. In making his innovations, he no more takes into consideration what is time honored than in his teaching he takes account of the vital needs of the society on whose fringes he places himself along with his friends and pupils. The laboratory in which he pursues his studies is supported for the most part by voluntary donations and owes its existence, moreover, to its relative seclusion and inconspicuousness. It is similar to a bubble that is connected to its surroundings only by a modest exchange of air. However, the precautions taken by the school are so insufficient and the restrictions on entrance so slight that outsiders can be allowed in, if they so desire, without close scrutiny of their fitness and can thereby become witness to the most shocking statements and arguments. Such as when the philosopher reveals to a neophyte in almost as many words that the supreme god who is honored in the political community not only does not exist but also does not deserve to be honored, and therefore is not a god.[1]

The picture I have briefly sketched of the pre-Socratic philosopher in the *Clouds* stands with reason at the beginning of my attempt to answer the question concerning what political philosophy is and to what end it is needed. For pre-Socratic philosophy not only precedes the turn to political philosophy historically but at the same time is prior to it in substance. In view of that turn, the *Clouds* has to be accorded a key role, regardless of whether the philosopher with whose name it is most intimately linked and who embodies the pre-Socratic philosopher in Aristophanes' comedy, that is, regardless of whether Socrates himself made that turn in advanced years or whether the turn from the pre-Socratic Socrates to the Socrates of political philosophy was carried out by Plato and Xenophon. In either case, one may justly attribute great importance to the catalytic effect the play had on a process of world-historical significance.[2] Here I am thinking primarily not of Socrates' conviction by the people of Athens in the year 399, although this event did contribute decisively to the unmistakable signature of political philosophy, and although Aristophanes almost literally anticipates both of the later charges in his comedy: Socrates does not believe in the gods in whom the polis believes but instead has introduced new divinities, and he corrupts the youth.[3] Where the historian may above all have the death of Socrates in mind, it is fitting that the philosopher give thought to the birth of political philosophy. And it is here that the poet of the *Clouds* deserves the praise proper to the midwife.

The critique to which the play subjects the pre-Socratic Socrates is not the critique of an enemy. If the comedy anticipates both of the charges brought in the trial before the people's court, then it does so with the telling difference that, on the one hand, Aristophanes includes himself among the new divinities of his Socrates, the clouds, lending them his voice and even placing himself at the head of the rest,[4] and, on the other

1 Cf. Aristophanes, *Clouds* 367.
2 In this connection, see *Socrates and Aristophanes*, 314.
3 Xenophon, *Memorabilia* 1.1.1; *Apology of Socrates to the Jury* 10; Plato, *Apology of Socrates* 24b–c; *Euthyphro* 2c–3b; Diogenes Laertius, *Lives of Eminent Philosophers* 2.40.
4 Aristophanes, *Clouds* (parabasis) 518–626.

hand, the youth whom Socrates "corrupts" in the *Clouds* is corrupted by his own father before everyone's eyes and brought to Socrates with a corrupt intention, before he ever falls under the dangerous influence of philosophical teachings. The course of the action of the comedy – beginning with the head of the school, who hovers in the airy heights and there devotes himself to his natural philosophical contemplations, and ending with the destruction of the entire *phrontisterion* or "thinkery" by a simple citizen who, driven by moral indignation, actively supported by a slave, and applauded by a god, burns down the house of Socrates and his companions – contains a clear warning. It is the warning of a friend, and Aristophanes gives it to Socrates well in advance. Whether concern for his friend or other considerations and motives were decisive for the poet need not occupy us here.[5]

For political philosophy, four points of the critique that Aristophanes in his way levels against the young Socrates[6] are of particular importance. The first, which the pre-Socratic philosopher lacks, is self-knowledge. He is wanting not only in the insight into what is good for him, or the Socratic *daimonion* that would keep him from getting involved with men and things that are not good for him. He lacks, above all, a clear awareness of the degree to which he and his friends are dependent upon the political community within whose walls they live and what consequences philosophical inquiry and teaching has or can have for the foundations of this political community, for the force of its laws and institutions, for the integrity of the family, for the political opinions and religious convictions of its citizens. Closely connected with the first point of criticism is, second, the apparent incapacity of the philosopher to argue convincingly for the philosophical way of life, and, third, the almost equally disturbing inability to defend it effectively. In all three respects – self-knowledge, the justification of one's own activity, and the protection from external attack – the poet lays claim to a position of superiority for himself since he knows how to steer the opinions of the citizens with his means, since he knows how to shape the political-theological reality in which the philosopher must assert himself. The poet's superior powers of formation are in the end grounded – and we thereby arrive at the fourth point – in a superior understanding of the *politika*, as well as in a better knowledge of human nature. Unlike Socrates and his pupils, who devote themselves in the

5 Cf. Plato, *Philebus* 48a–50a, and Strauss, *Socrates and Aristophanes,* 5–6.
6 Cf. Plato, *Second Letter* 314c.

seclusion of their *phrontisterion* to the study of the *physiologia*, Aristophanes and the other clouds, who in his comedy address the public, speaking to both the wise and the unwise, are aware of the diversity of human natures, of intellectual abilities and psychic needs. The word "soul" does not once cross the lips of Aristophanes' Socrates.[7]

The four points of Aristophanes' critique lead us on a straight path to the fourfold determination of political philosophy, which we wish to treat in what follows, or to the fourfold answer to the question of why philosophy must make the turn to political philosophy. The four moments of the answer concern firstly the object of political philosophy, secondly the political defense of the philosophical life, thirdly its rational justification, and fourthly political philosophy as the locus of the self-knowledge of the philosopher. As we shall see, the four moments are so intertwined with one another that together they constitute an articulated and internally dynamic whole. The rank of the critique that Aristophanes presents in what is in the poet's own judgment the wisest of his comedies[8] consists precisely in the fact that his critique requires one answer: it provokes a philosophical founding. This raises it above and beyond even the most penetrating confrontation in modernity with that "one turning point and vortex of so-called world history"[9] and distinguishes it from all other attempts to initiate the trial of Socrates anew that were inspired by Aristophanes' critique over more than two millennia. Nietzsche's critique of "theoretical man," which takes up Aristophanean motifs so as to turn them against the Platonic Socrates, is part of Nietzsche's own political philosophy. Intrinsically, it presupposes the philosophical founding of which we are speaking here and moves, not only historically, along the path that that founding marks out.[10] The political attack of a Sorel, by contrast, which takes aim at Socrates the citizen of Athens and is interested in the philosopher only insofar as he exerted influence as a public person, may appeal to the conservative spirit out of which Aristophanes' critique is held to have been born.[11]

7 ". . . he replaces soul by air"; *Socrates and Aristophanes*, 31. Here I refer the reader once more to Strauss's late work, the most significant philosophical commentary not only on the *Clouds* but also on Aristophanes' entire oeuvre.
8 Aristophanes, *Clouds* 522.
9 Nietzsche, *Die Geburt der Tragödie*, in *KGW*, III 1, 96.
10 Nietzsche, *Jenseits von Gut und Böse*, in *KGW*, VI 2, Vorrede, aphs. 28, 30, 40, 61, 190, 191.
11 Georges Sorel, *Le procès de Socrate. Examen critique des thèses socratiques* (Paris: Félix Alcan, 1889). "L'État transformé en Église, la force publique mise à la disposition des sectes, tel était l'idéal des Socratiques. Avec une pareille organisation, tout, dans les cités, tendrait vers le *bien*, tel que le comprendraient les chefs. 'La fraternité ou la mort!'

But it hardly approaches the force of a critique that, although or precisely because it breathes the spirit of friendship, is able to promote the most fundamental reflection and finally to compel a turn that makes a distinction in the whole.

A distinction in the whole is made by the turn to political philosophy insofar as philosophy can achieve the fulfillment of its reflexivity solely in political philosophy. The political philosophy at issue here is a special part and mode of philosophy, and we are speaking of it in constant consideration of the meaning it possesses for *philosophy tout court.* The fourfold determination of the cause that occupies us has only tangentially to do with the usage of the concept as it is commonly encountered today, where it is applied indiscriminately to political theories of any and every kind. It most certainly has nothing to do with the inflated use of the epithet "political philosophy" to describe arbitrary political opinions, programs, and convictions, as has recently become fashionable. Since the end of the ideologically established division of the world and the decline of the utopias that had prevailed until then, the appeal to "political philosophies" has experienced a boom. But even where fundamental questions of political theory are given thought or the foundations of the *res publica* are discussed with great seriousness, we still do not have political philosophy. Neither the competent theoretical approach to political questions and problems nor one's seriousness in dealing with them is, taken on its own, proof of political philosophy. It is no more equivalent to a *"philosophie engagée"* than to a "public philosophy" or to a *"Philosophie der bestehenden Ordnung."* Political philosophy achieves its ownmost task neither in establishing political meaning, in uplifting and edifying the public, nor in educating citizens in morality or in offering practical guidance for political action – regardless of how great or slight political philosophy's contribution in such matters may be considered. This task, which distinguishes it from all others, the task it possesses *as philosophy* and *for the philosopher,* is what we have in view when attempting to answer the question "Why political philosophy?"

hurlaient les hallucinés de 93" (p. 9). "Comme tous les sophistes, il [sc. Socrate] travaillait à ruiner les vieilles mœurs. La nouvelle génération trouvait ridicules toutes les œuvres qui avaient été tant admirées par les anciens. Les conservateurs, aussi bien qu'Anytus qu'Aristophane, pensaient que l'on ne pouvait former des générations héroïques que par la vieille méthode, en nourrissant la jeunesse des poèmes héroïques. Après les grands désastres de la guerre, tous les hommes sensés devaient partager cette manière de voir. Il fallait restaurer ou périr" (p. 235).

Political philosophy has as its object the political things: the foundations of the political community, the duties and rights of its members, the ends and means of their action, war and peace internally
and in relation to other political communities. Although political philosophy, as far as its subject matter is concerned, makes up merely
a part of philosophy, it by no means has a narrowly circumscribed
segment of human life as its object. Nor do we meet in this object,
say, an autonomous domain of life that exists alongside a number of
autonomous domains of life or "provinces of culture" of equal rank.
The central questions of political philosophy, the questions of the best
political order, of the right life, of just rule, of the necessary weight of
authority, knowledge, and force, can be properly raised only in con-
junction with those other questions of the nature of man, of his place
between beast and God, of the abilities of the human mind, the capac-
ities of the human soul, and the needs of the human body. The object
of political philosophy is thus the human things in the comprehensive sense, and the questions of political philosophy all lead back to a
question that is posed to man as man: the question of what is right.
If he wishes to answer *seriously*, if he seeks to gain clarity *for himself*, he
finds himself faced with conflicting claims. He is subject to the law of
the political community, the commandment of God or of man, and he
meets with answers that are advanced with the demand for obedience
or with the will to enforcement. The question of what is right is posed
to man, in other words, in the sphere of the political. In this way, both
the rank of the political is indicated and its urgency for philosophy is
designated.

But if the political does indeed have urgency, how is it to be explained
that philosophers could ever disparage or neglect the confrontation
with the political things? I shall limit myself here to three brief remarks
towards a possible answer: Precisely those conflicting political and theological claims that induce the philosopher to question the *nomoi* with
regard to what precedes or founds them, and that thereby lead him to
the discovery of *physis*, induce him to follow his own nature; the insight
into the conventional character of political institutions confirms him in
the rightness of his way of life, which is determined by his inclinations.
His thirst for knowledge and his thought are aimed at the whole; at first
glance, the political things do not seem to have any exceptional significance within it; contemplation of the unchanging, reflection on the first
principles, or even listening to the dispensation of Being seem, on the
contrary, to be worthy of far greater esteem than is the occupation with

the political or the merely human in all its frailness, irrationality, and uncertainty. And can the philosophical understanding of the political things not also be regarded as secondary, in the sense that knowledge of the most universal principles or laws of nature must come first since it is what first makes it possible to leave the shadow-world of opinions behind and lift the political into the realm of knowledge and accord it its proper place therein?

To these and similar considerations, which shed light on the sense in which philosophy precedes political philosophy, we respond: The political turn of philosophy occurs not least due to the insight that the expectations of philosophy and the valuations of philosophers must themselves be subjected to scrutiny, which can be carried out only on the path of confrontation with the political things. The notions of the sublime, the noble, or the beautiful, which are bound up with philosophy, must be questioned with regard to their dependence on the political, moral, and religious opinions within the political community that the philosophers seek to transcend, no less than must the desire for devotion to truth or the will to certainty, each of which is in danger, in its own way, of fostering a new dogmatism or a self-forgetfulness of philosophy. What is dearest to philosophy must be subjected to the most critical investigation. That holds also for the pre-Socratic belief that the political can be elucidated most compellingly in light of the first principles or that the opinions, conventions, institutions of the polis could be reconstituted on the basis of a preceding knowledge of the true being, a position that Plato recalls in the *Republic*'s image of the cave in order to follow it, with a critical intention, to its most extreme consequence, the postulate of the philosopher-king. This holds no less for the prospect of a *bios theoretikos* that finds its perfect self-sufficiency in the happy contemplation of the noble and most sublime things – likewise a pre-Socratic vision – for which Aristotle erected a monument in the tenth book of the *Nicomachean Ethics*.[12] This holds, in short, for an ideal of wisdom that dissociates a universal knowledge of principles from the philosopher's self-knowledge[13] or severs an allegedly pure knowledge

---

12 Aristotle, *Nicomachean Ethics* 10.6–9 (esp. 1177a12–28, b19–26, 1178b7–23); cf. 6.7 (1141 a16–20, 1141b1–8) and 1.3 (1095b19, 1096a4); cf. also *Protrepticus,* ed. I. Düring (Frankfurt a. M.: Klostermann, 1969), B 29, 50, 86.

13 The self-misunderstanding that is expressed in the view that the ideal of wisdom at issue here is to serve the philosophical life as a lodestar has been captured succinctly by Seth Benardete: "Wisdom is an idol of the cave." *Socrates' Second Sailing: On Plato's Republic* (Chicago: University of Chicago Press, 1989), 179; cf. 178 and 192.

from that knowledge which grows out of suffering[14] and is lent wings by joy.

Let us return to our argument. If the central questions of political philosophy are related to the question of what is right, and if this question is posed to the philosopher in the sphere of the political, then for political philosophy this means that it cannot evade the risk of the political. From the occupation with its object arises the necessity of political caution, just as possibilities of political influence are opened up. Put differently: Its object conditions its mode. From the beginning, political philosophy was also therefore always *political* philosophy, political action by philosophers, and was in fact forced by the prevailing circumstances to be primarily political action in the service of philosophy: the protection and defense of the philosophical life or an act of a politics of friendship that includes the interests of future philosophers. However, as we have seen, philosophy does not first require protection at the moment it publicly thematizes the question of what is right and enters into the more precise investigation of the political things. As a way of life, philosophy is in itself an answer to the question of what is right. It knows friendship and enmity. It is therefore – whether it accounts to itself for such or not – fundamentally in need of a political defense.

It is an error to assume that the discovery of nature could ever have been made in "political innocence." And it is no less an error – even if we have encountered it in recent times in philosophers – to believe that a move behind political philosophy, a step back to the pre-Socratic thought of *physis,* could be combined with the return to an "original harmony" from which political philosophy separated itself and us – as if the critique of the *nomos* had not been coeval with that thought.[15] Aristophanes' *Clouds* and the charge of impiety brought against Anaxagoras just a few years before its premiere, a charge that drove the Ionian philosopher of nature out of Athens, suffice to remind us that the study of the *physiologia* at times can be a highly political affair. The turn to the *politika* is made due to the precarious situation in which philosophy naturally finds itself. It enables the political defense of philosophy before the forum of the political community and, at the same time, the philosophical examination of the latter's political-moral-religious

---

14 Cf. Aeschylus, *Agamemnon* 178; *Prometheus* 585–86.
15 On this point see my epilogue, "Eine theologische oder eine philosophische Politik der Freundschaft?" in *Carl Schmitt, Leo Strauss und "Der Begriff des Politischen." Zu einem Dialog unter Abwesenden* (Stuttgart/Weimar: Metzler, 2d, expanded ed., 1998), 179–80.

law so as to influence a change for the better. How successful political philosophy has been in both respects is shown by the esteem that could be garnered for philosophy by Plato, Xenophon, and Aristotle in the Greek polis or by Cicero in Rome, the continued existence of the philosophical way of life that could be secured by Alfarabi, Avicenna, and Averroes in the Islamic world or by Maimonides in Judaism, and the protection by the state that the political philosophers of modernity, especially Machiavelli, Bacon, Hobbes, and Spinoza, were able to win for the freedom of philosophizing. The fact alone that the majority of the writings of the philosophers just mentioned have come down to us, whereas in the case of the pre-Socratics we must be satisfied with meager fragments, speaks eloquently.

Political philosophy, which in the spirit of a politics of friendship seeks to guarantee the political presuppositions of the philosophical way of life for both the present and subsequent generations, must attend no less to philosophy's beneficial effect on the political community than to the current, immediate protection of philosophy. Over time, however, the former aim may very well come into conflict with the latter. Likewise, the historical acquisition of institutionalized guarantees against political or religious persecution can nurture a false sense of security in philosophy and deceive it – not only to its own detriment – about the tension that exists in principle between it and the political community. The philosophical politics of friendship therefore requires a reflection on the necessities of philosophy, on the one hand, and on the necessities of the well-constituted political community, on the other. Such a reflection will keep a philosophical politics of friendship from allowing the political defense to degenerate into a mere apologetics for philosophy or from linking philosophy to a political status quo, placing it in the service of a historical moment, a religious mission, or a national uprising, in a word: from turning it into anyone's handmaid. What is good for the philosophical life need not be good for the political community, and what is suitable for philosophy is by no means simply on that account suitable for politics. The philosophical life has its raison d'être in the fact that it is grounded in unreserved questioning and stops at no answer that owes its authentication to an authority. The vital element of society is made up, by contrast, of opinions and faith; society draws its power from the fact that its basic principles are held to be true, its norms followed without question, its taboos regarded as matters of course, its institutions met with broad trust. Instead of doubt and the suspension of judgment, society requires resolute action and the courageous engagement, if not the enthusiasm of its citizens for the common good, which, however, remains a particular and partial good. The well-ordered political community is built on identification, on devotion and agreement, whereas the philosophical *eros* is "completely at home" nowhere but "in his homelessness."[16] The demand to live dangerously is as appropriate a maxim for the autonomous thinking of the philosopher as its application to politics has to be fatal;[17] and conversely, the maxim of the mean and measure, which makes complete sense for political praxis and for society as a whole, would, if appropriated by philosophy, result in the wings of philosophical *mania* being clipped before it had even begun its ascent in theory. A similar discrepancy arises in view of the chances for insight that the exception, in contradistinction to the rule, holds ready for philosophy, whereas the dangers for politics entailed in an orientation towards the exceptional case are obvious. To say nothing of the phases of institutional dissolution or epochs of social decline. The great political philosophers, from Plato to Rousseau, have given expression to the insuperable tension that exists between philosophy and the political community by assigning the best state for the species or for society and the best and happiest state for the individual or for the philosophical life to diverse ages or to different stages in the development of humanity.[18]

Philosophy needs political philosophy not only in view of its political defense but first and foremost with regard to its rational justification. Political philosophy addresses the theologico-political claims with which the philosophical life sees itself confronted. It concentrates its attention on that way of life by which its own answer to the question of what is right might be defeated. It turns to the commandments and prohibitions that compel philosophy to assert its right with reasons – if it is not to rest on the razor's edge of a mere decision or on an act of faith. For philosophy is able to justify its right and its truth only when it includes in the philosophical investigation the opinions and objections that are raised or can be raised against philosophy by appealing to a human or superhuman authority. That philosophy in this sense has to become *political* in order to acquire a *philosophically* sound

---

16 Benardete, *On Plato's "Symposium" – Über Platons "Symposion,"* 77.
17 Cf. Nietzsche, *Die fröhliche Wissenschaft,* in *KGW,* V 2, aph. 283.
18 Cf. Plato, *Statesman* 271d–273a, 274b–d; *Laws* 713a–e; Rousseau, *Discours sur l'inégalité,* ed. Meier, 166, 192–94, 256, 264–70, 342.

foundation is the decisive insight inherent in the Socratic turn.[19] Neither is the rational justification of the philosophical life to be achieved on the path of theoretical positings and deductions nor can it be made dependent upon the accomplishment of systematic efforts the conclusion and success of which lie in an uncertain future. Philosophy must demonstrate its rationality elenctically, in confrontation with its most powerful antagonists and with the most demanding alternative. And it must undertake this confrontation in the present. A confrontation that is *fundamental* for the philosophical life can be postponed no more than it can be delegated.

This is the context in which the critique of political theology gains its special interest for philosophy. For in its objection to philosophy, political theology appeals to no less an authority than the omnipotent God. Like political philosophy, political theology has the political things as its object. Both agree that the conflict over what is right, which arises in the sphere of the political, is the most important conflict and that the question "How should I live?" is the first question for man. Both distinguish themselves by being reflexive conceptions that aim at self-understanding, conceptions that demand, albeit for very different reasons, that they account for themselves: the thought and action of the philosopher, as well as of the theoretician who believes in revelation, therefore become the heart of political philosophy and political theology, respectively. In contrast to political philosophy, however, political theology claims to present a political theory or political doctrine that in the final analysis is based on divine revelation. Whereas political theology builds unreservedly on the answer of faith and hopes to find its security in the truth of revelation, which it attempts to interpret and apply, political philosophy raises the question of what is right – to speak with the Platonic Socrates – entirely on the ground of "human wisdom,"[20] in an effort to develop it here as fundamentally and comprehensively as man can while relying on his own resources. Political theology, which understands itself on the basis of the *obedience of faith*[21]

19 Cf. Plato, *Phaedo* 96a–100b; Xenophon, *Memorabilia* 1.1.11–16; and Marcus Tullius Cicero, *Tusculanae Disputationes* 5.10.

20 Plato, *Apology of Socrates* 20d–e; cf. *Persecution and the Art of Writing*, 107.

21 Calvin comments on the Pauline phrase in Romans 1:5 as follows: "Unde colligimus, Dei imperio contumaciter resistere, ac pervertere totum eius ordinem, qui Euangelii praedicationem irreverenter et contemptim respuunt, cuius finis est nos in obsequium Dei cogere. Hic quoque observanda est fidei natura, quae nomine obedientiae ideo insignitur, quod Dominus per Euangelium nos vocat: nos vocanti, per fidem respondemus. Si-

and wishes to place itself as theory in the service of the sovereign authority, considers itself to be obliged to historical action, political decision,
and the negation of a life that seeks to follow natural reason alone and
grants primacy to knowledge. In political theology, philosophy meets a
demanding alternative. It has every reason to confront a position thoroughly that not only can endanger it politically but also places its very
principle in question.[22]

The insight that a rational justification of the philosophical way of
life can be achieved only in the confrontation with the most demanding
alternative or on the path of a radical critique also remains determinative for those attempts at philosophical self-examination that go beyond

cuti contra, omnis adversus Deum contumaciae caput, est infidelitas." *Commentarius in
Epistolam Pauli ad Romanos,* ed. Parker, 16. Erik Peterson has presented the commandment of obedience as a positive entitlement of God, which is said to meet man in the
Gospel *jure divino* and is extended "into dogma and sacrament" ("The Gospel is, after
all, not any good news that is directed 'to everyone' – how could it then be distinguished
from the communist manifesto? – but rather it is a positive entitlement of God, who
out of the body of Christ meets each one of us concretely, specifically meets [each of
us] *jure divino.*") in order to objectify the obedience of faith in this way in the dogma of
the church. ("But only through the dogma does it also become visible that obedience
belongs to revelation. For in the obedience that the dogma demands, obedience to
Christ is fulfilled.") That he was able to rid himself of the problems thereby that the
commandment of obedience raises for historical action in general and for the historical
action of the political theologian in particular is, to be sure, doubtful. The question of
subjectivism and self-deception that follows the obedience of faith like a shadow and that
several of the most important political theologians of Christianity sought to grasp and to
domesticate for themselves in the conflict between grace and justice – this problematic
is only concealed or displaced, but not resolved, by the reference to the dogma that
"has subalternized all human knowledge" and by the flight to an intermediary authority.
(Erik Peterson, *Was ist Theologie?* [Bonn: Friedrich Cohen, 1925], 20, 23–24, 25; cf. 8,
16 [*Theologische Traktate,* ed. Barbara Nichtweiss (Würzburg: Echter, 1994), 13–14, 16;
cf. 4–5, 11]. The consequence that Peterson draws for theology from the subordination
of theology to church dogma should at least be mentioned here: "There *is* no theology
among the Jews and pagans; there *is* theology only in Christianity and only under the
assumption that the incarnate word of God has spoken. The Jews may engage in exegesis
and the pagans in mythology and metaphysics; there has been theology in the genuine
sense only since the incarnate has spoken of God" [18–19 (12)]. As far as I can see,
this pronounced, politically distinguishing concept of theology of Peterson's has not
received any attention from the authors who appeal to the famous concluding thesis of
his political-theological treatise, *Der Monotheismus als politisches Problem,* 99.)

22 Cf. here Heidegger's statement "that *faith* in its innermost core remains as a specific
possibility of existence the mortal enemy of the *form of existence* that belongs essentially
to *philosophy* and that is factually quite alterable. So absolutely that philosophy does
not even begin to want to fight that mortal enemy in any way!" The conclusion that
Heidegger draws in 1927–28 from the "*existential opposition* between faith and one's freely
taking one's entire existence upon oneself" sheds sudden light on the fundamentally
pre-Socratic position of his philosophy. Heidegger, *Phänomenologie und Theologie,* 32
(*Wegmarken,* 66).

a scrutiny in the light of the opposing theological and political positions in order to challenge philosophy before the tribunal of nature. We can grasp them as an answer to the historical course of development in which philosophy – not least as a consequence of its political turn – gained so much prestige and acted for social ends or allowed itself to be enlisted for them to such a degree that it sank to the level of a kind of higher matter of self-evidence. The historical success of philosophy's teaching and philosophy's influence on politics had the result that philosophical doctrines and conceptions increasingly impregnated the prevailing worldviews and left deep marks on the contrary theologico-political positions. The sharpening of its self-critique is one of the strategies of which philosophy can avail itself in order to counteract its social domestication, as well as its petrification in the tradition. If, in opposition to the biases of the humanistic tradition in favor of philosophy, Nietzsche wanted to "transpose man back into nature" and get down to the "eternal basic text *homo natura*,"[23] and if Rousseau attempted to go back from the idea of the *animal rationale,* which had long since become congealed into a general opinion, to man's first, solitary, bestial state of nature, we are not faced in either case with self-forgetful speculations of natural philosophical provenance, but with authentic pieces of their political philosophy that belong to the self-examination, self-critique, and self-understanding at issue here. Rousseau, who called philosophy most radically into question in the horizon of nature, knew as hardly anyone else that he had to adopt an eccentric position if he wanted, as a philosopher, to be himself in a self-centered whole.[24]

If at the beginning of our elaboration of the four determinations of political philosophy we said that political philosophy is a special part and mode of *philosophy* in order to delimit it from political theories of the most diverse kinds and origins, we are now in a position to refine that statement: Political philosophy is *the part* of philosophy in which *the whole* of philosophy is in question. For the three determinations that we have discussed thus far are, as it were, united into one in the fourth determination, namely, political philosophy as the locus of the self-knowledge of the philosopher. For the sake of his self-knowledge, the philosopher must make the political things the object of his inquiry and observation. And from the knowledge of the precarious political

23 Nietzsche, *Jenseits von Gut und Böse,* aph. 230; cf. aph. 259 and *Die fröhliche Wissenschaft,* aph. 109, as well as *Nachgelassene Fragmente,* in *KGW,* VIII 1, 130.
24 See my "Einführender Essay" to the critical edition of the *Discours sur l'inégalité,* lviii–lxviii, lxxvi–lxxvii.

situation in which philosophy finds itself as a matter of principle results the twofold task of the political defense and the rational justification of the philosophical life, a task that, in turn, is in both branches suitable for promoting the self-knowledge of the philosopher. The self-knowledge of the philosopher thus proves to be the comprehensive determination that binds together the other three and orders them in relation to one another. Beyond that, however, the fourth determination has its own function and significance.

This holds first of all in view of the philosophical life itself; its inner unity and concrete form are bound up with the knowledge of its distinct character, its limits, and its presuppositions. If it is true that men are naturally led to philosophizing and that philosophy, in the persistent effort to unlock the whole by questioning, merely makes its vocation that which grows out of the necessities of human life and human being-in-the-world, then it is no less true that the philosophical life rests on a discontinuity, on a conscious separation, and thus on a choice that determines this life thoroughly and that will be held fast in it in the face of all resistance. The awareness of the difference thus does not remain extrinsic to this life. The experience of detachment and departure that stands at the beginning of this life and marks a caesura can be illustrated by way of the image of the seafarer who sets out onto the open sea, not knowing if he will ever set foot on terra firma again. This and related experiences, which distinguish philosophy from a discipline that in principle can restrict the treatment of scientific problems to an enclosable sphere of life, become thematic in political philosophy, since in it the choice that is constitutive of the philosophical way of life and the authoritative objection against which it must assert itself become the central topic.[25] The insight into how much philosophy, as a distinct and conscious way of life, owes to that objection is not the least important fruit of self-knowledge that political philosophy holds ready.

The locus of self-knowledge is political philosophy, moreover, in the sense that it compels the philosopher to subject his opinions, convictions, and prejudices in things political, moral, and religious to precise scrutiny and thereby makes it possible for him to gain distance from what is dearest to him due to his origin, on the basis of his inclinations,

---

25 In 1933, an important theologian captured the objection raised from the standpoint of faith in revelation in the sentence: "Faith can judge the choice of the philosophical existence only as an act of the self-founding freedom of the man who denies his subordination to God." Rudolf Bultmann, *Theologische Enzyklopädie,* ed. Eberhard Jüngel and Klaus W. Müller (Tübingen: Mohr, 1984), 89.

or in view of what are supposedly matters of self-evidence in his age. For the individual philosopher no less than for philosophy in general, it holds that what is dearest requires the most critical investigation. When as a philosopher he confronts the political things, he will not spare his "personal opinion" from unreserved examination. On the contrary, there is every reason to expect that he will attest the truth of Plato's *Republic,* according to which the ascent of philosophy begins with the political opinions that are obligatory or binding for the individual and is consummated as the insight into their nature or their limits. The experience of separation and departure, which we tried to capture in the archetypal image of the seafarer, receives its individual expression for the political philosopher in his taking leave of the nationalist hopes or the socialist dreams of his youth, in his wresting himself free of the resentments cultivated by his family or the class from which he stems, in his distancing himself from the belief that the power of the government is a God-given institution or that the history of humanity has reached its goal in liberal democracy, and other such views. As for what weight is to be attributed to political philosophy regarding this fourth moment, it becomes conspicuous when one considers more closely those philosophers who have not made the turn to political philosophy – who therefore have remained "pre-Socratics" in a precise sense. Heidegger would have to be mentioned here.[26] Likewise, the diaries of Wittgenstein and Frege provide some examples.[27]

26 More instructive than the much-discussed errors and illusions that accompanied the "uprising" (*Aufbruch*) in the sphere of the political, which was as sudden as it was short-lived, when Heidegger believed himself to have been called in the "historical moment" of the year 1933 to act politically and to be able to "lead the leader" (*den Führer führen*), are the expectations (verging increasingly on the metaphysical) placed on politics on which that action was based and the devout charging of his philosophy, which after the failure of his political hopes in the present was redirected towards an event that would bring about the all-decisive reversal in the future. (Cf. *Beiträge zur Philosophie, Gesamtausgabe* 65 [Frankfurt a. M.: Klostermann, 1989], 11–13, 28, 369–70, 399–400, 411, 412–14.) The absence of political philosophy becomes visible particularly clearly where Heidegger seems to pursue a political intention and speaks of political things or avails himself of a political language. On this cf. "Abendgespräch in einem Kriegsgefangenenlager in Russland zwischen einem Jüngeren und einem Älteren," in *Feldweg-Gespräche (1944– 45), Gesamtausgabe* 77 (Frankfurt a. M.: Klostermann, 1995); consider, on the one hand, 208–9, 215–16, 235–36, 242, 240, and, on the other hand, 216–17, 224–25, 227, 231, 233–34, 237, 244, 240.

27 Ludwig Wittgenstein, *Geheime Tagebücher 1914–1916,* ed. Wilhelm Baum (Vienna: Turia & Kant, 1991), 21 (9/12/1914), 49–50, 70, 71, 72 (5/27/1916); *Denkbewegungen. Tagebücher 1930–1932, 1936–1937,* ed. Ilse Somavilla, 2 vols. (Innsbruck: Haymon, 1997), I: 39–40 (65), 43 (75), 51 (95), 54 (102), 75 (160–61), 78 (167), 80 (174), 91

In its core, the turn to political philosophy is a turn and reference of philosophy back to itself. The political critique that confronts philosophy with its own questionableness causes a reversal of the original, first, and dearest direction of inquiry. The resistance the philosopher runs up against when he allows himself to be led by his *eros*, the objection he must confront if he follows his nature, keeps him from losing sight of himself when investigating the world. The answer that the Socratic-Platonic-Xenophontic turn gives in the form of political philosophy to Aristophanes' critique links the question of philosophy back to the question of the good; it links knowledge back to the self-knowledge of the philosopher. It is for that reason that the Platonic attempt to articulate the whole by means of the "What is?" question occurs in the horizon of the question "What good is it?" The linkage of both questions establishes the connection of philosophical inquiry and philosophical life in the particular case and gives expression to the reflexivity of philosophy in the concrete object[28] – and the most important applications of the "What is?" question concern the central objects of political philosophy.[29] The linkage proves itself no less with respect to the concept of political philosophy itself, and it is thus no accident that our four-fold determination answers both questions: "What is political philosophy?" and "What good is it?" It thereby gives an account of the cause of political philosophy, for which the comprehensive determination of the self-knowledge of the philosopher is of constitutive significance. To

(204), 96 (217–18), 99 (225–26), 101–2 (232–33). Cf. his *Vermischte Bemerkungen*, in *Werkausgabe* 8 (Frankfurt a. M.: Suhrkamp, 1989), 495–96 and 497. Frege's "Political Diary" shows us an author who at the end of his life gives expression to hopes, opinions, and resentments *in politicis* that we could have predicted with some likelihood in a contemporary of his origin, education, and social background – so long as we were to disregard, in other words, the fact that we are dealing with a philosopher. Gottlob Frege, "[Tagebuch]," ed. Gottfried Gabriel and Wolfgang Kienzler, in *Deutsche Zeitschrift für Philosophie* 42, no. 6 (1994), 1067–98; see esp. 1075, 1078 (4/3/1924), 1080, 1081–82, 1083 (4/13/1924), 1087 (4/22/1924), 1088–89, 1091, 1092 (4/30/1924), 1094–95, 1096–97. The final sentence of the diary reads: "A life of Jesus, as I imagine it, would have to have, I believe, the effect of establishing a religion, without its coming to the fore as an intention" (1098).

28 In his commentary on Plato's *Statesman*, Seth Benardete indicates the fundamental character of this reflexivity when he writes: "Socrates refuses to separate the way of understanding from what is understood, so that the question 'What is it?' is always accompanied by the question 'What good is it?'" *The Being of the Beautiful: Plato's Theaetetus, Sophist, and Statesman* (Chicago: University of Chicago Press, 1984), III, 69; cf. *Socrates' Second Sailing*, 44, 163.

29 Cf. my "Eine theologische oder eine philosophische Politik der Freundschaft?" 170, 179–80, 189, and *The Lesson of Carl Schmitt*, 50–51, 86–87.

that extent, one can characterize the fundamental structure of political philosophy as Platonic.[30]

Political philosophy, which is determined by the four moments sketched above, proves in the respective forms in which we encounter it to be an internally dynamic and changeable whole. It is internally dynamic since the four moments interlock with and affect one another. We can speak of a changeable whole since the weighting of those moments is variable within a given political philosophy and, as a result, their organization within one whole can differ considerably from that in another. The dynamics that the quadrilateral – *confrontation with the political things, political defense and rational justification of philosophy, self-knowledge or self-examination of the philosopher* – harbors within itself recedes behind the statics of the firmly established and often artfully articulated presentation of political philosophy to such an extent that it is all too easy to lose sight of it. As interpreters, we can attempt to do justice to the internal dynamics of political philosophy solely by setting out from the level of the doctrinal presentation and inquiring back to the intention of the author in order to involve ourselves in the movement of thought that took place within that quadrilateral and takes place in it ever anew.

In the weighting of each of the moments, the individual abilities and experiences of the philosopher find expression as much as his diagnosis of the present, his assessment of the situation of philosophy, and his stance towards the philosophical tradition come into play there. Thus, for example, in times of severe political persecution, not the rational justification but instead the political defense of philosophy will stand in the foreground of the teaching. With respect to a well-ordered political community – whether one actual in the present or one possible in the future – the political defense will avail itself in turn of a rhetoric that is clearly distinct from the rhetoric that may appear appropriate to the defense in view of a society that is in decline and to a high degree worthy of critique. Where there are powerful enemies of or strong reservations about philosophy, it will look different than where the appeal to philosophy has become fashionable. Whereas the defense in the one case will exhibit the healthy political influence and the great social utility of

---

30 That all political philosophy in the sense specified here can be called Platonic may have induced Leo Strauss to give the last book that he himself planned the title *Studies in Platonic Political Philosophy*, a collection containing fifteen studies, only two of which are expressly concerned with Plato.

philosophy, or will at least assert its compatibility and harmlessness, in the other case it is more likely to emphasize the oppositions, draw out the basic distinctions, and stress the need to justify philosophy in order to protect it from being usurped, losing its contours, or being leveled.

Correspondingly great is the multiplicity of phenomenal shapes that we can observe in the long history of political philosophy since the Socratic turn. In Aristotle we encounter the first attempt on the part of philosophy to assign an independent domain of knowledge to the political things. Assuming and at the same time distancing himself from Plato's founding of political philosophy, he delimits a teachable and learnable political science that can be implemented by the citizens and with which he can win over future statesmen as allies of philosophy, elevating the strict precedence of the philosophical life over the political life to an integral component of the political-philosophical teaching and, as it were, positivizing it for the tradition. From this eminent act of a politics of friendship, we move with historical seven-league boots to Machiavelli's endeavor to regain the *libertas philosophandi* on the path of a radical politicization of philosophy. He, too, attempts to win allies with the aid of a practical science. The alliance he strives for with the sovereign – the prince or the people – is to guarantee the lasting protection of philosophy by means of the effective separation of politics and theology. He subjects the presentation of his political philosophy so thoroughly to the requirements of spiritual warfare that he not only rejects or avoids all the notions, conceptions, and theorems deriving from the philosophical tradition that could offer the adversary a foothold or that could contribute to the softening of future philosophers, but he even refrains from expressly thematizing what the entire undertaking aims at, namely, the philosophical life itself. It would be a mistake, however, to conclude from Machiavelli's concentration on the knowledge of the political things and their political presentation that the other two determinations of the cause lack significance for his political philosophy. Much the same holds for the political philosophies with which Alfarabi and Maimonides answer the challenge of revealed religion six and four centuries before Machiavelli, respectively. They take the changed situation of philosophy into account by moving the foundations of faith in revelation into the foreground. Returning to Platonic political philosophy, they grasp the divine law, providence, and the prophets as subjects of politics. When, with a view to founding the "perfect city," Alfarabi and Maimonides concern themselves with the philosophical justification of the law as founders and lawgivers, they too by no means follow exclusively political ends. For the philosophical justification of the law is for them the place where the question of the right of the philosophical way of life is raised most acutely and thus where the rational justification of philosophy is at stake.

A thoroughly altered situation arises for philosophy out of the historical change ushered in by the alliance with the political sovereign that Machiavelli and his successors inaugurated so as to achieve the systematic conquest of nature and the rational reorganization of society. What began as the emancipation of politics from theology leads, after the successful unleashing of a world of increasingly purposive rationality and growing prosperity, to a state in which the demands of politics are rejected with the same matter-of-factness as those of religion. In pursuing an undertaking that was intended to bolster peace and security, philosophy loses the demanding alternatives that compel it to engage in a serious confrontation. Its contours are blurred in the multiplicity of merely personal concerns, in which everything appears to be compatible with everything else. For political philosophy, the question thus arises whether under such conditions the philosophical transgression, the philosophical ascent, must be preceded more than ever by a counterfounding whose originator is the philosopher himself, a founding that reinstills an awareness of the rank of the political, makes the dignity of the political life visible, and leads those who are the fittest to philosophy – by giving their dissatisfaction with the prevailing situation another orientation. In this sense, Rousseau, Hegel, and Nietzsche, for example, advanced political counterprojects in the eighteenth and nineteenth centuries in answer to a process that, according to their diagnoses, led to the rise of the "bourgeois" or of the "last man," to the dominance of an existence that closes itself to all claims that aim at the whole. While taking the political and philosophical consequences of previous counterprojects into consideration, Strauss attempts in the twentieth century to "repeat" the historical foundings and the *querelles célèbres* of political philosophy, that is, to expound their fundamental principles and the intellectual experiences congealed in them in such a way that they gain a new actuality in the present and draw renewed attention to the question of the one thing needful. The emphasis placed on regions of life and provinces of culture by the "philosophy of culture" then predominant had "relativized" that question to such an extent that philosophy ultimately had to fail to answer the question: "Why philosophy?"

Just as little as philosophy marks a province in the realm of culture, but rather is by its natural sense a way of life, likewise political philosophy does not mark a field in the garden of philosophy. It represents instead, as we have seen, a special turn, a shift in the direction of regard and inquiry that for philosophy makes a difference in the whole. Political philosophy enriches and deepens the philosophical life to the degree that the growth in self-knowledge is able to enrich and deepen life. And it casts the philosophical life in toto in a different light. This may be illustrated by way of one of the most famous descriptions of philosophical self-sufficiency and philosophical happiness left to us by a political philosopher. I am speaking of the *cinquième promenade* in Rousseau's *Les rêveries du Promeneur Solitaire.* At first glance the philosopher – who follows his "solitary reveries" while letting himself, stretched out in a boat, be carried along by the drift of the water, who watches the flux and reflux of the waves from the banks of Lake Bienne, and who listens to the aimless lapping of a beautiful river or a brook against the shore – seems to be no less remote from any thought of a political philosophy than Aristophanes' pre-Socratic Socrates hanging high above in his basket. Even if we recall that, in the case of Plato's and Xenophon's Socrates, the citizen of Athens by no means absorbs the philosopher, that the new Socrates does not abandon his study of nature, and that Xenophon shows us at one point a Socrates who dances alone and is sufficient unto himself [31] – even if we take all this into consideration, the contrast between the citizen of Geneva, who calls for virtue and points the way to a well-ordered political community, and the philosopher, whom we encounter in the solitude of his leisurely walks, looks to be astonishingly great at first. Whereas the *législateur* Rousseau did all he could to elevate the political life by elaborating his political theory, as well as by working out the constitutional projects he was asked to outline for republics in his day, the *promeneur* Jean-Jacques depicts the bliss of a private, secluded, solitary existence, and he praises the pleasure it would have given him to occupy himself with collecting and studying plants and writing a *Flora petrinsularis* to the end of his days. The perfect happiness he achieved in his "*rêveries solitaires*" Rousseau describes as a state of continuous, fulfilled, timeless present, a state in which the soul finds a solid-enough base on which to rest itself entirely and on which it can gather its whole being. "What does one enjoy in such a situation?" Rousseau asks. "Nothing external to oneself, nothing besides oneself and one's own existence; as long as this state lasts, one is sufficient unto

---

31 Xenophon, *Symposium* 2.19.

oneself, like God."[32] In the same breath, however, Rousseau adds not only that this state is "little" known to "most men" but also that it "would not even be good" for them "in the present constitution of things" since it would spoil the "active life" for them. It offers Rousseau, by contrast, "compensations" for the persecution that he suffered and that brought him to such isolated places as St. Peter's Island. Just as Rousseau keeps himself in view when occupied with the political things,[33] likewise when he points to his supreme happiness, he does not for a moment immoderately disregard the political references. And no one will be able to disclose the significance *philosophy* has for Rousseau's *"bonheur suffisant, parfait et plein,"* no one will be able to disclose that in which *his* soul finds its "solid enough base," if one stops with the poetic presentation of the *cinquième promenade* and does not seek to pursue the argument step by step that Rousseau unfolds on his walks before and after it. For the *Rêveries,* which Rousseau died writing, prove on careful inspection to be a masterpiece of political philosophy. The defense of philosophy, the confrontation with the most demanding alternative, and the self-knowledge of the philosopher are unified in this work in a special way, enchanting both philosophers and nonphilosophers. Of its rank are few.

---

32 Rousseau, *Les rêveries du Promeneur Solitaire* V, *OCP* I, 1043, 1045, 1046–47.

33 On this see the concluding chapter of *Du contrat social* (IV, 9; *OCP* III, 470), on which Hilail Gildin has splendidly commented in *Rousseau's Social Contract: The Design of the Argument* (Chicago: University of Chicago Press, 1983), 190–91. The first word of the *Contrat social* is *je,* the last *moi.*

APPENDIX

TWO UNPUBLISHED LECTURES BY LEO STRAUSS

THE LIVING ISSUES OF GERMAN POSTWAR PHILOSOPHY (1940)

Introductory remark

Both the intellectual glory and the political misery of the Germans may be traced back to one and the same cause: German civilisation is considerably *younger* than the civilisation of the West. The Germans are, strictly speaking, less civilized than the English and the French, i.e., they are to a lesser degree citizens, *free* citizens. This is one aspect of the matter. The other aspect is that German philosophy is more apt to take a critical attitude towards civilisation, towards the *tradition* of civilisations, than Western philosophy is.[2] We may go so far as to say that,[1]generally speaking,[1] German philosophy *implies* a more or less radical criticism of the very idea of civilisation and especially of modern civilisation – a criticism disastrous in the political field, but necessary in the philosophical, in the theoretical field. For if civilisation is distinguished from, and even opposed to, what was formerly called the state of nature, the process of civilisation means an increasing going away from the *natural* condition of man, an increasing *forgetting* of that situation. And perhaps one must have a living knowledge, [3]an acute recollection[3] of that situation if one wants to know, i.e. to understand in its full meaning, the *natural*, the basic problems of philosophy.

Criticism of modern civilisation is related to a longing for some past, for some antiquity. An English acquaintance of mine told me that what struck him most, and what was most incomprehensible to him, when he was talking to Germans, was their longing for their tribal past. Now, longing for the

Teutonic past is only the most crude and unintelligent, the most ridiculous[4] form of a[5] deep dissatisfaction with modern civilisation. In its most enlightened form, it is a longing for classical antiquity, especially for Greek antiquity. In a famous aphorism, Nietzsche has described German thought as one great attempt to build a bridge leading back from the modern world to the world of Greece. One has only to recall the names of Leibniz, Lessing,[I] Goethe, Schiller, Hölderlin and Hegel to see that Nietzsche's remark is based on some evidence. This much is certain: Nietzsche's own philosophy, the most powerful single factor in German postwar philosophy, is almost identical with his criticism of modern civilisation in the name of classical antiquity.

The backbone of modern civilisation is modern *science*. German criticism of modern civilisation is therefore primarily criticism of modern science, either in the form of a limitation of its bearing or in a still more radical form. That criticism was expressed by the German philosophic movement of the end of the 18th and of the beginning of the 19th century, by the movement culminating in Hegel, in the form of the opposition of *history* as the realm of *freedom* vs. *nature* as the realm of (mathematical or mechanical) *necessity*, or of the opposition of organic growth or dialectical process vs. rational construction. This interpretation of the criticism of modern[6] civilisation naturally was an important factor in German postwar philosophy. But it was not *characteristic* of the latter. The slogan which expressed the attitude characteristic of postwar Germany towards modern civilisation, is, *not* history vs. unhistorical naturalism, or the grown vs. the made, *but* life or existence vs. science, science being *any* purely theoretical enterprise. The science criticized[7] in the name of life or existence, comprises both natural science and history.[II] The German postwar criticism is directed as much against Hegel and romanticism as

I "Kritik so verstanden, Gelehrsamkeit so betrieben, ist der Weg, auf dem Leibniz der geworden ist, der er ist, und der *einzige* Weg, auf dem ein denkender und fleissiger Mann sich ihm nähern kann." ["Critique understood in such a way, scholarship pursued in such a way, is the path on which Leibniz became the man he is and is the *sole* path on which a thinking and industrious man can approach him."]

II Nietzsche's 2. *Unzeitgemässe*.

against Descartes. The originator of that criticism was Nietz-sche who had made it its principle to look at science from the point of view of art, and to look at art from the point of view of life. |

As is implied in what I have already said, German post-war philosophy is only to a certain extent postwar-philosophy. The large majority of the older generation and a considerable part of the younger generation naturally continued traditions which had been established in the 19th century or earlier without being disturbed by the upheaval of the war and of its aftermath. We may call this type of men the merely academic philosophers. Public opinion of postwar Germany was deter-mined not by them, but by those men who were in contact with the revolution of thought – either as its exponents or as its originators –, by thinkers who felt that the traditions of the 19th century *could* not be continued and did not *deserve* to be continued. Of these thinkers one may distinguish two kinds: thinkers who had a direct and revolutionizing effect on the more open-minded and excitable part of the academic youth, and thinkers who in relative secrecy discovered, or rediscov-ered, a basis more in accordance with the nature of things than that underlying the preceding[8] period had been. For the purpose of a general discussion, I believe it to be better if I limit myself to a reasoned sketch of the more superficial movements which, however, were[9] influenced by, and influ-encing in their[10] turn, the deeper movement, that deeper movement being practically identical with the development of phenomenology. In doing this, I shall base myself not only and not even mainly on printed books or articles. Certain lec-tures and conversations and discussions which I remember, revealed to me the tendencies of the world in which I then was living, much better than the so-called final statements which I could read later on in print.

[1]One more word before I start: I speak of what *other people* thought – I do not necessarily approve of these thoughts – but my purpose is exclusively to give you sound information.[1]

The intellectual situation of Germany immediately after the war shows itself most clearly in two memorable publications: Spengler's *Decline of the West* and Max Weber's *Science and Learning as a Vocation*. The meaning of these publications

1 verso

may be described as follows: Spengler's work was a most ruth-
less attack on the validity or the value of modern science
and philosophy (and indeed of science and philosophy altogether), and Weber's public lecture was the most impressive
defence, offered in postwar Germany, of modern science and
philosophy.

I. Radical historicism and the impulse toward radical historical understanding, toward interpretation of texts

a) To appreciate the bearing of Spengler's teaching, one
must remind oneself of the original claim of modern science and philosophy: they originally had[1] claimed to teach
the truth, the truth valid for all men and indeed for all intel-
ligent beings (Voltaire's *Micromégas*). That science and philosophy was declared by Spengler to be no more than the
expression of a specific soul, of a specific *culture*, the Faustic
culture –, and only one form of its self-expression, no less
but no more significant than art, economy, strategy and what
not. The claim of mathematic[s] and logic, e.g., to be absolutely true was dismissed: there is no logic or mathematic[s],
but there are various logics and mathematics in accordance
with the variety of cultures to which they belong. The same
holds naturally true of ethics. Modern science or philosophy is no more *true* than, say, the[1] Chinese system of
administration.

The only consequence which a theoretical man, a philosopher, could draw from this was that *the* task of philosophy is to
understand the various cultures[11] as expressions of their souls.
This would be certainly more philosophic than to elaborate
still further modern logic, e.g., modern logic being nothing
other than the expression of a specific soul. Spengler as it were
replaced theory of knowledge or metaphysics by the understanding of the souls producing the various cultures, of these
souls which are the *roots* of all "truth." |

2 recto   The understanding of cultures naturally has a standard of
truth. But it does not claim to be *absolutely* true. For whatever
truth may be – it certainly must be meaningful. Now, historical studies are not meaningful for, they are not even understandable to, cultures other than the Faustic culture: historical

truth, the most radical truth, we might say: the only truth left, *exists* exclusively for Faustic man.

b) Prepared by the idealistic interpretation of science:

α) if reason does not *discover* the laws of nature, but if it is reason which *prescribes* [to] nature its laws, truth is the *product* of reason. Reason has its *history*. And that history is not necessarily determined by the exigencies of reason itself.

β) Science consists in organizing sense-data – but there are various ways of organizing sense-data – Newton and Goethe (Cassirer) – Simmel's various "planes."

c) Spengler seemed to represent the extreme of historicism; but it was soon seen[12] that he had not gone to the end of his way.

α) The philosophic deficiency of Spengler's teaching: it required as its basis an elaborate philosophy of man, of human existence as being essentially historical; a philosophy showing that man as *the* historical being is the origin of all meaning; and this presupposed an analysis of truth, an analysis showing that truth is essentially relative to human existence. Such a philosophy was elaborated by *Heidegger*.

β) Spengler had emphasized certain features common to *all* cultures: static (art, science, politics, religion) and dynamic (growth including decay) laws of culture, we may say. He had thus acknowledged the distinction between the essence of culture as such and the peculiar features of the individual culture, between unhistorical and historical elements of culture. But is it possible to make such a[1] distinction, as it is implied in the use of the very term "culture"? Is not "everything" historical? Is not the most abstract categorical system still historical, applicable to one culture only? More precisely: are the categories used by Spengler, really applicable to the phenomena which he tries to interpret? If it is crazy to interpret Brutus in terms of the French revolution, it is still more crazy for a historicist to talk of Greek *states*, of Greek *religion* etc., i.e. to apply categories which are not Greek to Greek phenomena. If it is true that each "culture" is unique, it has a categorical system of its own, and that system must be discovered out of the phenomena of that culture itself. We must then study the various cultures directly, and not, as Spengler largely had done, the *literature on* these cultures. We must study the *documents*. This, however, primarily means *interpreting texts*[13], seeing that the interpretation of other documents, e.g. statues[14], is much more open to subjective interpretation than are explicit statements.

Thus Spengler gave to historical studies an infinitely greater significance than they previously had[1] had. For he had practically reduced philosophy itself to understanding of the historical phenomena. [1](Prewar historicism had acknowledged at least logic and theory of knowledge as nonhistorical disciplines.)[1] It was[15] now no longer historians, but philosophers who studied the past with no other interest than to understand the past.

γ) If philosophy is reduced for one moment to understanding texts, the philosophic interest has to be focussed on the phenomena of interpretation, generally speaking: of understanding other people's thoughts. That is to say: *hermeneutics* takes on a central significance. Study of hermeneutics, of the principles underlying understanding ≠ explaining paves the way for a philosophy as an attempt to *understand* the phenomena, as distinguished from a philosophy which attempts to *explain* the phenomena. |

2 verso   δ) The turning to the texts themselves implies a profound distrust of the initial categories of interpretation, of the categories we use before having *submitted* ourselves to the [1]test of the[1] past. That distrust is directed especially against the term "culture" which is the product of the[16] Faustic soul. More elementary, less sophisticated terms are required if we want to give an accurate and adequate account of the thoughts and interests guiding the life of earlier people. [1]We must get rid of the whole conceptual apparatus created by modern philosophy or science, and indeed by the older traditions of philosophy or science; we must return to a[1] pre-philosophic or a[1] pre-scientific language if we want to arrive at an adequate understanding of pre-philosophic "culture."[1]

Whoever tried seriously to understand the past along these lines discovered certain *basic* facts and interests which have *not* changed and which are not subject to change. Therewith the historical interest turned into a philosophic interest, into the interest in the eternal nature of man. And that turn was backed by historical studies as distinguished from a general philosophy of history. Finally, it became clear that members of all "cultures", ¹being *men*,¹ may understand each other, whereas the "Faustic" historicist understands none, because he does not see the eternal nature of man, ¹because he does not see the wood for the trees.¹

Besides, familiarity with earlier thought provides[17] the experience of the *practicability* of an essentially *unhistorical* approach: radical historicism awakes a passionate interest in the past and therewith a passionate interest in the[18] unhistorical approach characteristic of man up to the 18th century.

II. Demand for evident justification of historical studies in general and of each individual historical study in particular

The assumption underlying the tendency under discussion is the view that philosophy is self-knowledge of man in his historicity. Such philosophy takes on the form of historical study. Philosophy or history thus understood is essentially and purely *theoretical*. Now, a purely theoretical approach to history is open to an objection which had been raised by Nietzsche in the '70s, in his essay "Vom Nutzen und Nachteil der Historie für das Leben", but which was not appreciated very much before the war. The objection may be put this way: historical knowledge, as self-knowledge of man, as *reflection*, is dangerous to spontaneity; human life and human history are essentially spontaneous; therefore, the total victory of historical consciousness, of history *understood*, would be the end of history itself, of history *lived* or *done*. (If the philosophers of the past had been historians, there would be no history of philosophy. Or, the other way round: if we want to *understand* the philosophers of the past, we must be guided by the same basic interest which guided them: the interest in *the* truth, in the truth about the whole, and not ¹the *historical* interest,¹ the interest in the opinions of other people). Historical consciousness ought then not to be left to itself, it ought to be limited by, and made subservient to, the forces which *make* history: historical studies ought to be in the service of *life*. Life means the *present*. Historical consciousness left to itself, historical consciousness ruling supreme, would mean the unlimited rule of the past over the present. The consequence is: we must no longer take it for granted that historical knowledge and historical studies are useful, pleasant and necessary. For experience shows that mankind lived at almost all times without the famous historical sense ("the sixth sense"). |

3 recto   Of course, we find historical interest, historiography, very early in the development of mankind. But never before the 18th century did history take on a *philosophic* significance. The view that history has such a significance – this view underlying the very term "philosophy of history" – has to be considered a *prejudice,* as long as we have not understood thoroughly why present-day life, why present-day philosophy, as distinguished from that of earlier periods, *needs* historical consciousness. And that *need,* that *necessity* has to be shown not merely in general, but, moreover, no individual historical study can be considered significant, if it is not undertaken with perfect clarity as to *its* "existential" necessity.

If radical historicism changed the character of historical studies profoundly[19], in so far as it engendered a new *passion* for historical studies, indeed an *extreme* passion for such studies, Nietzsche's criticism of historicism (and also the philosophy of existence) enlightened that passion by compelling people to make perfectly clear to themselves the *motives* of historical studies in general and of each individual historical study in particular. It was apt to direct historical studies towards the interpretation of such texts as were relevant to the solution, or understanding, of our most urgent immediate problems. And it led up to the fundamental question of the meaning of historical consciousness by raising the question why and how far historical consciousness is a necessity.

III. The reasons characteristic of our time which make historical consciousness a necessity

The question of the reason why and how far historical consciousness is a necessity, is itself a *historical* question. Nietzsche's question and answer had been unhistorical: he had explained out of human nature as such why *man* needs history. He naturally had seen that there is a basic difference between all earlier historical interest and that radical historical interest which had developed since the 18th century.[20]

He had *objected* to that radical historical interest; but he had not attempted to *understand* the *necessity* underlying it. Thus, Nietzsche's question had to be made more precise: why does *modern* man need historical studies, why is *modern* man compelled to be historically minded in a way in which no earlier age had been? Why do *we* need history?

Three answers were given to that question.

a) Human life is essentially historical, i.e., man naturally needs a *tradition* which guides him, which makes possible communication and mutual understanding. *The* tradition, the tradition based upon Greek science and Biblical religion, had been gradually undermined since the 16th century. For modern man attempted to be free from all prejudices, i.e. from all traditions. But the fact that man does need tradition is shown by this, that the very same modern man who undermined all traditions was compelled to take refuge in history: history is the modern surrogate for tradition. |

b) It is not true that modern man has no tradition; each generation necessarily grows up in a tradition, even if it grows up in a tradition of anti-traditionalism. Tradition is *always* a decisively determining *power*. That power cannot be disposed of by a decision to doubt once in one's life one's prejudices; Descartes' fate shows clearly that such a wholesale liberation from the prejudices does not work; to[21] free our minds from the shackles of tradition which prevent us from looking at things with our own eyes, in an unbiased and independent way, we must first *know* the power we are up against; we cannot get rid of the prejudices but after having *understood* them from their roots, from their *historical* roots. Now, it would be an error to assume that the destruction of tradition, attempted since Descartes, actually achieved its purpose. It could not achieve its purpose, because its attack on *tradition* was bound up with belief in actual or possible *progress*. Now, progress at its best is the establishment of a true and sound tradition, but at any rate the establishment of a new *tradition*. For "progress" means that certain questions, the *basic* questions can be settled once and for all, so that the answers to these questions can be taught to children, so that the subsequent generations simply can build up on the solutions found out by earlier generations, without bothering any longer about the basic questions.

3 verso

I.e.: "progress" implies that the answers to the basic questions can be taken for granted, that they can be permitted to become *prejudices* for all generations after that of the founding fathers. Accordingly, the process of intellectual development during the modern centuries consists in this, that each generation *reacts* to the preceding generation and to the preceding generation *only*, without raising the question whether the whole basis on which the discussion takes place – that basis discovered by the founding fathers – is valid. Hegel's view that the historical process is a sequence of thesis, antithesis and synthesis, a sequence which necessarily brings to light the truth, is only an expression of the actual procedure of the modern centuries. That process may be sketched as follows: Descartes attacks and refutes late scholasticism, Locke refutes Descartes, Berkeley refutes Locke, Hume[III] refutes Berkeley, Kant refutes Hume, Hegel refutes Kant etc.; but the foundation laid by Descartes is never truly tested, because the root of the pre-modern position, the philosophy of Aristotle, the alleged refutation of which is the basis of modern philosophy, is never adequately discussed. For all discussions of Aristotle make use of modern conceptions, of conceptions the use of which decides beforehand the outcome of the discussion.

Robert Musil in his novel *The Man Without Qualities* expressed the criticism of the then still prevalent view by saying that the process of history, far from being guided by the exigencies of reason, actually is a process of muddling through ("Weiterwurschteln"). The outcome of a discussion depends, not on reason, but on "history," and the verdicts of history are what we believe to be established truths. To counteract that tendency, a radical revision at least of the causes célèbres, allegedly[1] decided by *history*, is indispensable. And *we* are in need of such a revision much more than the former generations, since I the anti-traditionalism characteristic of modern thought is apt to make us blind to the fact that we are the *heirs* of a *tradition* of anti-traditionalism, and since historical research shows us more and more how much we still are under the spell of the medieval *tradition* of Aristoteli[ani]sm

4 recto

III His criticism of causality takes into account exclusively Hobbes, Clarke and Locke – not: Aristotle.

and Biblical *authority*. The *ballast* of tradition has *not* become *smaller* since the days of Descartes, it has become *greater*.

c) Historical studies are the most urgent necessity, if present day man does not happen to *know* of fundamental facts which were known to earlier generations, in other words, if we have *teachers* in the past and none in our time. Historical studies are necessary because of the *bankruptcy* of modern man. That bankruptcy was asserted by a large number of people – it implied a less fatalistic view of the same facts which had given birth to the title "Decline of the West." To mention one example only: Yorck von Wartenburg in his correspondence with Dilthey which was published in 1926, had said: modern man is finished and just fit to be buried; the movement which had begun in the Renaissance or earlier, has come to its close; enthusiastic pupils of Heidegger said that *Martin* Heidegger marks the end of the epoch which was opened by another Martin, Martin Luther. The feeling[22] that we were witnessing an end, that modern man was at his wit's end, was the most important motive for historical studies, for a turning to the thought of the past. "We are sold out completely as regards knowledge – we know nothing – this ignorance of ours is then, and then only, not utterly unbearable if we are willing to *learn* something; i.e. if we are willing to open the old in-folios, to *read* – but to read not with that astonishing detachment and indifference with which the preceding generations used to read those books, but with the consuming interest of him who wants to be taught, who wants to receive a teaching" (Ebbinghaus).

In a less dogmatic form, that view may be expressed as follows: it is after all *possible* that the truth, or the right approach to the truth, has been found in a remote past and *forgotten* for[23] centuries.

IV. The bankruptcy of the present: the turning from reason to authority

The bankruptcy of modern man seemed to become obvious in the crisis of modern science. The expression *Grundlagenkrisis* (crisis of the foundations of all sciences and studies) became a slogan. Of course, the existence of such a crisis was denied with regard to the continuing progress of the natural sciences as well as of historical research. But the critics of modern science pointed to the fact that science as a whole had lost that *significance*, that *human* significance which it certainly had [had] up to the end of the 19th century and even up to the last war. The controversy over Darwin's *Origin of Species* had been of immediate concern to every thinking person; even the controversy over du Bois-Reymond's *Die Grenzen der naturwissenschaftlichen Erkenntnis* had a wide echo; but the scientific discoveries of postwar time (except those of immediate bearing on technology and medicine) were important only to specialists.

The enormous loss of prestige which science, the scientific spirit, had suffered, revealed itself nowhere more clearly than in the most significant *defence*, offered in postwar Germany, of the scientific spirit: Max Weber's *Science and Learning as a Vocation*. Weber had an unusually high qualification to state the case of traditional science before the younger generation: he enjoyed a very high reputation as a scholar (he was not merely a theoretician of the social sciences, but he had enriched the social sciences themselves) as well as a teacher, and he understood the aspirations as well as the frustrations of the younger generation. During the turmoil of the year 1919, when the thinking part of the academic youth was more eager than ever before the war for genuine *knowledge*, for real *science* as regards the basic principles or ends of human actions, |

4 verso

Weber declared that no science of that kind is possible, that no genuine *knowledge* of the true aims of human life can be expected of science or philosophy. To the question of what the more than technical meaning of science or scholarship or philosophy is, Weber gave this answer: the views that science etc. is the way to the true being or to nature or to God or to happiness, are "illusions" which no one but "great children" can accept any longer. Science can teach us many things as regards the *means* leading to the various ultimate ends which are possible; it can even elucidate the *meaning* of these ends or values; but it cannot settle the conflicts between the different values: which value of the various conflicting values is to be preferred, can*not* be said by science or philosophy. The conflict which cannot be settled by *argument*, must be settled by the free *decision* of every individual. This is, according to

Weber, the distinction between the man of science and the prophet: that the prophet can and must recommend on the basis of his decision what he considers to be the right aim, whereas the man of science must refrain from any such recommendation. Weber went to the end of this way by asserting that science or philosophy, far from being able to settle the fundamental question of the right life of man as man, is itself ultimately based on an "irrational" decision: the opposition to the scientific spirit, to the scientific approach as such, cannot be *refuted*[24], cannot be shown to be absurd, by *science*.

Weber's thesis amounted to this: that reason and argument are intrinsically incapable of giving to life a real guidance. Reason and argument cannot bridge the gulf which separates the different groups each of which is guided by a star, a value-system, of its own. Now, every human community needs some degree of agreement at least as regards the basic moral questions. Such an agreement may be supplied by a tradition; but in Germany, traditions were losing their force more and more. If reason and argument are incapable of supplying people with the minimum of mutual understanding required for living together,[25] if mutual understanding as regards the practical basis of common life cannot be reached by reason and argument, people had no choice but to turn away from reason to *authority*.

The most visible kind of authority – most visible at least in Germany – is the *State*. In an essay *Der Begriff des Politischen* (What is political?), Carl Schmitt indicated the following chain of thought: there is not one ideal, but a variety of conflicting ideals; therefore, ideals cannot have an obligatory character; more precisely, any value judgment is a free decision, which concerns exclusively the freely deciding individual himself; it is essentially a private affair; therefore, no one can expect of any other man that that other man sacrifice[26] anything for the first man's ideal; but no political community can exist without asserting that there are *obligations* which can overrule any private decision; whatever may be the ultimate source of these obligations, they cannot be derived from free decisions of the individual, or else they could be no more than *conditional* obligations, not *absolute* obligations, the obligation to sacrifice life itself. For, Schmitt asserts, if we analyse political obligation, and above all the meaning of "political," we find that we mean by "political" any fact which is related to the distinction of friend and enemy of the group to which we belong, that distinction originating in the possibility of *war*. The basic fact of the possibility of war sets an absolute limit to all freedom of decision: it creates *authority* and therewith it gives all members of the community a generally valid guidance. |

5 recto

A more radical expression of this view is to be found in an essay by Ernst Jünger "On pain" (in: *Blätter und Steine*). Jünger asserts that in our period all faiths and ideals of earlier times have lost their force and evidence. Consequently, all standards with reference to which we can judge ourselves and others are no longer valid. But there is one standard left: the ability or inability to stand pain, physical pain. Fortitude or courage is the only virtue which is still evident, the only virtue left – and this not without reason: ἀνδρεία is *the* original virtue.

However highly people might think of the State, the remembrance was not lost that the State can never be an *absolute* authority. An absolute authority must be superhuman, the authority of God. Since the beginning of this century, people had spoken of a religious revival after the positivistic indifference of the 19th century. That revival was always accompanied by the opinion that an unreserved return to the teaching of the Bible was impossible, because of the achievements of modern science and criticism. After the war, however, such an unreserved return to the Bible as the document of *revelation* became a serious possibility for many people. The age-old distrust of revelation and theology was replaced by a distrust of religion. A remarkable philosophic writer of predominantly theological interest was fond of the fact that the very term "religion" did not occur once in his work. The belief that the unmodified and unmitigated teaching of the Bible had been refuted by modern science and criticism, lost its power. Karl Barth in particular insisted upon the fact that what had been refuted in the 17th and 18th centuries[27] was a weak kind of apologetics, but never the doctrine of Calvin and Luther themselves.

The development under discussion may be described in the following terms: [the] theory of knowledge had raised the question of what science is. It had *not* raised the more fundamental question of Nietzsche "*Why* science?" The question "why science" [28]seems to imply[28] that there is a standard higher than science with reference to which science as such can be judged. According to Nietzsche, that standard is "life." But life, human life, is not intrinsically superior to science, human science: the philosopher is always free to answer "pereat vita, vivat philosophia," and therewith to reject the authority of "life." The [1]evidently necessary[1] question "why science" becomes compelling[29] only with regard to something which is superior to everything human: the question "why science" calls science before the tribunal of the authority of revelation. Science is not necessary: man may choose it or reject it (this is implied in the very question "why science?"). An absolute necessity cannot be found but in divine command.

The inability of modern science or philosophy to give man an evident teaching as regards the fundamental question, the question of the right life, led people to turn from science or reason to authority, to the authority of the State or the authority of Revelation. Politics and theology, as distinguished from science of all kind[s], appeared to be much more closely connected with the basic interests of man as man than science *and all culture:* the political community and the word of the living God are basic; compared with them everything else is derived and relative. *"Culture" is superseded by politics and theology, by "political theology."* We have travelled a long road away from Spengler.

In that situation, a pupil of Max Weber, Karl Mannheim, made an attempt to save argument and reason against the doubt, expressed by his teacher, that argument and reason are incapable of leading[30] to agreement as regards the fundamentals. Mannheim believed that such an agreement could be reached on the basis of the fact that all divergent opinions worth considering are related to, or produced by, the *present situation.* Consciousness of our belonging to the same situation may lead to a solution of our most urgent problem: discussion between the various opposed groups leads to a dialectic synthesis of the divergent opinions. This suggestion, if meant as a philosophic and not merely as a political suggestion, (and there is reason for believing that it *was* meant to be a philosophic suggestion) seems to be absurd: a dialectic

synthesis of atheism and theism, e.g., cannot even be imagined. Mannheim probably would answer that theism is today
nothing[31] more than an obsolete ideology, | since it is not
genuinely related to the present situation. At any rate, this *was*
asserted by many people: Nietzsche's statement that the greatest event in the recent history of Europe is the death of God
was explicitly or implicitly adopted by a considerable number
of writers (Spengler, Scheler, Hartmann, Heidegger). According to that view, the present age is the first radically atheistic
epoch in the history of mankind. Thus, reflection on the specific character of the present age leads indeed to the discovery of an ideal potentially common to all present-day men or
at least Europeans. That ideal ¹which is¹ in accordance with
the characteristic assumption of our time will be an atheistic
morality.

The new atheism is opposed not only to the belief in a
personal God and to pantheism, but equally to the *morality* of
the Bible, to the belief in progress, in human brotherhood
and equality, in the dignity of man as man, in short to all
moral standards which, [32]as it believed,[32] lose their meaning
once they are separated from their religious basis. – Also: the
new atheism does no longer believe (as the Greeks did) in the
κόσμος: therefore the attitude, underlying Greek science, of
admiring the κάλλιστος κοσμος is replaced by the attitude of
courage and Standhalten. – Moreover: 19th century atheism
had tried to replace God by mankind or man; it thus had
deified man, who, however, is a finite being. The new atheism
insists on the finiteness of men: deification of mankind is no
genuine atheism.

People[33] were then confronted with an atheism, much
more radical than e.g. Marxist atheism can be, on the one
hand, and ¹an attempt at¹ a restoration of the belief in Divine
revelation on the other. That is to say, they[34] were confronted
with a situation which had not existed in Europe for[35] many
generations. Naturally, their[36] conceptual instruments (if I
may say so) were utterly insufficient to tackle the new or
rather old problems. It was hard not to see that the question of
the existence or non-existence of a personal God, Creator of
Heaven and Earth, was a serious question, more serious even
than the question of the right method of the social sciences. If

the question should be answered, if it should even be understood as a meaningful question, one had to go back to an age
when it was in the center of discussion – i.e. to Pre-Kantian
philosophy.

For: 1) atheism was no longer proved – it was asserted that
God is dead, i.e. that people no longer believe in
the Biblical God – which is clearly no proof. For
the view[37] that Biblical belief had been "refuted" by
modern science and criticism presupposed[38] belief
in that science and criticism, a belief utterly shat-
tered in the period in question.

2) as regards Biblical theology of Gogarten, Rosenzweig etc.: it was no longer the Biblical theology
of the Bible or of Calvin and Luther – was it then a
Biblical theology at all?

Return to the philosophy of the Enlightenment, or more
precisely to the philosophy of the 17th and 18th centuries[39],
seemed to be recommended by yet another consideration.
The urgency of a convincing, generally valid moral teaching,
of a moral teaching of evident political relevance, was clearly
felt. Such a moral teaching seemed to be discernible in the
natural law doctrines of the 17th and 18th centuries[39] rather
than in later teaching[s]. (Troeltsch had asserted time and
again that the political superiority of the Anglosaxons was
due to the fact that that natural law tradition had not been
superseded, to the same extent as in Germany, by historicism.)
For the natural law teachers of the 17th and 18th centuries
had spoken of laws and obligations, and not merely of ideals
and values. |

V. The return to reason and the final liberation
from historicism

6 recto

The tendencies just mentioned imply, as you doubtless have
noticed, a *reaction* to the defeatism which had led to the turning from reason to authority. But that reaction, that return to
sanity, was *not* a return to 19th century or 20th century positivism or neo-Kantianism. That positivism and neo-Kantianism
was inseparable from the belief in progress and therewith
from a philosophy of history. It was as inseparable from a

philosophy of history as was its opponent (authoritarianism and historicism). But the rationalism posterior to historicism returned from Turgot and his pupils to Montesquieu or the 17th century philosophers. For that new rationalism was engaged in the quest for *eternal* truths and *eternal* standards, and it clearly realized that eternal truths and eternal standards are indifferent in themselves to any theory as to the sequence in which they are discovered or put into practice. "History" became again the realm of *chance;* i.e. "history" ceased to be a realm of its own, a field in the way in which nature is said to be a field. Historicism was about to be overcome definitely.

Let me explain this somewhat more fully. The view that truth is eternal and that there are eternal standards, was contradicted by historical consciousness, i.e. by the opinion that all "truths" and standards are necessarily relative to a given historical situation, and that, consequently, a mature philosophy can raise no higher claim than that to express the spirit of the period to which it belongs. Now, historical consciousness is not a revelation; it claims to be *demonstrably* superior to the unhistorical earlier view. But what does the historicist really *prove?* In the best case, that all attempts hitherto made by man to discover *the* truth about the universe, about God, about the right aim of human life, have not led to a generally accepted doctrine. Which is clearly not a proof that the question of *the* truth about the universe, about God, about the right aim of human life is a meaningless question. The historicist may have proved that in spite of all the efforts made by the greatest men, we do not know the truth. But what does this mean more than that[1] philosophy, quest for truth, is as necessary as ever? What else does it mean but that no man, and still less no sum of men, is wise, σοφος, but only, in the best case, φιλοσοφος? Historicism refutes all systems of philosophy – by doing this, it does the cause of philosophy the greatest service: for a system of philosophy, a system of *quest* for truth, is non-sense. In other words, historicism mistakes the unavoidable *fate* of all philosophers who, being men, are apt to err[40], for a refutation of the *intention* of philosophy. Historicism is in the best case a proof of our *ignorance* – of which we are aware without historicism – but by not deriving from the insight into our ignorance the urge to seek for knowledge, it betrays a lamentable or ridiculous self-complacency; it shows that it is just one dogmatism among the many dogmatisms which it may have debunked. |

Philosophy in the original meaning of the word presupposes the liberation from historicism. I say, the *liberation* from it, and not merely its[41] refutation. Refutations are cheap and usually not worth the paper on which they are written; for they do not require that the refuting writer has *understood* the ultimate motives of the adversary. The liberation from historicism requires that historical consciousness be[42] seen to be, not a self-evident premise, but a *problem*. And it necessarily is a *historical* problem. For historical consciousness is an opinion, or a set of opinions, which occurs only in a certain period. Historical consciousness is, to use the language of that consciousness, itself a *historical* phenomenon, a phenomenon which has come into being and which, therefore, is bound to pass away again. Historical consciousness will be superseded by something else.

The historicist would answer: the only thing by which historical consciousness can be superseded is the new barbarism. As if historicism had not paved the way to that new barbarism. Historical consciousness is not such an impressive thing that something superior to it should be inconceivable.

What was[43] required was[43] that *history should be applied to itself*. Historical consciousness is itself the product of a historical process, of a process which is barely known and certainly never adequately, i.e. critically studied. I.e.: historical consciousness is the product of a *blind* process. We certainly ought not to accept the result of a blind process on trust. By bringing that process to light, we free ourselves from the power of its result. We become again, what we cannot be before, *natural* philosophers, i.e. philosophers who approach the natural, the basic and original question of philosophy in a natural, an adequate way.

VI. Return to reason as a return to Plato and Aristotle

A return to reason *which implies or presupposes a critical analysis of the genesis of historical consciousness*, necessarily is a return to reason as reason was understood in pre-modern times.

For it would be a mistake to think that historical consciousness is a product of romanticism only. Romantic historical
consciousness is only a correction of the historical consciousness of Enlightenment (criticism of the present vs. satisfaction
with the present and its potentialities). At the very beginning
of the modern period, in the 16th century, we observe for
the first time the turning of *philosophers* to history as history
(≠ facts recorded by historians). But when *studying* the genesis of historical consciousness, we *judge* it, we look at it with
critical eyes: we [44]are in[44] the first steps and the imperfect
beginnings of something wonderful, but the first step away
from the right approach: for we know from experience the
ultimate result[45] to which that first step led. I.e., when studying the genesis of historical consciousness, we look at it with
the eyes of pre-modern philosophy – we stand on the other
side of the fence. Only by doing this, shall we be enabled to
find the *right* name of that which *we* call history (Geschichte
≠ Historie).

Why has such a return become a necessity? In attempting
to answer that question, I shall have to summarize a number
of remarks which I made before in different connections. |

7 recto   Modern philosophy has come into being as a *refutation*
of traditional philosophy, i.e. of the Aristotelian philosophy.
Have the founders of modern philosophy *really* refuted Aristotle ? Have they ever *understood* him[46]? They certainly understood the Aristotelians of their time, but they certainly did not
understand Aristotle himself. But it might be said that the refutation not adequately done by the founding fathers, has been
done in the meantime. By whom? He cannot have been *refuted,*
if he has not been *understood.* And this was perhaps the most
profound impression which the younger generation experienced in Germany during the period in question: under the
guidance of Heidegger, people came to see that Aristotle and
Plato had *not* been understood. Heidegger's interpretation of
Aristotle was an achievement with which I cannot compare
any other[47] intellectual phenomenon which has emerged in
Germany after the war. Heidegger made it clear, not by assertions, but by concrete analyses – the work of an enormous
concentration and diligence – that Plato and Aristotle have
not been understood by the modern philosophers; for they

read their own opinions into the works of Plato and Aristotle; they did not read them with the necessary zeal to know what Plato and Aristotle really meant, which *phenomena* Plato and Aristotle had in mind when talking of whatever they were talking [about]. And as regards the classical scholars, their[48] interpretations too[1] are utterly dependent on modern philosophy, since the way in which they *translate*, i.e. *understand*, the terms of Plato and Aristotle is determined by the influence on their mind of modern philosophy. For even a classical scholar is a modern man, and therefore under the spell of modern biases: and an adequate understanding of a pre-modern text requires, not merely knowledge of language and antiquities and the secrets of criticism, but also a constant *reflection* on the specifically modern assumptions which might[1] prevent us from understanding pre-modern thought, if we are not constantly on our guard. If Plato and Aristotle are not understood and consequently not refuted, return to Plato and Aristotle is an open possibility.

That possibility exercised a certain appeal on all people who had become dissatisfied with modern philosophy. For a return to scholasticism was not so much considered in Germany as it was in France. And this [was so] not only because Germany is predominantly Protestant, but also because the *derived* nature of scholasticism as compared with the *original* philosophy of Plato and Aristotle was too keenly felt.

Heidegger was not the only man who drew the attention of the younger generation to Greek antiquity as *the* truly classical period. Werner Jaeger's activity had a similar effect. I think it was in the environment of Jaeger that the term "third humanism" was coined. "Third humanism" would be a movement which continues in a most radical way the second humanism, the humanism of the German classics, of Schiller, e.g., who in his essay *On Naive and Sentimental Poetry* had described the relation of the moderns to the ancients in these terms: the Greeks *were* nature, whereas for modern man, nature, being natural, is only an ought, an *ideal*; modern man[49] has a *longing* for what was *real* in Greece.

The discussion concerning science, concerning the specific features of the scientific approach, had led to [50]a point[50] where this general impression of what the Greeks were could take on a more definite meaning. It had been an implication of phenomenology to distinguish between the *scientific* view of [the] world (the view, elaborated by *modern* science) and the *natural* view of the world, the idea being that that natural view is prior to, and the[1] basis of, the scientific view: the scientific view of the world | emerges out of the natural view by virtue of a specific modification of approach. Now it became clear that that basic view, the starting point of the view elaborated by modern[1] science, more precisely: that the world as it is present for, and experienced by, that natural view, had been the subject of Plato's and Aristotle's analyses. Plato and Aristotle appeared to have discussed adequately what had *not* been discussed by the founders of modern philosophy, nor by their successors. For Hegel had indeed attempted to understand "the concrete," the phenomena themselves, but he had tried to "*construct*" them by starting from the "abstract." Whereas this was precisely the meaning of the Socratic turning: that science must *start* from the known, from the "known *to us*," from what is known in ordinary experience, and that science *consists* in *understanding* what is known indeed, but not understood adequately. (E.g. to deny motion, is "madness," for δῆλον ἐξ ἐπαγωγῆς; but τί ἔστι κίνησις – *that* is the question). Platonic and Aristotelian terms appeared to have a directness, and they appeared to have that direct relation to "impressions" which Hume had demanded and which he could not find, indeed, in the *modern* concept of cause and effect to which he limited his discussions – a directness, I say, absent from the modern concepts which all presuppose that *break*, effected by Descartes and continued by all his successors, with natural knowledge.[IV] Therefore, if we want to arrive at an adequate understanding

7 verso

IV Cf., e.g. Hegel: "Im allgemeinen ist zu bemerken, dass das Denken sich auf den Standpunkt des Spinozismus gestellt haben muss; das ist der wesentliche Anfang alles Philosophierens. Wenn man anfängt zu philosophieren, so muss man zuerst Spinozist sein. Die Seele muss sich baden in diesem Äther der einen Substanz, in der alles, was man für wahr gehalten hat, untergegangen ist." ["In general it should be noted that thinking had to take the standpoint of Spinozism; that is the essential beginning of all philosophizing. If one begins to philosophize, then one has to be a Spinozist first. The soul has to bathe in the ether of the one substance in which everything that one has held to be true has perished."]

of the "natural" world, we simply have to *learn* from Plato and Aristotle.

But however this may be, whatever may be the final result of our studying Plato and Aristotle, whether or how far we can adhere ultimately to their analyses in all respects or not – what is decisively important is that we first learn to grasp their intention and then that their results be *discussed*. La querelle des anciens et des modernes must be renewed – it must be repeated with much greater fairness and greater *knowledge* than it was done in the 17th and 18th centuries.

Heidegger's interpretation of Aristotle, which is not more than a beginning, would not have been possible without *Husserl's* phenomenology. As regards Husserl's work, I can only say that I believe that it surpasses in significance everything I know of, which was done in Germany in the last 50 years. Such an analysis as that of the transformation of geometry underlying Galileo's physics, as we find it in one of his latest publications, is the model for any analysis[51] concerning the basic assumptions of modern science and philosophy. |

But Husserl was not the only superior mind who was responsible for the great change we have been witnessing. At least as influential in this respect was the work of *Nietzsche*. Nietzsche changed the intellectual climate of Germany and perhaps of the whole continental Europe in a way similar to that in which Rousseau had changed that climate about 120 years before. And I do not think that a comparable change of the intellectual climate had occurred in the time between Nietzsche and Rousseau. The work of Nietzsche is as ambiguous as was that of Rousseau. And there is therefore a quite understandable difference of opinion as to what the real meaning of Nietzsche's work is. If I understand him correctly, his deepest concern was with philosophy, and not with politics ("philosophy and State are incompatible"); and that philosophy, in order to be really philosophy, and not some sort of dogmatism, is the sake of *natural* men,[52] of men capable and willing to live "under the sky," of men who do not need the shelter of the cave, of *any* cave. Such a cave, such an artificial[53] protection against the *elementary* problems, he described, not only in

8 recto

the pre-modern tradition (of providence), but likewise in the modern tradition. It was against "history," against the belief that "history" can decide any question, that progress can ever make superfluous the discussion of the primary questions, against the belief that history, that indeed any human things, are the elementary subject of philosophy, that he reasserted hypothetically the doctrine of eternal return: to drive home that the elementary, the natural subject of philosophy still is, and always will be, as it had been for the Greeks: the κόσμος, the world.

Text-Critical Notes

[] contains additions by the editor.
<> indicates deletions by Leo Strauss.

1. Inserted or added by Leo Strauss between the lines or in the margins.
2. Ms.: than is Western philosophy.
3. [Insertion in ink in the margin. LS first wrote *an acute remembrance.* Then he made the correction in pencil: *recollection.*]
4. the most < petty-bourgeois and > ridiculous
5. < that >
6. < western >
7. < attacked >
8. < preceded >
9. < was >
10. < its >
11. cultures < and their >
12. Ms.: seen soon
13. < the > *texts*
14. Ms.: statues e.g.
15. Ms.: were
16. < a specifically >
17. Ms.: provides with
18. < that >
19. < radically >
20. [Noted in the margin in pencil:] But see Nietzsche, 2nd Unzeitgemässe, p. 61.
21. < to prev >
22. < fact >
23. Ms.: since
24. *refuted* < by science >
25. together, < people had no choice but to *turn away from reason to authority.* >

26. Ms.: sacrifices
27. Ms.: century
28. < implied >
29. compelling < and meaningful >
30. Ms.: incapable to lead
31. < no >
32. < allegedly >
33. < We >
34. < we >
35. Ms.: since
36. < our >
37. < fact >
38. < implied >
39. Ms.: century
40. < be mistaken >
41. < the >
42. Ms.: is
43. < is >
44. < observe >
45. < reason >
46. < that >
47. other < impression >
48. Ms.: they
49. Ms.: modern modern has
50. < a position >
51. < studies >
52. [The English formulation *is the sake of natural men* is explained and
    is to be understood as a rendering of the German expression *ist die
    Sache natürlicher Menschen,* is the task or subject matter of natural
    men.]
53. artificial < , if for all practical purposes necessary, >

REASON AND REVELATION (1948)

1. To clarify the issue, we replace "reason – revelation" by
"philosophy – revelation."
By the problem of reason and revelation I understand the
problem of *philosophy* and revelation. "Reason" is neutral: the
rights of reason [2]would seem to be[2] recognized by believers in
revelation and by unbelievers alike. We rise above the level of
neutrality, or of triviality, we enter the arena of conflict, if we
confront revelation with a particular *interpretation* of reason –
with the view that *the* perfection of reason and *therefore the* perfection of man is philosophy. *Philosophy* is incompatible with
revelation: philosophy must try to *refute* revelation, and, if not
revelation, at any rate theology must try to *refute* philosophy.

2. Revelation must try to prove the absurdity of philosophy.
Speaking as a non-theologian to theologians, I shall not pre-
sume to define *revelation*. Only one point must be made.
Regardless of whether revelation is understood as revelation
of a *teaching* or as a *happening*, the claim of revelation becomes
noticeable first through a *teaching based* on revelation. Faith in
revelation necessarily issues in preaching or proclaiming the
message of revelation and therefore ultimately in a teaching –
if in a teaching which always falls short of its task. Those who
present that teaching cannot *disregard* the claim of philosophy which is incompatible with the claim of revelation. And
they cannot leave it at[1] anathem[at]izing or at forbidding

Lecture to be delivered at Hartford (Theological Seminary) on January, 8, 1948.

philosophy: they have to refute its claims. This necessity creates a serious problem. If we assume on the basis of the account of the Fall that *the* alternative for man is philosophy *or* obedience to God's revelation, a refutation of philosophy would seem to be tantamount to a *proof* of the truth of revelation. But such a proof is considered by the most radical theologians as incompatible with the very idea of revelation. The response to revelation is faith, and faith is knowledge, if a particular kind of knowledge. Every attempt, not merely at *replacing* the certainty of faith by any other certainty, but even at *supporting* the certainty of faith by any other certainty, contradicts the nature of faith; every attempt of this kind amounts to substituting trust in flesh for trust in God. There cannot be any evidence in favor of revelation but the *fact* of revelation as known through faith. Yet this means that for those who do not have the experience of faith, there is *no shred of evidence* in favor of faith; the unbelieving man has *not the slightest reason* for doubting his unbelief; [3]revelation is nothing but a factum brutum; the unbeliever[3] can live in true happiness without paying the slightest attention to the claim of revelation: the unbeliever is excusable – contrary to what Paul clearly teaches. One cannot leave it then at the notion that there is no shred of evidence outside of the fact of revelation in favor of revelation. While a *direct* proof of revelation contradicts the nature of revelation, an *indirect* proof is | inevitable. That indirect proof consists in the proof that the philosophic position is *inconsistent*, i.e. *absurd*. This proof that is not based on faith, does not do away with the difference between the knowledge of faith and merely human knowledge. For the alternative: "philosophy or obedience to revelation" is not complete: the third alternative is escapism or despair. The refutation of the claim of philosophy leads, not to faith, but to despair. The transformation of despondent man into a believing and comforted man is the action, not of man, but of God's grace.

1 verso

3. What philosophy is, cannot be directly known to-day.

It is more appropriate for me to try to explain what *philosophy* is. It seems to me that the idea of philosophy which is presupposed in present-day discussions by theologians as well as by others, blurs the decisive features. As a consequence, the philosophic challenge to theology is underestimated. People are led to believe that all serious philosophers rejected atheism explicitly or implicitly and since all philosophic doctrines of God are obviously insufficient, the desirability, if not the fact, of revelation seems to become a foregone conclusion for every honest person. Of course, no one can help admitting that there is a philosophic atheism, but that atheism is declared to be a *modern* phenomenon, a *post-Christian* phenomenon which *therefore* presupposes Christianity and is an indirect witness to the Christian faith. Indeed a case can be made for the view that all specifically modern ideas are merely secularised versions of Biblical ideas and therefore untenable without Biblical support.

But the question is precisely whether there is no alternative to Biblical faith on the one hand, and *modern* unbelief on the other. Only if it is realized that there *is* such an alternative, will[4] the philosophic challenge to theology be properly appreciated. The alternative which I have in mind, is exactly philosophy in its original or pre-modern meaning.

To-day, we do not have a direct access to what philosophy originally meant. Our concept of philosophy is derived from *modern* philosophy, i.e. a *derivative* form of philosophy. Modern philosophy did not start from a reactivation of the original motivation of philosophy, but it took over the idea of philosophy as an *inheritance.* What is being done by a better type of historians of philosophy to-day, is nothing other than the attempt to make good for a sin of omission perpetrated by the founders of modern philosophy. These historians try to transform a mere inheritance into a living force. Hitherto, this historical work has had little effect on the general notion of philosophy which is still derived from modern philosophy. Accordingly, it is frequently assumed, e.g., that philosophy is essentially a *system*; it is forgotten that if this were so, philosophy as love of wisdom, | or *quest* for wisdom, or quest   2 recto
for the truth, were superfluous. Philosophy was originally not systematic in *any* sense. The idea of system presupposes, as Hegel has seen, that the philosophizing individual finds "the abstract form," i.e. a context of *concepts*, "ready made." But philosophy in its original form consists in *ascending* to the

abstract form, or to conceptual clarity, or in *acquiring* concepts. Or, to turn to a more simple example, according to the view of philosophy which to-day is generally accepted, a distinction has to be made between philosophy and science. This distinction, wholly unknown to philosophy until the later part of the 18th century, amounts, for all practical purposes, to the admission of an unscientific philosophy and of an unphilosophic science. Of these two pursuits, science enjoys naturally the highest prestige. For who can have anything but contempt for an unscientific philosophy, a thing as unworthy of esteem as justice not backed by the will to *fight* for justice. This unphilosophic science does no longer aim at what philosophy originally aimed, viz. at *the final* account of the whole. Science conceives of itself as *progressive*, i.e. as being the outcome of a progress of human thought beyond all earlier human thought and as being capable of still further progress in the future. There is an appalling disproportion between the exactness of science and the self-consciousness of science as essentially progressive as long as science is not accompanied by the effort, at least *aspiring* to exactness, to prove the *fact* of progress, to understand the conditions of progress and thus to guarantee the possibility of still further progress in the future. I.e.: modern science is necessarily accompanied by the *history* of science or the history of human thought. That history now takes actually, if silently, the place formerly occupied by philosophy. If the history of human thought is studied in the spirit of science, one arrives at the conclusion that all human thought is historically conditioned or historically determined, or that the attempt to liberate one's mind from all prejudices or from all historical determination is fantastic. Once this has become a settled conviction constantly reinforced by an ever increasing number of new observations, a final account of the whole – an account which as such would be beyond historical determination – appears to be impossible *for reasons which can be made clear to every child.* Thereafter, and we are living in this Thereafter, there exists no longer a direct access to philosophy in its original meaning as quest for *the* true and final account of the whole. Once this state has been reached, the original meaning of philosophy, the very *idea* of philosophy, is accessible only through recollection

of what philosophy meant in the *past*, i.e. through *history* of
philosophy. |

4. *The original meaning of philosophy.*

What then is the original meaning of philosophy? Philosophy
is originally the quest for truth, for *the* truth – for *the* beginnings of all things: In this, philosophy is at one with myth. But
the philosopher is fundamentally different from the teller, or
inventor, of myths. What separates the philosopher from the
mythologist, is the discovery of φύσις: the first philosopher
was the discoverer of φύσις. Φύσις had to be *discovered*: man
does not know without further ado that there is such a thing
as nature. Cf. O.T.[1] Nature was discovered when the quest
for the beginnings became guided by these two fundamental
distinctions:

a) the distinction between hearsay and seeing with one's
own eyes – the beginnings of all things must be made manifest,
or *demonstrated*, on the *basis* of what all men can see always in
broad daylight or through *ascent* from the visible things.

b) the distinction between man-made things and things
that are not man-made – the beginning of artificial things is
man, but man is clearly not the first thing, *the* beginning of
all things. Hence those things that are *not* man-made, lead
more directly to the first things than do the artificial things.
The production of artefacts is due to contrivance, to forethought. Nature was discovered when the possibility was realized that the first things may produce all other things, not by
means of forethought, but by blind necessity. I say: the possibility. It was not excluded that the origin of all things is forethought, *divine* forethought. But this assertion required from
now on a *demonstration*. The characteristic outcome of the

I [Noted in pencil at the bottom of the page with an asterisk:] Nature *not*
totality of phenomena. The pre-philosophic equivalent of φύσις: custom or
way; the permanent way = the right way; right = old, ancestral, one's own –
right way necessarily implies account of ancestors – of first things; ancestors
must be *gods;* variety of codes – *contradiction* –; *quest* for the right code by
right account of first things – how to *proceed*: a) ακοη – ὄψις (→ man is the
measure of all things) – examination of all alleged superhuman knowledge
in the light of *human* knowledge – *highest* superhuman knowledge is τέχνη;
b) τέχνη – φύσις.

discovery of nature is the demand for rigorous demonstration of the existence of divine beings, for a demonstration which starts from the analysis of phenomena manifest to everyone. Since no demonstration can *presuppose* the demonstrandum[5], philosophy is *radically* atheistic. The difference between Plato and a materialist like Democritus fades into insignificance if compared with the difference between[1] Plato and any doctrine based on religious experience. Plato's and Aristotle's attempts to demonstrate the existence of God far from proving the religious character of their teachings, actually disprove it. |

3 recto   This state of things is obscured by the *language* of Plato and of many other pre-modern philosophers. The *principle* underlying this particular kind of *speaking* has never been properly explained. Permit me therefore to say a few words about it.

Philosophy as the quest for the true beginnings of all things is the attempt to replace *opinions* about these beginnings by genuine *knowledge*, or *science*, of them. Now, it is by no means certain that this is a *legitimate* pursuit. Not only was there a popular prejudice against the attempt at prying[6] into the secrets of the gods, but strong reasons suggested the view that opinion, and not knowledge, is the very element of human or social or political life. If opinion is the element of political life, philosophy which questions opinions as such, dissolves the very element of social life: philosophy is essentially subversive (corrupting the young). From the point of view of philosophy, this is no objection to philosophy, since quest for the truth is infinitely more important than political life: philosophizing is learning to die. Still, the philosopher has to meet the legitimate claims of society or to shoulder his own responsibility as a citizen. He does this by refraining from publicly teaching what he considers *the* truth in so far as the truth could become dangerous to society. He hides his true teaching behind a socially useful exoteric teaching.

This view of the relation of philosophy to life, i.e. to society, presupposes that philosophy is essentially the preserve of the very few individuals who are by nature fit for philosophy. The radical distinction between the wise and the vulgar is essential to the original concept of philosophy. The idea that philosophy as such could become the element of human life

is wholly alien to all pre-modern thought. Plato demands that the philosoph*ers* should become kings; he does *not* demand that philosoph*y* should become the ruler: in his perfect polity, only 2 or 3 individuals have any access whatever to philosophy; the large majority is guided by noble lies.[II] The[7] quest for knowledge implies that in all cases where sufficient evidence is lacking, assent must be withheld or judgment must be suspended. Now, it is impossible to withhold assent or to suspend judgment in matters of extreme urgency which require immediate decision: one cannot suspend judgment in matters of life and death. The philosophic enterprise that stands or falls by the possibility of suspense of judgment, requires therefore that all matters of life and death be settled *in advance*. All matters of life and death can be reduced to the question of how one ought to live. The philosophic enterprise presupposes that the question of how one ought to live be settled in advance. It is settled by the pre-philosophic proof of the thesis that the right way of life, the one thing needful, is the life devoted to philosophy and to nothing else. The pre-philosophic proof is later on confirmed, within philosophy, by an analysis of human nature. However this may be, according to its original meaning, philosophy is *the* right way of life, *the* happiness of man. All other human pursuits are accordingly considered fundamentally defective, or forms of human misery, | however splendid. ¹The moral life as moral   3 verso
life is *not* the philosophic life: for the philosopher, morality is nothing but the condition or the by-product of philosophizing, and not something valuable in itself. Philosophy is not only trans-social and trans-religious, but trans-moral as well.¹ Philosophy asserts that man has ultimately no choice but that between philosophy and despair disguised by delusion: only through philosophy is man enabled to look reality in its stern face without losing his humanity. The claim of philosophy is no less radical than that raised on behalf of revelation.

Philosophy stands or falls by the possibility of suspense of judgment regarding the most fundamental questions. That is to say, philosophy is as such sceptical: in the original meaning

II [Noted in pencil between the lines:] Idea of the enlightenment implied in current notion of philosophy: *harmony* between philosophy and society.

of the term. σκέψις means *looking* at things, *considering* things. Philosophy is concerned with understanding reality in all its complexity. Its complexity may preclude demonstrative answers to the fundamental questions: the arguments in favor of the various incompatible answers may be inconclusive. This would not make the philosophic enterprise futile: for the philosopher, full understanding of a *problem* is infinitely more important than any mere answer. What counts from the philosophic, i.e. the theoretical, point of view, is the articulation of the *subject matter* as an articulation supplied by the argument in favor of two contradictory answers rather than the answers themselves. Philosophy in its original sense is disputative rather than decisive. Disputation is possible only for people who are not concerned with decisions, who are not in a rush, for whom nothing is urgent except disputation. The anarchy of the systems, the pudenda varietas philosophorum is no objection whatever to philosophy.

When the philosophers say that the only possible happiness consists in philosophizing, they do not mean that philosophy can *guarantee* human happiness; for they know that man is not the master of his fate: εὐημερία, sunshine in the shape of food, shelter, health, freedom and friendship – a sunshine that is not *produced* by philosophy, is *required* for philosophizing and hence happiness, although it does not *constitute* happiness. In religious language: σὺν θεῷ = ἀγαθῇ τύχῃ. |

4 recto **5. The *alternative to philosophy is revelation – philosophy must try to prove that revelation is impossible*.**[8]
The legitimacy of philosophy does not seem to be a serious problem for the philosopher as long as he is confronted only with the pagan myths and laws. For those myths and laws essentially antedate the awareness of the problem posed by the contradictions between the various divine laws, i.e. the problem whose realisation immediately precedes the emergence of philosophy. The situation of philosophy becomes fundamentally changed as soon as philosophy is confronted with the *Bible*. For the Bible claims to present a solution to the very problem which gave rise to philosophy, and the Biblical solution is diametrically opposed to the philosophic solution. The

Bible questions the view that philosophy is the only alternative to myth; according to the[1] Bible, the alternative to myth
is the revelation of the living God. The Biblical account of the
first things, especially the account of what happened in the
period from the creation of heaven and earth to Abraham's
acts of absolute obedience, can best be understood within the
present context, as an attempt to explain why one particular
possible code can be the only divine code that ever was and
ever will be. The same account rejects as illegitimate the possibility which came to its maturity in Greek philosophy: the
possibility that man can find his happiness, or his peace, by
eating of the fruit of the tree of knowledge. What to the classical philosophers appeared as the perfection of man's nature,
is described by the Bible as the product of man's disobedience
to his Creator. When the classical philosophers conceive of
man's desire to know as his highest natural desire, the Bible
protests by asserting that this desire is a temptation. To the
philosophic view that man's happiness consists in free investigation or insight, the Bible opposes the view that man's happiness consists in obedience to God. The Bible thus offers
the only challenge to the claim of philosophy which can reasonably be made. One cannot seriously question the claim
of philosophy in the name, e.g., of politics or of poetry. To
say nothing of other considerations, man's ultimate aim is
what is really good and not what merely *seems* to be good,
and only through *knowledge* of the good is he enabled to find
the good. But this is indeed the question: whether men can
acquire the knowledge of the good, without which they cannot
guide their lives individually and collectively, by the unaided
efforts of their reason, or whether they are dependent for that
knowledge | on divine revelation. Only through the Bible is   4 verso
philosophy, or the quest for knowledge, challenged by *knowledge*, viz. by knowledge revealed by the omniscient God, or by
knowledge identical with the self-communication of God. No
alternative is more fundamental than the alternative: human
guidance or divine guidance. *Tertium non datur.* The alternative between philosophy and revelation cannot be evaded by
any harmonization or "synthesis." For each of the two antagonists proclaims something as the one thing needful, as the
only thing that ultimately counts, and the one thing needful

proclaimed by the Bible is the opposite to that proclaimed by philosophy. In every attempt at harmonization, in every synthesis however impressive[9], one of the two opposed elements is sacrificed, more or less subtly, but in any event surely, to the other: philosophy which means to be the queen, must be made the handmaid of revelation or *vice versa*. If it is confronted with the claim of revelation, and only if it is confronted with the claim of revelation, philosophy as a radically free pursuit becomes radically questionable. Confronted with the claim of revelation, the philosopher is therefore compelled to *refute* that claim. More than that: he must prove the *impossibility* of revelation. For if revelation is *possible*, it is possible that the philosophic enterprise is fundamentally wrong. |

4a recto

6. *Philosophy cannot refute revelation.*

You will not expect me to give a comprehensive and detailed appraisal of the philosophic critique of revelation. I shall set forth briefly the chief lessons to be learned from a critical examination of *Spinoza's* critique of revelation. I choose Spinoza because his is the most *elaborate* critique of revelation.

Spinoza rejects revelation because of its *imaginative* character. Since it is the imagination, and not the intellect, which is the vehicle of revelation, revelation cannot supply the truth. The Biblical facts to which Spinoza refers, doubtless prove that imagination *cooperates* in the act of revelation, but they do not disprove[10] the possibility that in that act imagination may be in the *service* of genuine superhuman illumination. He disposes of this possibility, in other words, he proves that divine revelation is nothing but human imagination by showing that the decisive features of revelation are identical with those of human imagination pure and simple. Imagination is essentially uncertain: we can never be certain as to whether what we imagine is actually taking place, or will take place, or not. Now, revelation is also uncertain as is shown by the fact that signs or miracles are required in order to establish the fact of revelation which without these signs and miracles would be absolutely uncertain. Secondly, imagination as such does not disclose the truth. Now, revelation as such does not disclose the truth. This is shown by the contradictions in the

Bible, i.e. by the contradictions of statements which are all allegedly based on revelation. Divine revelation is then nothing but human imagination. This is confirmed by the kinship between Biblical revelation and pagan divination. Traditional theology explains the difference between genuine revelation and pagan divination by tracing the former to God and the latter to demons or to the devil. Accordingly, belief in revelation would imply acceptance of belief in demons or in the devil. The whole fabric of the teaching based on revelation stands or falls by the acceptance of these and similar superstitious notions.

The deficiencies of this argument are obvious. It is based throughout on rigid and stupid limitation to that literal sense of every passage which is equally accessible to the believer and unbeliever. Spinoza does not consider the fundamental difference between carnal and spiritual understanding of the Bible. If his argument is to be of any significance, it must comprise a more radical consideration. Spinoza says that revelation requires confirmation by miracles; this again may be questioned. But he [11]is on safe ground when he asserts[11] that revelation in the Biblical sense is itself a miracle. His critique of miracles is the core of his critique of revelation.

A miracle is a supra-natural event. In order to be certain that a given event *is* supra-natural, and not e.g. a natural delusion of the imagination, one would have to know that it can*not* be natural. I.e.: one would have to know the *limits* of the power of nature. This would require that we have a *complete* knowledge of nature, or that natural science is *completed*. This condition is not fulfilled | and cannot be fulfilled. Accordingly, if we are   4a verso
confronted with an event that we cannot explain naturally, we can merely say that the event has not *yet* been explained, that it has not been explained *hitherto*. Miracles can never be *known* to be miracles.

This argument is obviously defective. It presupposes that *everything* would be possible for nature, and Spinoza himself is forced to admit that there are things which are impossible by nature. The crucial example is resurrection from the dead. Spinoza disposes of the difficulty by raising this question: *how* do we know of these events which are impossible by nature? We know them, not from seeing with our own eyes, but from *reports. Who* reported them? Trained scientific observers who looked at the facts in question dispassionately or people without any scientific training and attitude? Obviously people of the second type. Is it an accident that miracles do not happen in societies quickened by the spirit of science? The assertion of miracles is essentially relative to the pre-scientific stage of mankind. Divine revelation is human imagination as it can be active only in the pre-scientific stage. Divine revelation is identical with the prejudice of an ancient nation.

Spinoza derives further confirmation of his view from the results of his[12] criticism of the Bible. If Moses is not the author of the Pentateuch, the Mosaic miracles are reported, not only by untrained observers, but by people of a much later age who knew of the happenings in question only through the medium of oral tradition, i.e. of legends.

The whole argument tends to show that the belief in revelation essentially belongs to a pre-scientific, or mythical, mind. No one can deny that there is an element of truth in Spinoza's assertion. But this element of truth is inconclusive. For we are justified in retorting that man is more capable of dimly *divining* the truth of revelation before he has cut[13] himself loose from the roots of his existence by limiting himself to the scientific approach than after that. That the pre-scientific horizon is more favorable to belief in revelation than is the scientific horizon, does not yet prove that revelation is absolutely bound up with a mythical horizon.

Spinoza's reasoning remains defective as long as it is not supplemented by an account of the *motivation* of the alleged revelation in terms of the unbelieving reason. For Spinoza, belief in revelation is one form of *superstition*. Superstition is the way of acting and thinking in which man's pre-philosophic life protects itself against its breakdown in despair. The pre-philosophic life is the life swayed by the imagination and the emotions; in that life, man attaches himself with all his heart to finite and perishable things; their actual or foreseen loss drives him to despair of his own power to secure his happiness; he is unable to look reality in its face, to recognize with equanimity the utter insignificance of his fate and of his more cherished objects; he craves comfort; | he demands passionately that his fate be of cosmic significance, and his unchecked imagination

5 recto

obeys the demands of his desires by producing the required images.

For the time being, we limit ourselves to noting that Spinoza completely disregards what the Bible and theology teach regarding the specifically religious sentiments. When speaking of the crucial importance of fear e.g., he does not say a word about the difference between servile fear and filial fear. He seems to discredit himself completely by saying that he does not understand the Bible.

The best one could say about his kind of argument is that it drives home how unevident or uncertain revelation is without previous *faith* in revelation. But since this is admitted by theology, an extensive[1] argument which suffices for protecting unbelief against the demands of revelation seems to be almost insipid. In other words, even if the unbeliever could explain satisfactorily how belief in revelation *could* develop as a delusion, he would not have proved that revelation is *impossible*. Indeed, all philosophic questioning of the *demonstrability* of revelation becomes relevant only if it transforms itself into a demonstration of the *impossibility* of revelation, or of miracles.

To prove that revelation or miracles are impossible, means to prove that they are incompatible with the nature of God as the most perfect being. All proofs of this kind presuppose that there is a natural theology. Hence to-day, when the possibility of natural theology is generally denied, a refutation of the belief in revelation is not even imaginable. On the other hand, however, a *hypothetical* natural theology, a theology arguing for the mere *notion* of a most perfect being, would suffice. For it is hard to deny for anyone that, if there is a God, he must be absolutely perfect. The purely philosophic doctrine of God, i.e. the only theology which is unequivocally *natural* theology, was based on the analogy of the wise man: the most perfect being as known from experience, the wise man, gives us the only clue regarding the most perfect being simply. E.g., a wise man would pity the fools rather than wax indignant about their criminal or monstrous actions; he would be kind to everyone, he would not care particularly for anyone except for his friends, i.e. those who are actually or potentially wise. Accordingly, God cannot be conceived to condemn men[1] to eternal damnation. He cannot even be conceived as exercising individual providence. He cannot be conceived as *loving* men, i.e. beings who are infinitely inferior to him in wisdom. [1]But at this point a most serious difficulty arises for natural theology.[1]

A God[14] who is infinitely superior to man in wisdom, may

be said to be *inscrutable:* He is *mysterious.* All the | difficulties against which natural theology seemed to protect men, come in again: a mysterious God may well be the God of revelation. There is therefore only one way of disposing of the possibility of revelation or miracles: one must prove that God is in no way mysterious, or that we have adequate knowledge of the essence of God. This step was taken by Spinoza. His whole argument stands or falls by his denial of the legitimacy of any analogical knowledge of God: any knowledge of God that we can have, must be as clear and as distinct as that which we can have of the triangle e.g.

The question is how he secured this fundamental dogma. The usual answer is that he bases his doctrine on an intuitive knowledge of the idea of God. But it can be shown that Spinoza's intuitive knowledge is, not the beginning, but the end of his philosophy, or, in other words, that Spinoza's intuitive knowledge is knowledge, not of God, but of nature as *distinguished* from God. Spinoza arrives at his doctrine of God by freely forming a clear, distinct idea of God as[15] the fully intelligible cause of all things: his methodical demand for clear, distinct knowledge, and no proof of any kind, disposes of the mysteriousness of God. What one might *call* a proof is supplied by the fact that the clear and distinct idea of God leads to a clear and distinct idea of all things or of the whole, whereas every other idea of God leads to a confused account, e.g. to the account given in the Bible. We may say that Spinoza's theology is a purely hypothetical doctrine which could become more than a hypothesis only if it actually led to a clear and distinct account of the whole. But it can never lead to that result: it can't lead to an account of the *whole* because it arbitrarily excludes those *aspects* of the whole which can't be understood clearly, distinctly.

The limitations of Spinoza's teaching are of general significance for the following reason: that teaching presents the most comprehensive, or the most ambitious, program of what

modern science could possibly be. To realize that Spinoza has failed to refute revelation means therefore to realize that modern science cannot have refuted revelation. Modern science is much more modest in its claims than Spinoza's philosophy, because it has divorced itself from natural theology; hence no objection whatever to the teaching of revelation can be based on modern science. To mention only one example: it is sometimes asserted that the Biblical account of the creation of the world has been refuted by modern geology, paleontology etc. But: all scientific accounts *presuppose* the impossibility of miracles; presupposing this, they prove that the age of the earth, or l of life on the earth etc. is millions of years; but what   6 recto
natural processes could achieve only in such periods, could be done in a moment by God miraculously.

To conclude: philosophy may succeed in proving the impossibility of demonstrating the fact of revelation to unbelievers; it may thus succeed in defending the unbelieving position; but this is absolutely irrelevant seeing that revelation is *meant* to be accessible only to faith, or on the *basis* of faith. The *experiential* knowledge of the *fact* of revelation remains absolutely unshaken.

7. The impression of a refutation of revelation by philosophy is created by the influence of philosophic critique on modern theology: this seems to show that the radical position of revelation is possible only in mythical horizons.
We could leave it at that but for the fact that modern theology has abandoned many positions of traditional theology under the influence of the philosophic and scientific attack on revelation. This fact seems to show that the belief in revelation is not as unassailable as it would appear on the basis of the general consideration that I have sketched. The modern theologians claim of course that by abandoning certain traditional positions they bring out the pure and central meaning of revelation more clearly than traditional theology has done. They claim that what they have abandoned are merely peripheral elements of theology and that they limit themselves to the central or essential theological teaching. But the question arises whether this distinction is tenable, i.e. whether the peripheral

elements are not necessary consequences, or implications, of
the central thesis – and therefore whether modern theology
which abandons the peripheral teaching, is consistent. The
apparent inconsistency of modern theology has led Nietzsche
among others to hurl against modern theology the charge
that it lacks intellectual honesty.

Many present-day theologians subscribe without hesitation
to Spinoza's thesis that the Bible is not everywhere truthful
and divine. They reject therefore the belief in the verbal inspiration of the Bible and in the historical authenticity of the
Biblical records. They reject especially the belief in miracles.
They admit that the Bible abounds with mythical notions.
They would say that in revealing himself to earlier generations God allowed them to understand this revelation within
their mythical horizon because that horizon does not prevent
at all the faithful or pious understanding of revelation. The
change from the mythical world-view of the past to the scientific world-view of the modern age is completely indifferent
as regards the intention of revelation. But since the mythical
outlook has become discredited, one does the greatest disser-
vice to faith by keeping the message of revelation | within the
mythical shell in which the record of early revelation has been
transmitted to us.[16]

Modern theology stands or falls by the distinction between
the central or true and peripheral or mythical elements of
the Bible. The Biblical basis, or point d'appui, for this distinction is the distinction between the spiritual and the carnal,
or between God and flesh. Blessed is the man who puts his
trust in God, cursed is the man who[1] puts his trust in flesh.
Revelation is revelation of God Himself as the Father, Judge
and Redeemer – and nothing else. The response to revelation is faith in God Himself – and in nothing else. But man is
always tempted to put his trust, not in God, but in flesh. He
substitutes worship of his own works, or idols, for the worship
of God. He substitutes faith in something tangible, in something which he can control by his sense-perception, reason
or action, for pure faith which has no support outside of the
direct self-communication of God. Hence he tries to secure
belief in God by belief in facts such as traditions or books or
miracles. This has happened in traditional theology and this

6 verso

has been corrected radically in modern theology. The true
understanding of faith demands that a radical distinction be
made between theology which is nothing but soteriology and
true knowledge simply which is nothing but knowledge of the
world, or cosmology. Natural theology, which is neither soteriology nor cosmology, must be rejected. The idea that the Bible
contains anything relevant to faith that can be contradicted or
confirmed by science, must be dismissed as absurd. Faith does
not presuppose any definite view of the world as preferable
to any other. It does not require any knowledge of facts which
are not an integral part of the experiential-existential knowledge of God as the Redeemer. Revelation and faith "are," i.e.
they are meaningful, only in and for decision, whereas facts
as facts are independent of any decision. The very *manner of
being* of revelation and faith is therefore fundamentally different from the manner of being of any fact, or of the world as
world. There cannot be any conflict between revelation and
knowledge of facts because revelation does not say anything
about facts except that they are worldly or fleshly. All knowledge that is equally accessible to the believer and unbeliever,
is absolutely irrelevant to the assertions of faith, and therefore
science[17] is perfectly free: the notion that philosophy or science ought[18] [to] be the handmaid of theology, is based on a
radical misunderstanding.

It seems to me that this kind of theology identifies the genuinely Biblical distinction between the spirit and the flesh with
apparently similar, but actually entirely different distinctions
that originate in modern philosophy: the distinction between
mind and nature, between history and nature, between the
existential and the merely real (i.e. between the being of
responsible and responsive beings and the being of facts or
things or affairs). Using the distinction between history and
nature, a modern theologian has said that faith in revelation |
requires the truth of certain *historical* facts and that therefore   7 recto
a conflict between historical criticism and Biblical faith is at
least possible, whereas faith in revelation implies no assertion
regarding *nature*, and therefore no conflict between science
and Biblical faith is possible.

The solution suggested by many present-day theologians
is apt to lead to the consequence that the assertions of faith

have a purely *inner* meaning, that the truth ascribed to them is a purely emotional and moral truth, and not truth simply. There exists therefore the danger that only the intrinsic *value* of the experience of faith distinguishes that experience from any hallucination or delusion. However this may be, the legitimate distinction between the spirit and the flesh, or between God and the world, does not justify the distinction between the central and the peripheral – at least as that distinction is frequently practised to-day. What I am driving at is this: while faith is not *of* the world, it necessarily issues, not merely in actions *in* the world, but in assertions *about* the world. Faith implies the assertion that the world is *created*. In consequence of the distinction between God and the world, Gogarten has tried to limit[19] the thesis of creation to the creation of *man*: [20]the thesis of[20] creation does not say anything about extra-human beings. This is an obvious absurdity. He also has asserted that God speaks to man only through other men, especially through the preaching of the Gospel. But certainly the OT prophecies contain many cases in which God spoke to human beings directly. Bultmann has denied that the resurrection, as distinguished from the crucifixion, can be understood as a phenomenon in the world, as an event which took place at a given moment in the past. He does not deny of course that the crucifixion was a phenomenon in the world. Considering the connection between crucifixion and resurrection, Bultmann's distinction is unconvincing and is obviously due to his unwillingness to assert an unambiguous miracle. The fact that the cross is visible to everyone, whereas resurrection is only to the eyes of faith, does not do away with the fact that to the eyes of faith resurrection is visible also as an event in the past, and not merely as belonging to the eschatological Now.

There cannot be faith in God that is not faith in[21] our being *absolutely* in the hands of God, and this means that is not faith in God's *omnipotence*, and therefore in the possibility of *miracles*. It is true that miracles cannot be the *basis* of genuine faith; but it is quite another thing to say that genuine faith does not *issue* in belief in miracles, or that it is incompatible with belief in miracles. But if the admission of the possibility of miracles is of the essence of faith, there is no reason whatever for making an arbitrary distinction between [what] one is tempted to call intelligible miracles (especially the resurrection) and unintelligible miracles (the sun stands still in the vale of Ajalon). If we are truly convinced of our utter insufficiency and of God's hiddenness, we will prefer humbly to | confess that a given Biblical account does not touch us, or does not edify us, rather than to say that the account in question can be rejected as untrue, or as a mythical residue. 7 verso

But modern theology becomes inconsistent not only by making an arbitrary distinction between the miracles which it admits, and those which it rejects; it also obscures the meaning of miracles as such. According to the traditional view, miracles are supranatural actions of God, or actions that interfere with, or interrupt, the natural order. Brunner[III] e.g. rejects this view. He explains the miracles by employing the analogy of how life uses inanimate matter: the life processes do not interfere with the processes of inanimate matter, or put them out of action, but use them for a purpose alien to inanimate matter. Analogously, revelation "does not break into the sphere of human existence in such a way that it either pushes the human element aside or puts it out of action; but it enters by using the human in its service. Jesus Christ is a human being, 'born of a woman' etc. He is 'true man', as the dogma says." (303)[1] In Christ, the divine and the human interpenetrate: the human is not removed. (304)[1] Statements such as these seem to evade the real issue. Jesus is born, not simply of a woman, but of a virgin; above all, he is not begotten by a human father. If this is not an interruption of the natural order, I do not know what it is. If man is essentially, as Aristotle asserts, generated by man, Jesus as the Christ could not be a true man. The dogma stands or falls therefore by the fact that a being can be a human being without being begotten by human parents. The Scriptural proof of this possibility is

III [Emil Brunner, *Offenbarung und Vernunft. Die Lehre von der christlichen Glaubenserkenntnis* (Zürich: Zwingli-Verlag, 1941). In the following, Strauss cites Olive Wyon's translation *Revelation and Reason: The Christian Doctrine of Faith and Knowledge* (Philadelphia: The Westminster Press, 1946). The passages that Strauss cites or to which he refers are found in the original German edition on pp. 256, 276, 277, 280, 299, 300, 323, 329, 419, 420.]

Adam. And the parallel between Adam and Christ is basic for Christian theology also in other respects.

I would like to dwell for a moment on the theology of Brunner because Brunner is [22]unusually conservative and sober.[22] To mention only one example: Brunner rejects Kierkegaard's thesis according to which the Christian faith requires not more than the Apostolic reports that they believed that in that and that year God showed himself in the form of a servant, that he lived, taught and died. Brunner soberly admits that "the credibility of the Gospel narrative in its main features is the necessary foundation of real Christian faith." Yet even Brunner abandons[23] essential theological positions. His principle is that "the Scriptures are the word of God, because, and in so far as, they give us Christ," i.e. that the essential teaching of the Bible is soteriological, not cosmological, and[24] he rejects therefore without any misgivings all cosmological theses of the Bible. He admits that the Christian faith "does contain certain historical statements." But he obviously thinks that no historical assertions, essential to faith, have cosmological

8 recto   implications. While insisting most strongly on the historicity of the life of Jesus and of the resurrection, he rejects the historicity of Adam and of the whole Biblical account of the origins of mankind. But does not[1] the Biblical eschatology stand in strict correspondence to Biblical *poetology*, or account of the beginnings? Just as the eschatology of unbelief (the notion that human life will one day perish from the earth without leaving any traces and without Last Judgment) corresponds to the poetology of unbelief (the evolutionism of modern science). If one accepts evolution, does one not admit that man was not created perfect? are then man's greatest failings not due to the imperfect form in which human beings made their first appearance on earth? is man then not excusable – contrary to Paul's assertion: how could early man *know* God's law if he was not created perfect and dwelling in Eden, but poorly equipped mentally and materially? are his polytheism, his idolatry, his moral monstrosities not necessary errors as distinguished from *sin*? But, one might object, regardless of when[25] primitive man *became* a real human being: *in that moment* he had the choice between obedience and sin: *in that moment*, however frequently repeated, the fall took place and

is taking place. But what shall we say[26] of the *inheritance* of *excusable ignorance* with which real man starts his career, if the evolutionary account is right – i.e. if man was not really created, but "cast on this globe" and owes all his humanity to his revolutionary efforts? I fail to see how one can avoid the dilemma: either a perfect beginning followed by sin, or an imperfect beginning and hence *no* original sin. By denying the historicity of the fall, Brunner repeats the typical mistake for which he upbraids so severely the idealistic theologians in regard to incarnation and resurrection: he replaces a unique fact by an external concept or symbol.

Observations of this kind may be fatal to modern theology; they are ultimately of no consequence whatever. The inconsistency of modern theology does not improve in the least the position of philosophy. For even if the philosopher would have succeeded in tearing to pieces every *theology*, he would not have advanced a single step in his attempt to refute *revelation.* |

8. *Revelation cannot refute philosophy.*

8 verso

Let us now look at the other side of the picture. Let us see how philosophy fares if it is attacked by the adherent of revelation. I have said that the theologian is compelled to refute philosophy. For if he fails to do that, the philosopher can say that there is no shred of evidence against the view that the right way of life is the philosophic life: revelation is nothing but a factum brutum, and in addition an uncertain one. Our[27] first impression is that all theological arguments directed against philosophy are defective, because they are circular: they are conclusive only on the *basis* of faith.

Take Pascal's famous argument of the misery of man without God, i.e. without the God of Abraham, Isaac and Jacob, an argument which is meant to be conclusive "par nature." This argument does not in any way refute Plato's thesis that the philosopher, as exemplified by Socrates in particular, lives on the islands of the blessed. If Pascal would say that Plato did not have Pascal's Christian experience, Plato could answer with equal right that Pascal obviously did not have Plato's experience of philosophic serenity. Pascal might answer that all

philosophers underrate the power of evil, that they are superficial or optimistic. He might refer to the manner in which
Lucretius opens his poem devoted to the exposition of Epicurean philosophy by praising the beneficent power of earthly
love. But Lucretius could answer that this edifying prayer is
only the beginning: the poem ends with the description of a
most terrible plague: philosophic equanimity is beyond the
conflict between optimism and pessimism.

Yet, the theologian would continue, evil is not primarily
physical evil, but *moral* evil. The philosophers are blind to the
fact, and the power, of *sin*. "Philosophic ethics... knows less
of (moral) evil than the man in the street" (Brunner 327). But
for this blindness, the philosophers could never have elaborated, and used, their natural theology which is based on the
analogy of the wise man. The philosopher who[1] complacently
asserts that God could not visit men with eternal punishment,
because he, the philosopher, would never take sins of less wise
beings as seriously, merely shows by this argument his callous-
ness, or at best he reveals his dim notion that he would be lost,
if God were to take sins seriously.

To this the philosopher would answer by questioning the
decisive and ultimate significance of *moral* criteria. All theological attacks on the laxity of all philosophic morality could[28]
be rebutted by the demand for a demonstration that *the* cos-
mic principle, or *the* first cause, is in any way concerned with
9 recto   morality. | No evidence supporting this view has ever been
advanced: The man in the street is no authority: for is not theology the ultimate source of what he thinks and even feels? In
other words, the philosopher would say that sin presupposes
a moral *law*, and he would deny that there *is* a moral law.
He would deny what Luther e.g. considered an indubitable
fact, viz. that every human being experiences something of
the reality of God who confronts him in the conscience which
judges him according to the moral law. He would refer to
what Aristotle says on αἰδώς (sense of shame): that it befits
only young people, mature people simply must not do anything of which they would be ashamed. And as regards the
intentions (≠ actions), the βουλησεις are ἄδηλοι. There is no
"synderesis" in Aristotle. ¹The open secret of the Philebus: the
highest good: θεωρια plus ἡδονη.¹

The theologian: but it is inconsistent of the philosopher not to admit the strictest moral demands; for philosophy claims to be love of *truth*, and every relaxation of morality amounts to admitting the right of self-assertion or self-seeking or eudemonism which is incompatible with the radical self-denial that is implied in every real quest for truth. Philosophy is inconsistent because it would *require* a rebirth, a regeneration, but excludes it.

The philosopher: denies that human self-assertion and love of truth are incompatible. For we have a *selfish need* for truth. We *need* the eternal, the *true* eternal (Plato's doctrine of ἔρως). The kinship between φιλοσοφία and φιλοτιμία: *lasting* fame possible only through knowledge of the *truth*. The most far-sighted selfishness transforms itself into, nay, reveals itself as, perfect unselfishness.

The theologian: philosophy is self-deification; philosophy has its root in *pride*.

The philosopher: if we understand by God the most perfect being that is a *person*, there are no gods but the philosophers (Sophist[29] in princ: θεος τις ἐλεγκτικος). Poor gods? Indeed, measured by imaginary standards. – As to "pride," who is more proud, he who says that *his* personal fate is of concern to *the* cause of the universe, or he who humbly admits that his fate is of no concern whatever to anyone but to himself and his few friends.

The theologian: the philosophic understanding of man is *superficial*; they have not fathomed the depths of man, his despair, what is hidden in his craving for distraction and in that mood of boredom which I reveals more[30] of man's reality   9 verso
than all his rational activities.

The philosopher: these and similar phenomena reveal indeed the problematic character of all ordinary human pursuits of happiness which are not the pursuit of the happiness of contemplation. The philosopher as philosopher never craves distraction (although he needs relaxation from time to time), and he is never bored. Theological psychology is such a psychology of *non-philosophic man*, of the *vulgar*, as is not guided by the understanding of the natural aim of man which is contemplation. If the philosophers do not stress certain most "interesting" aspects of men, they are guided by a most noble pedagogic intention: it is better for men to be reminded of what is noble and reasonable in them than to be depressed by moving and effeminating pictures of the seamy side of life.

Philosophy cannot explain[31] revelation – ?

Perhaps the most impressive theological argument is taken from the insufficiency of the philosophic *explanation* of the belief in revelation. Philosophy *must* interpret revelation as a *myth*. I.e. it must overlook the essential *difference* between myth and revelation.

Myth		Revelation
Polytheism	–	One omnipotent God
Gods controlled by impersonal fate	–	the *actions* of God
recurrent phenomena	–	absolutely unique, unrepeatable events – *decision*, History
no distinct relation to historical events	–	essential relation to historical events (OT history; "Crucified under Pontius Pilatus")

Brunner 259: "In *all* forms of religion, in addition to fear, there is reverence; as well as the human desire for happiness, there is also a real longing for divine perfection; in addition to social usefulness, there is also a genuine striving after communion with the deity, and a genuine submission to a higher, holy command; and behind all that rank fantasy growth[s] of affective thought there is an element which cannot be derived from fantasy at all: the knowledge of something which is unconditioned, ultimate, normative, supra-mundane, supra-temporal." |

10 recto   Reasons why philosophic explanation *seems* to be insufficient:

a) the philosopher's unwillingness *openly* to identify the very core of the Biblical teaching with superstition – hence no real *open* discussion of the *difference* between Bible and other superstition (myth).

b) Tr. IX. 42 bg., 60 end[IV]: the extremely rare psychological phenomena as alien as possible to the typical experiences of the philosopher – hence imperfect description of the phenomena by the philosopher.

Now as regards the philosophic interpretation – the philosopher would admit the essential difference between Bible and myth: the Bible presupposes, just as philosophy itself, the realization of the *problem* of myth[V]: myth – philosophy / myth – revelation.

Myth and revelation belong together: not predominance of the critical-sceptical spirit.

Myth and philosophy belong together: not predominance of morality.

The starting-point of philosophic explanation[32] of *revelation* would therefore be the fact that the foundation of belief in revelation is the belief in the central importance of *morality*.

(Brunner 424[33]: according to the NT, "this despairing knowledge of distress and need, that is, the awareness of sin," comes from the law which only makes demands. The law in question "*belongs absolutely to that which man can tell himself*" – i.e. it is meant to be accessible to man as man.

333: "it is a fact to which the Scripture[s] and the best teachers of the Church bear witness with one voice: that *man as man knows the law of God*... indeed that this knowledge of the law is the *center of [the] natural human existence* and the natural self-understanding of man.")

The task of the philosopher is to understand how the original (mythical) idea of the θεῖος νόμος is modified by the radical understanding of the moral implication and thus transformed into the idea of revelation.

IV [Benedictus Spinoza: *Tractatus theologico-politicus*, IX, ed. Bruder § 42 beginning, § 60 end: "Nescio quid superstitio suadere potuit, et forte inde factum est, quia utramque lectionem aeque bonam seu tolerabilem aestimabant, ideoque, ne earum aliqua negligeretur, unam scribendam et aliam legendam voluerunt." "...neque enim scire teneor, quae religio ipsos moverit, ut id non facerent."]

V σημεῖον: the "historical" character of large parts of the Bible – cf. the insistence of *truth* in Greek ἱστορίη ≠ myths, poetry.

1) Need of man → society, or else sociability was irreducible: need for *law*.

2) [need] for *good* law: original criterion for goodness: ancestral.

   Rational basis: a) tested things, b) concern with stability.

3) the law depends on the ancestors = the *father* or fathers, *the* source of one's being, loving (beneficent) and demanding obedience (cf. Fustel de Coulanges).

4) absolute superiority of the ancestors: superhuman[34] beings, *divine* beings – *divine law.* the first things, | the sources of our being are *gods*.

5) contradiction between various divine laws: only *one* divine law.

6) *full* obedience to the law: the law must be the source of *all* blessings → the god must be *omnipotent* → there can be only *one* God – Maker, Creator ≠ Generator.

7) *full* obedience to the law: obedience not merely a duty to be fulfilled in order to get something *else* as reward: full obedience is *love* of the one God with all one's heart, all one's soul and all one's power.

8) *full* obedience to the law: no human relation is left to irresponsible arbitrariness → love of *all* men. God is the father of all men, and all men are brothers. בצלם אלהים [in the image of God – Gen. 1,27].

9) *full* obedience to the law: not only external actions, but the right *intention*: purity of the heart (loving God with *all* one's heart) – impossibility for man of achieving this: *sin*: need for *mercy*: the loving God forgiving sin more important than God as Judge.

10) full obedience to the law: rejection of ὕβρις, self-assertion in *any* sense: critique of cities, arts, kings – *especially* of science which is *the* vehicle of human self-assertion. A unique final revelation which has taken place in the past is *the* correlative of absolute obedience, absolute surrender.

   No science: no universals – goodness a derivative from a *particular, individual* phenomenon (goodness = being Christian, Jew . . .). *The* guidance is not knowledge of universals, but the record of the deeds of the mysterious God.

11) full obedience to the law: the *required* law must be the *gift* of God: *God* must purify our heart, if our heart is to be pure – *God* must open our lips if our mouth is to proclaim His praise. God must communicate *Himself* to man → He must come *close* to him: Incarnation.[VI] |

Objections: 11 recto

a) The problem of the presence, the call – not characteristic of the *Bible.* The presence of Asclepius e.g. – what was it? Hallucination – Cf. also C. F. [Meyer],[VII] Heidegger: God is death.

b) the explanation cannot account for the *fact* of real love of God and neighbour – but it is a *question* whether these are *facts*, and not *interpretations* of facts – what has to be explained, is merely the *demand* for such love.

c) the explanation is based on the Bible of theologians – it *utilizes* them → it *presupposes* them: if the explanation were valid, philosophers should have been able to devise the whole claim independently of the Bible, – i.e., for all practical purposes, in classical antiquity. But: why should philosophers who were going to the opposite direction as the Biblical teachers have been *capable* of discovering what only an entirely different human type bent on the anti-philosophic possibility *could* discover or invent?

VI [Strauss grouped points 5 and 6 with a brace. He either wanted to stress thereby that they belong together or he intended to reduce the eleven steps of his genealogy to ten.]

VII [The reference in the Ms. "Cf. also C. F., Heidegger: God is death," which is rendered obscure by an obvious omission, is to a parallel between Conrad Ferdinand Meyer's novella *Die Versuchung des Pescara* and the significance that Heidegger accords death: In chapters 3 and 4 of the novella, Pescara calls death his divinity. In this connection, consider Leo Strauss, "Preface to Spinoza's Critique of Religion" (1965) in *Liberalism Ancient and Modern* (New York: Basic Books, 1968), n. 23.]

Notes on Philosophy and Revelation

N 1 recto ***The Biblical argument.***

1) *Two* considerations guiding Biblical account of creation: God giving *names* to things, *and* his *seeing* that things created by him are *good*. In the light of these considerations → depreciation of heaven and heavenly bodies → Bible opposes the admiring contemplation of heaven – Babylon seat of astronomy: *tower* of Babel – philosophy.

2) Only things not explicitly called good in Genesis 1 are: heaven and *man*. Connection between problematic goodness of heaven and of man: heaven *tempts* man. Why and how? Question answered by Gen. 2, 3 (story of the fall).

3) Prohibition against eating of "knowledge" = depreciation of heaven → rejection of philosophy

Man created to live in child-like *obedience,* in *blind* obedience: *without* knowledge of good and evil. To devote himself to the *earth,* to his *life* on earth (≠ heaven): man *names, rules* only earthly things. Knowledge of good, evil = knowledge *simply* (God's knowledge of the completed work = knowledge of its being *good*). Eating of "knowledge" = irreconcilable with eating of "life": not naturally, but because God has *willed* it so. For *this* reason, man has to be *forcibly* prevented from eating of "life" after eating of "knowledge" (expulsion from garden).

4) *How* did man fall? Account of fall explains under what conditions could there be human knowledge of good and evil, and why that condition is impossible of fulfillment.

Eve, not Adam, tempted at once (she adds "touching" to "eating" – more stringent than God). But decisive: intervention of *serpent.*

168

Serpent says the *truth* – allegedly it contradicts God's word: you will *not* die... Why is the serpent right? By virtue of *reasoning: for* God knows that on the *day* you eat thereof you will be like Gods... God *cannot* kill you, because he *knows* – his *knowledge* limits his power – his knowledge of something *independent* of his will → μοῖρα (Deum fato subicere), ideas, ἀνάγκη, φύσις.

The fact that serpent is *right*[35] shows that there is something to it – but the sequel (the expulsion) shows that the serpent is *decisively* wrong: something[36] *unexpected* happens. |

True statement of serpent is *decisively* wrong, because the N 1 verso *reason* on which it is based, is wrong: limitation of God's power is proved by the limited character of *manifestations* of God's power. Serpent is blind to the *hidden, reserved* power of God. Serpentine principle is: denial of divine omnipotence.

5) That *this* is decisive point, is shown by *punishment* of serpent. Although unexpected: ¹serpent was created *good* – its *slyness* is good,¹ serpent was not *forbidden* to tempt Eve – its punishment a clear case of poena, crimen sine lege – serpent tacitly identifies God's law with his *promulgated* law – and it is *punished* for it. Just as God's *works* do not reveal God's full¹ power, his[37] revealed word does not reveal his full *will.*

Connection with Genesis 1: The serpentine conclusion from the *regularity* of heavenly movements etc. to their *intrinsic necessities.*

6) Ascription of the attitude which fully developed is that of philosophy or science, to the *serpent.*

Brutish: man's dignity or nobility consists, not in his knowledge-begotten freedom, but in the simplicity of his obedience. ¹Also: *woman.*¹ This is not to deny that it is a *real* serpent.

7) Self-assurance of serpent based on blindness to God's unpromulgated law. On the other hand, radical obedience → *divination* of God's unpromulgated law. Abraham's bargains with God for the salvation of [38]the few just[38] in the condemned cities. (Contrast with Cain – guardian of his brother – and Noa[h]'s indifference to victims of deluge). – Abraham's action is a *climax.* ¹More important than עקדה [the binding of Isaac – Gen. 22,9] which is maximum obedience to *revealed* law.¹

8) Story of fall, especially punishment of serpent → man cannot know what God will do – *This* is the meaning of "I shall be that I shall be" (= I shall be gracious to whom I shall be gracious). *Hidden* God – "the Lord hath said that he would dwell in the[39] thick darkness." Man cannot know what God *is* (he cannot *see* God): if he could know what God is, he would know what God *will be*. God will be all he will be, and not what he *is*, i.e. *known* to be, *now*. What man can know of God, he owes to God – to his free revelation – freedom or *grace* → particular revelation, [1]*contingent* revelation (≠ eternal revelation)[1] → *particular* law is *the* divine law, *the* absolute law.

9) Story of fall not last word of Bible about knowledge. General principle of Bible: things rebelliously devised by man, are finally accepted by God, [1]transformed into vehicles of grace[1] (city, agriculture, arts, kingship ...). The same applies to *knowledge*. God *gives* knowledge: his law, becomes[40] the tree of knowledge which is the tree of life for all those who cling to it. After the fall, man can no longer live in uninstructed obedience. He needs now wisdom, understanding: but not philosophy, but divine revelation. |

N 2 recto   10) *Final conclusion*: Bible grants to philosophers that they would be right if there were no God who can and does reveal himself. Only philosophy, not art, morality etc. etc., is *the* alternative to revelation: human guidance or divine guidance. Tertium non datur. If God had not forbidden it, eating of tree of knowledge = ὁμοίωσις θεῷ would be *the* highest human possibility. Myth of *Politikos*: if there is no divine guidance, *human* guidance is *the* one thing needful. Philosophy and Bible agree as to this: *the* alternatives are[1] philosophy or divine revelation.

Philosopher's answer to Biblical argument.
Philosophers would not be impressed by it: reminded of pagan stories of envious gods – since God would not be envious, he would not forbid man to become like him by understanding good and evil.

Biblical[41] insistence on man's *faith*, on *trust*, in God would be ridiculed as implying a gentleman's view of the first cause: every gentleman is offended if one does not believe him or his word (Cyrop. VII 2, 15–17) – a[42] wise being[43] would not be offended by doubt, but would *encourage* doubt of everything not evident.

Above all: νόμος and μῦθος. Bible[1] in some respects better, in some worse than other νομοι and μῦθοι.

The *inevitable alternative: philosophy or revelation.*

1) Alternative cannot be avoided by ascribing to philosophy and revelation different spheres or planes – for: they make assertions about the *same* subject: about the world and human life. (Cf. the controversies about Darwinism, biblical criticism etc.: conflict is, not only possible, but actual.)

2) Alternative not contradicted by fact of harmonizations which abound throughout Western history. For: [1]fact is *attempt* at harmonization, not harmonization *itself.*[1] In every harmonization one is sacrificed, subtly, but surely, to the other.

[1]*Philosopher accepts revelation.*[1] If there is revelation, faith is infinitely more important than philosophy – philosophy ceases to be *the* way of life – by accepting revelation, the philosopher ceases to be a philosopher – *if* he does not transform revelation into philosophy (Hegel) and thus sacrifice revelation to philosophy.

[1]*Theologian accepts philosophy*[1] – can do it, if he believes that philosophy is *permitted,* that it is justified on the *basis* of revelation. Philosophy thus permitted, thus admitted, is necessarily a humble hand-maid of theology, and not *the* queen of the sciences. |

Nature of alternative allows only of *sub*ordination, *not* of coordination. *One* demand is right or wrong: for each claims to be *the* one thing needful.   N 2 verso

3) *Objection*: does philosophy not imply unbearable dogmatism? does it not imply *a limine* rejection of revelation? of faith? is philosophy not love of truth, and is a limine rejection not sign of insincerity? Philosophy *is* love of truth, i.e. of *evident* truth.

Precisely for this reason, it is of the essence of the philosopher to *suspend* his judgment, and *not* to assent, in all cases in which assent would be based on insufficient evidence.

Whoever is incapable of suspending his judgment in such cases, of *living* in such suspense, whoever fails to know that *doubt* is a good pillow for a well-constructed head, cannot be a philosopher.

But *life* requires *decisions* – this is not exact: *action* does – but who said that the life of philosophy is a life of action? The philosophic answer to the pragmatist objection was given by Goethe: der Handelnde ist immer gewissenlos – *quâ* acting man (or as Aristotle says: quâ *merely* human beings) we have to accept unevident premises – but this merely shows the inferiority of action.

Transition to the decisive difficulty.

Philosophy could accept revelation only if revelation were an evident, demonstrable fact. For all practical purposes: if revelation could be proved by *historical* evidence.

But revelation cannot be proved by historical evidence.

Coincidence of the teaching of the Reformers with modern historical criticism.

Modern historical criticism has not refuted belief in revelation – but it has refuted historical *argument* allegedly proving the fact of revelation. But this it has really done. |

N 3 recto ### Revelation cannot refute philosophy.

A large number of arguments – I shall mention here only the most popular ones.

Political argument: *social* need of revelation > stable order; inability of philosophy to establish moral standards (Socrates cannot refute Callicles etc.) –

Proves *at best* necessity of *myth* of revelation (noble lie).

[44] *Misery of man without God*: but – Socrates (consolation, not M[isery] due to envy, limited to Epicurus, Stoics).[44]

Moral argument: inferiority of philosophic morality as compared with Biblical morality (its eudemonism; placere sibi ipsi ≠ placere Deo; self-assertion vs. self-denial – to love God with all one's heart vs. to love with all one's heart the perfection of one's understanding).

Yet: the criterion *itself* can be questioned – viz. the *radical* moral demand, the insistence on absolute purity of intentions.

All arguments of faith against philosophy *presuppose* faith: they are circular.

Revelation has no support other than revelation: the only book written in defense of the Bible is the Bible itself (Lessing) [1]Or: Newman's "I know, I know."[1]

Since revelation has no support outside itself, since its arguments are circular, philosophy can disregard revelation.

Philosophy cannot refute revelation.

Again limited to most popular aspects. Fundamental difference between: refutation of *adherents* of revelation (= human beings) and refutation of revelation (= God) – cf. Calvin: se nobiscum litigare *fingunt*.

The famous refutation of Genesis 1 by modern geology – the *wrong* answer is: the Bible is not a scientific book, but concerned only with matters of faith and manners – for: faith and science overlap, e.g. in the question of miracles – if the Bible is not to be taken seriously in matters concerning physical world and events in it, may be the Biblical reports go back to people incapable of exact observation etc.[45] The good and decisive answer is this: all scientific arguments against the Biblical account of creation etc. *presuppose* the impossibility of miracles (events which according to science must have required billions of years, are miraculously possible in a split second) – i.e. they beg the question.

Or: Biblical criticism – the arguments *presuppose* the impossibility of verbal inspiration: it was impossible for *Moses* to describe[46] events occurring centuries after his death, but not for God to inspire to him the truth etc.

The multiplicity of revelations – they refute each other – a particularly shallow argument: for|

1) if una est religio in rituum varietate, if every revealed N 3 verso religion is a *human* interpretation of the call of God, the variety of human interpretations does not do away with the fact that a personal God freely and mysteriously calls men to Himself. It is true, this would presuppose an attitude of radical *tolerance.* But this is not even necessary; for:

2) scandals *must* come, heresies *must* come – it is of the essence of revelation to be constantly challenged by pseudo-revelations, heresies etc.

Why revelation cannot refute philosophy, and vice versa.
Generally:

a) human knowledge is always so limited that the *possibility* of revelation cannot be refuted[47], and *need* for revelation cannot be denied.

b) revelation is always so uncertain that it can be rejected, and man is so constructed that he can find his satisfaction, his happiness, in investigation, in the progress of clarity.

Conclusions to be drawn from this state of affairs.
First suggestion – neutrality is superior to the alternatives –
neutrality means:

a) our thesis can be proved to both, whereas neither of the 2 opposed theses[48] – right of revelation and right of philosophy – can be proved to the other.

b) attempt to *understand,* to do *justice* to both positions.

Deplorable state of mutual appreciation. Believers are rightly shocked by what philosophers say, or intimate, regarding revelation, and philosophers can only shrug their shoulders about what believers say about philosophy.

(Cf. Spinoza on Bible; Pascal on Epicureans – Stoics; Nietzsche on Bible as resentment; Kierkegaard on Socrates as distinguished from Plato. As regards Thomas, a *problem* is shown by Luther's dissatisfaction with scholastic theology.)

One could say that the very fact that each side has tried to refute the other, reveals[49] a[50] deep misunderstanding.

But: neutrality is a *philosophic* attitude > victory of philosophy.

The very insight into the *limitations* of philosophy is a victory of philosophy: because it is an *insight.* |

N 4 recto   Yet:

Second suggestion: Problematic basis of philosophy is revealed by
its inability to refute revelation.
Revelation or faith is *not* compelled, by its principle, to *refute* philosophy. But philosophy is – threatened by the very possibility of revelation which it cannot refute: philosophy cannot leave it at a *defence;* it *must* attack.

Why is philosophy threatened by the very possibility of revelation?

I a. *The* alternative is philosophy or revelation, i.e. what *ultimately* counts is either divine guidance or human guidance; *if* there is no divine guidance, human guidance is *the* One Thing needful.

The other way round: if there is revelation, philosophy becomes something infinitely unimportant – the *possibility* of revelation implies the *possible meaninglessness* of philosophy. If the possibility of revelation remains an open question, the *significance of philosophy* remains an open question.

Therefore, philosophy stands and falls by the contention that philosophy is the One Thing Needful, or the highest possibility of man. [1]Philosophy cannot claim less: it cannot afford being modest.[1]

b. But philosophy cannot refute the possibility of revelation. Hence, philosophy is *not* necessarily the One Thing Needful; hence the choice of philosophy is based, not on evident or rational necessity, but on an unevident, a fundamentally *blind* decision. The claim of philosophy is plausible, but not cogent; it is verisimile, but not verum.

The *claim* of philosophy that it[51] wisely suspends its judgment, whereas faith boldly or rashly decides, is untenable; for philosophy *itself rests* on a decision.

If philosophy cannot justify itself as a rational *necessity*, a life devoted to the quest for evident knowledge rests *itself* on an unevident assumption – but this confirms the thesis of faith that there is no possibility of *consistency*, of a *consistent life* without faith or belief in revelation. |

II. One might suggest this way out: philosophy does not N 4 verso have to prove the *impossibility* of revelation; for the possibility of revelation is so remote, so infinitely remote that it is not a practical proposition.

This argument is becoming for business-men, but it is a disgrace – I do not say for philosophers – but for anyone who claims ever to have come [with]in hailing distance of philosophy or science.

Philosophy cannot prove that revelation is impossible; hence it cannot prove *more* than that revelation is most *improbable* or radically *uncertain*. But this is so far from being a refutation of revelation, that it is not even *relevant*: it is the very *boast* of revelation to be a *miracle*, hence most improbable and most uncertain. [1]Philosophy implies the refusal to accept, or to adhere to, whatever is not *evident*; but revelation is per se inevident; ergo philosophy does not *refute* the claim of revelation; it begs the question; it rests on a *dogmatic* assumption. No specific *argument* of philosophy, but simply the philosophic criterion of truth *settles* the issue. Philosophy presupposes *itself*.[1]

Philosophy rejects revelation because of its uncertainty – but uncertainty is of the *essence* of revelation – revelation *denies* the philosophic criterion of truth (everything which is incapable of being made manifest, is suspect; αὐτοψια; evident necessity . . .). Philosophy rejects revelation, philosophy asserts its own *necessity*, on the *basis* of the philosophic criterion of truth: the justification of philosophy is *circular* – i.e. it is a scandal.

On the basis of its initial *hypothesis* (that philosophy is the highest possibility of man), philosophy can maintain itself *easily* against the claim of revelation – but it cannot deny that this basic premise is, and is bound to remain, a *hypothesis*.

I conclude: the fact that revelation cannot refute philosophy and vice versa, decides in favor of revelation. Or: the impossibility of neutrality between revelation and philosophy decides in favor of revelation.

[1](Consider this: revelation cannot be proved – but philosophy can be proved: it can be proved that man does philosophize: the *fact* of philosophy can be proved, whereas the fact of revelation can *not*.)[1]

N 5 recto   *Consequence for philosophy*: appears if we restate the problem as follows: Philosophy is the highest possibility of man, if there is no revelation; but there is no revelation, because there can never be evident *knowledge* of the fact of revelation. The argument presupposes the tacit identification of "being" with "evidently knowable." Philosophy is essentially "idealistic" (Laberthonnière, L'idéalisme grec et le réalisme chrétien[VIII]).

VIII [The title that Strauss cites from memory reads: Lucien Laberthonnière, *Le réalisme chrétien et l'idéalisme grec* (Paris 1904) – cf. letter to Gerhard Krüger from March 14, 1933, *Gesammelte Schriften* 3, p. 427.]

It is *this* fact which gave rise to Kant's Critique of pure reason, to his distinction between the phenomenon and the Thing-in-itself: Kant's "idealism" is an *attack* on the "idealism" of classical philosophy. ¹But cf. Plato on ἀσθένεια τοῦ λόγου.¹

A philosophy which believes that it can refute the possibility of revelation – and a philosophy which does not believe that: *this* is the real meaning of la querelle des anciens et des modernes.

The consequence for philosophy: radical revision of fundamental reflections of classical philosophy (man = animal rationale – his perfection = philosophy etc.) along the lines of Kant's Critique of Pure Reason.

Third suggestion⁵² – the Greek philosopher would answer along *these* lines –

Philosophy does not need revelation, but revelation needs philosophy: philosophy refuses to be called before tribunal of revelation, but revelation *must* recognize the tribunal of philosophy. For adherents of revelation may *say* credo quia absurdum, they cannot *mean* it; they can be forced to admit that the objects of faith must be *possible* – but the elaboration of what is possible or not, is the sake of *philosophy*.ᴵˣ

But the cognizance of philosophy is not limited to *possible* things, for there is human knowledge of actual things. Since both philosophy and faith make assertions about *actual* things, there is a possibility of *conflict* and of *refutation* of one by the other. ¹Faith as faith *must* make assertions which can be *checked* by unbelievers – it *must* be based at⁵³ *some* point on alleged or real *knowledge* – but that "knowledge" is *necessarily* only *alleged* knowledge, owing to the *basic* fallacy, of faith, the attribution of *absolute* importance to *morality* (the pure heart).¹

To *exclude* the possibility of refutation radically, there is only one way: that faith has no basis whatever in human knowledge of actual things. This view of faith is not the Jewish and the Catholic one. It was prepared by the Reformers and reaches its climax in Kierkegaard. Whereas the Reformation stands and

IX [The English phrase "is the sake of philosophy" is explained and is to be understood as a rendering of the German "ist Sache der Philosophie" (is the task or subject matter of philosophy).]

falls by the absolute truth of the Bible, i.e. of a book which is
subject to various kinds of human investigations, *Kierkegaard*
took away this last link between the realm of actual knowledge
N 5 verso   and the realm of faith. | He says (*Philosophical Fragments* 87):
for faith it would have been more than enough if the generation contemporary with Jesus had[54] left nothing behind than
these words: "We have believed that in such and such a year
God appeared among us in the humble figure of a servant,
that he lived and taught in our community, and finally died."
If we disregard the difficulty that one would have to *know* that
"this little advertisement" *really* goes back to the contemporaries of Jesus, can faith on *such* a basis be defended against
the objection that "assentire his quae sunt fidei, est levitatis"
(S.c.G. I 6)? And if this is so, must we not admit the possibility of refutation of one by the other and hence start the
discussion all over again? or rather, *begin* the discussion by
taking up the *concrete* problems to which I could barely allude
tonight?[55]

In conclusion, I would like to name[56] that man to whom I
owe, so to say, everything I have been able to discern in the
labyrinth of that grave question: Lessing. I do not mean the
Lessing of a certain tradition, the Lessing celebrated by a certain type of oratory, but the true and unknown Lessing. Lessing's attitude was characterized by an innate disgust against
compromises in serious, i.e. theoretical, matters: he rejected
Socinianism, enlightened Christianity (of which one does not
know where it is Christian and where it is enlightened) and
deism, and he would have rejected German idealism as well
(as Jacobi vs. Schelling shows). He admitted only[1] this alternative: orthodoxy (in his case Lutheran, of course) or Spinoza
(i.e. philosophy, for there is no philosophy other than that of
Spinoza). He decided in favor of philosophy. – Why he took
this step, he has indicated in more than one passage of his writings – but in none, I think, more clearly than in this (*Antiqu.
Briefe* 45 end) with which he concludes his discussion of the
different treatment of 'perspective in ancient and in modern
painting'[1]:

"We see more than the ancients; and yet our eyes might
possibly be poorer than the eyes of the ancients; the ancients
saw less than we; but their eyes might have been more[57]

discerning than ours. – I fear that the whole comparison of the ancients and the moderns would lead to this result."

[1]Possibility of refutation of revelation implied in Platonic-Aristotelian philosophy. What their specific argument is, we cannot say before we have understood their whole teaching. Since I cannot claim to have achieved this, I must leave the issue open.[1]

Text-Critical Notes

[] contains additions by the editor.
<> indicates deletions by Leo Strauss.

1. Inserted or added by Leo Strauss between the lines or in the margins.
2. < are >
3. < he >
4. < can >
5. < demonstration >
6. Ms.: preying
7. < According to its original me[aning] > The
8. [The title and the beginning of point 5 first read as follows and then were immediately discarded by LS:] < 5) *Philosophy must assert that revelation is impossible.* Philosophy asserts that the one thing needful is philosophizing. This assertion is contradicted by the teaching of revelation. The philosopher must therefore *refute* the teaching of revelation. More than that: he must prove the *impossibility* of revelation. For if revelation is *possible*, it is possible that the philosophic enterprise is fundamentally wrong. >
9. < subtle >
10. < prove >
11. < implies >
12. his < literary > < textual >[1]
13. < divorced >
14. < Also, > a God
15. as < the cause of all things the fully[1] intelligible >
16. us. < They would say the thing >
17. < it >
18. < can >
19. limit < creati >
20. < creation as >
21. in < God >
22. < less than most other theologians >
23. < admits >
24. and < that >
25. < whether >

26. say < in this case >
27. < My contention is th >
28. < will >
29. < (Theaet. in pri >
30. more < than >
31. < *refute* >
32. explanation < would therefore be >
33. Ms.: 423
34. < divine >
35. *right* < that >
36. < the >
37. his < word is >
38. < the just >
39. the < dark >
40. < the tree > becomes
41. < It would be ridiculed as gentleman's view > [Then in a new line:] Biblical
42. < Bible seems to apply this to God. > – a
43. < man >
44. [Inserted between the lines in pencil. The first four words in the brackets are especially difficult to decipher, particularly as *M.* looks to be only an abbreviation. The commas after *consolation* and *envy* have been added by the editor so as to allow the thought, which Strauss noted for himself in an extremely condensed form, to become more comprehensible.]
45. etc. ¹< Applied to >¹
46. describe < this to >
47. < denied, and >
48. Ms.: thesis
49. < shows >
50. < that >
51. it < suspends >
52. [In the Ms. *Third suggestion* is underlined, unlike in the case of *First suggestion* and *Second suggestion* previously, not once, but twice, and thus is given special emphasis.]
53. Ms.: on
54. had < nothing >
55. [Noted in this connection in the lower margin and then crossed out:] < Die kleinen Zettel a) und b). > [= Small slips of paper a) and b).]
56. < mention >
57. < better >

INDEX OF NAMES

Tertullianus, Quintus Septimius Florens, 20, 84
Troeltsch, Ernst, 131
Turgot, Anne Robert Jacques, 132

Varro, M. Terentius, 79
Voltaire, 118

Weber, Max, 117, 118, 126, 127, 129
Wittgenstein, Ludwig, 105, 106

Xenophon, xii, 15, 24, 25, 27, 51, 92, 99, 101, 110, 170
Yorck von Wartenburg, Paul, 125

For EU product safety concerns, contact us at Calle de José Abascal, 56–1°,
28003 Madrid, Spain or eugpsr@cambridge.org.

www.ingramcontent.com/pod-product-compliance
Ingram Content Group UK Ltd.
Pitfield, Milton Keynes, MK11 3LW, UK
UKHW010251140625
459647UK00013BA/1784